Chicago Manual

BROWN v. BOARD OF EDUCATION

ALSO BY JAMES T. PATTERSON

America's Struggle Against Poverty in the Twentieth Century
(Harvard University Press, 2000)

America in the Twentieth Century: A History
(Harcourt Brace, 1999)

Great Expectations: The United States, 1945–1974
(Oxford University Press, 1996)

The Dread Disease: Cancer and Modern American Culture
(Harvard University Press, 1987)

Mr. Republican: A Biography of Robert A. Taft
(Houghton Mifflin, 1972)

The New Deal and the States: Federalism in Transition
(Princeton University Press, 1969)

Congressional Conservatism and the New Deal
(Kentucky University Press, 1967)

PIVOTAL MOMENTS
IN AMERICAN HISTORY

Series Editors

David Hackett Fischer

James M. McPherson

BROWN v. BOARD OF EDUCATION

A Civil Rights Milestone and
Its Troubled Legacy

JAMES T. PATTERSON

OXFORD

UNIVERSITY PRESS

2001

OXFORD
UNIVERSITY PRESS

Oxford   New York

Athens   Auckland   Bangkok   Bogotá   Buenos Aires   Calcutta
Cape Town   Chennai   Dar es Salaam   Delhi   Florence   Hong Kong   Istanbul
Karachi   Kuala Lumpur   Madrid   Melbourne   Mexico City   Mumbai
Nairobi   Paris   São Paulo   Shanghai   Singapore   Taipei   Tokyo   Toronto   Warsaw

and associated companies in
Berlin   Ibadan

Copyright © 2001 by James T. Patterson

Published by Oxford University Press, Inc.
198 Madison Avenue, New York, New York 10016

Oxford is a registered trademark of Oxford University Press

Library of Congress Cataloging-in-Publication Data
is available
ISBN 0-19-512716-1

1 3 5 7 9 8 6 4 2

Printed in the United States of America
on acid-free paper

To my students and colleagues at Brown University,
especially my long-time friends
Howard Chudacoff, Jack Thomas, and Gordon Wood

CONTENTS

EDITORS' NOTE

This volume is the first in a series called Pivotal Moments in American History. Each book will examine a large historical problem through the lens of a particular event and the choices of individual actors. The design of the series reflects the current state of historical writing, which gives growing attention to the experiences of ordinary people, increasing sensitivity to issues of gender, class, and ethnicity, and deep interest in large structures and processes. We seek to combine this new scholarship with old ideas of history as a narrative art and traditional standards of sound scholarship, mature judgment, and good writing.

James T. Patterson's *Brown v. Board of Education* is an appropriate choice for the beginning of our series. Much of America's history has been made in its courts. In this republic of laws, judicial decisions have often become events of high moment—none more so than the two rulings in *Brown v. Board of Education of Topeka* that came down from the Supreme Court on May 17, 1954, and May 31, 1955.

Few rulings have ever been so extravagantly praised and condemned. The historical literature has also been deeply divided. Richard Kluger's *Simple Justice* (1975) and J. Harvie Wilkinson's *From Brown to Bakke* (1979) saw *Brown* as strongly positive. In the 1990s, academic revisionists argued that *Brown* did more harm than good: the "backlash" thesis. James T. Patterson, one of the leading historians of modern America, looks again at the subject from a longer perspective and in a larger context and sees the story afresh.

A theme of our Pivotal Moments is the important of contingency:

people making choices, and choices making a difference, often in unexpected ways. The history of *Brown* is a sequence of contingencies in that sense. It began with Oliver Brown and many other black parents who chose to fight for the education of their children, with high courage and often at heavy personal cost. Many other people made critical choices as the case progressed. Chief among them was Thurgood Marshall, head of the NAACP's Legal Defense Fund, later Solicitor General of the United States, and the first black justice on the Supreme Court.

The choices that followed in Washington, local courthouses, and the streets were often surprising. Nobody could have predicted that Earl Warren would have united a broken court, or that Lyndon Johnson would have become the staunchest presidential supporter of integration, or that the conservative Burger court would have decided to give strong support to *Brown*, or that the second black justice on the Court would have invoked the *Brown* case in opposing affirmative action.

The book is also about the consequences of this long chain of events: a backlash of unimagined power, and yet strong evidence of sweeping change—the end of Jim Crow, a revolution in attitudes toward race, and a great expansion of opportunity for American children. James T. Patterson shows that the legacy of *Brown* has been fiercely contested from the day it was handed down. That it continues to be contested today shows us just how pivotal a moment it was.

David Hackett Fischer
James M. McPherson

PREFACE
Contesting the Color Line

Shortly before the Supreme Court announced *Brown v. Board of Education of Topeka* on May 17, 1954, the historic decision that struck down state-sponsored racial segregation of America's public schools, Chief Justice Earl Warren decided to spend a few days visiting Civil War sites in Virginia. His black chauffeur drove him south out of Washington, D.C.

At the end of the first day Warren checked into a hotel where he had made advance reservations. He assumed that his chauffeur would locate lodgings of his own. The next morning, however, he realized that his chauffeur had spent the night in the car. Warren asked why.

"Well, Mr. Chief Justice," the chauffeur replied, "I just couldn't find a place—couldn't find a place to . . ."

The Chief Justice had heard enough: it was obvious that there were no decent accommodations to be had for a black man in that racially segregated region. "I was embarrassed, I was ashamed," he said later. He cut short the trip and returned immediately to Washington.[1]

Warren recalled this experience as evidence of the formidable edifice of racial discrimination in the United States in 1954. He identified *Brown*, a unanimous ruling, as a huge stride in the direction of knocking it down. Many contemporaries agreed that the Court had courageously contested America's durable color line. Thurgood Marshall, chief attorney for the black families who launched the litigation, had fought against racist school practices for many years. When Warren delivered the decision, Marshall could not restrain his joy. "I was so happy," he said of his feelings during a long night of celebration, that "I was numb."[2]

Marshall, however, had struggled long enough against racial discrimination to know that *Brown* would arouse furious controversy. That it did—no ruling in the twentieth century was more hotly debated. The complicated issues that *Brown* tried to resolve in 1954 still torment Americans half a century later. This book explores these issues and tries to identify the most important legacies of the decision in our own times.

Many black people shared Marshall's elation in 1954. "The Supreme Court decision is the greatest victory for the Negro people since the Emancipation Proclamation," Harlem's *Amsterdam News* exclaimed. "It will alleviate troubles in many other fields." The *Chicago Defender* added, "this means the beginning of the end of the dual society in American life and the system . . . of segregation which supports it." The writer Ralph Ellison captured the sentiments of many when he wrote a friend, "The court has found in our favor and recognized our human psychological complexity and citizenship and another battle of the Civil War has been won. The rest is up to us and I'm very glad. . . . *What a wonderful world of possibilities are unfolded for the children.*"[3]

People like Marshall and Ellison had ample grounds for expressing grand expectations such as these, for many other "possibilities" already seemed "wonderful" to Americans by 1954. Only recently the United States had helped to defeat militaristic enemies and had marched to the forefront of the "Free World" in the Cold War. It was by far the most powerful country on the planet. Though it had failed to win the Korean War, and though a Red Scare soured political life, America—that is, white America—was in most respects a stable, optimistic culture, and it was becoming an ever more fantastically prosperous nation. Its boisterously confident experts, predicting wonders in science, technology, and economic growth, seemed capable of conquering all frontiers. In a culture of high expectations, the considerable betterment of race relations, too, appeared not only possible but probable. For hopeful liberals in 1954, *Brown* promised to become only the first step toward reaching that long elusive goal.

Brown did seem likely to have huge social consequences. In 1954, seventeen southern and border states required the racial segregation of public schools, and four others—Arizona, Kansas, New Mexico, and

Signs at an ice cream parlor and a bus station, Durham, N.C., 1940. *(Library of Congress, Prints and Photographs Division)*

Thurgood Marshall in front of the Supreme Court. *(Library of Congress, Prints and Photographs Division, New York World-Telegram & Sun Collection, 1958 photo)*

Wyoming—permitted local districts to impose it. Segregated schools had prevailed in the District of Columbia since the Civil War. Americans who grew up prior to the 1950s had assumed that such practices were all but immutable. David Dellinger, a constitutional scholar, recalled, "Segregation was a fact about my universe. It seemed no more 'right' or 'wrong' than the placement of the planets in the solar system. It simply was." The *Brown* decision promised to sweep all that away—to integrate 11.5 million black and white school-age children in 11,173 school districts in the segregating states. They were nearly 39 percent of America's 28,836,000 public school students.[4]

Supporters of *Brown* were especially excited because segregation in public education had powerfully buttressed Jim Crow, the state-sponsored, constitutionally protected system of racial discrimination and segregation that deliberately disadvantaged more than 10 million black people in the South and parts of the border states. The system stigmatized them, cut them off from avenues of opportunity, and in most cases consigned them to inferior social, economic, and political status.[5] It also dumped black children, two-thirds of whom still lived in southern and border states, into poorly funded, often ramshackle schools. In 1940, public spending per pupil in southern black schools had been only 45 percent of that in white schools. In South Carolina, Georgia, and Alabama it was only 33 percent; in Mississippi, it was 15 percent. At that time, white officials in hundreds of heavily black counties in the South authorized little or no high schooling for blacks. By 1954 public expenditures for black schools had increased, reflecting belated efforts by white officials to deflect mounting legal challenges to segregation. But public funding per pupil for southern black schools in 1954 was still only 60 percent of that for southern white schools, which in turn received only 60 percent of spending per pupil in the nation as a whole.

Advocates of desegregation were certain, above all, that racially mixed schools, more than any other institutions, would facilitate the cherished American dream of equal opportunity. In this belief they reflected long-standing assumptions about the powerful role of education in life. Insofar as blacks were concerned, there seemed to be no doubting the logic of this assumption. Black schools under Jim Crow were not only inferior in terms of facilities. As Marshall emphasized, segregation was as damaging as inequality—perhaps even more so. It shunted black students from the mainstream, isolating them and depriving them from association or competition with whites. A people set apart, blacks in the South could not be sure how bright, how competent, how worthy they might be. Some clearly wondered: were they, as whites maintained, inadequate or inferior?[6]

Neither Marshall nor anyone else was sure in the early 1950s how desegregated schools might work in practice. Ever more expectant as they drove toward success in the courts, they could not easily predict the extent of resistance that mixing in schools was to provoke among whites. But they had come to believe that desegregation of schools would lead—*had* to lead—to some larger betterment of conditions for black people. So it was that they had long ago singled out schools as prime targets of their litigation.

In so doing they fired their legal guns at the most sensitive citadels of the Jim Crow system. Although this system separated the races in virtually all walks of southern life, not only schools but also restaurants, hotels, theaters, waiting rooms, buses and trains, rest rooms, beaches, parks, cemeteries—even drinking fountains and telephone booths—it was anchored on segregation in schools. White parents (like all parents) understandably cherished their children above all. Those who believed blacks to be inferior, were certain that racial mixing in the classroom would impede the learning process. Mixing in the classroom, they also feared, could lead to mixing out of class, and even (a horror scarcely to be imagined) to interracial dating or marriage. For these reasons, the struggle over school segregation was often to become the most impassioned and bitter of all the battles for racial change in America after the 1950s. But it was a battle that Marshall and others believed they had no choice but to fight.

Marshall, Warren, and others also had high expectations that the decision would strike a sharper blow against racial prejudice. To this extent, they were social engineers, heirs of John Dewey and other educational reformers who had argued that public schools could be—indeed, should be—laboratories for the shaping of more egalitarian values. Bringing blacks and whites together in schools, they thought, would weaken hateful stereotypes and promote interracial understanding among the young—and in time among society at large. Some day, white people might respond to black people as individuals, not as racial symbols— or, as the Reverend Martin Luther King, Jr., was to say, judge them by the content of their character instead of by the color of their skin. Delivered from racist oppression, blacks would become proud and confident; whites, too, would be liberated from the curse of racist perceptions. As President Harry Truman's Committee on Civil Rights had argued in 1947, there was "incontrovertible evidence . . . that an environment favorable to civil rights is fostered whenever groups are permitted to live and work together."[7]

Those who have hailed the Court's opinion later advanced other arguments. *Brown*, they declare, stimulated the Court to emerge as a stalwart warrior in a wide range of subsequent crusades for social change: the ruling, says the historian David Garrow, "singlehandedly marks the advent of the 'modern' or present-age Supreme Court." Like Garrow, admirers of *Brown* emphasize that the decision ultimately reached far beyond the schools. Robert Carter, who helped Marshall litigate the case, stressed later that the Court's intervention had "side or fallout effects" that in time accelerated not only a dramatic civil rights movement for blacks but also inspired rights-consciousness among many other groups. "*Brown*," he said, "allows us to take pride in ourselves and in the greatness of the nation we live in, and to stand tall and apart from most of the other countries of the world." John Salmond, a historian of civil rights, agrees: "After *Brown*, nothing could ever be the same."[8]

Of course, some Americans denounced the decision. Loudest among them were white defenders—mainly southern—of segregation. May 17, 1954, many of them believed, was Black Monday. A Mississippi judge, Tom Brady, wrote a pamphlet with that title stressing that the Court's decision would endanger "blue-eyed, golden-haired little girls" by placing them in the same classrooms with black children. Bryant Bowles, a thirty-four-year-old white man, quickly organized a National Association for the Advancement of White People (NAAWP). During nasty confrontations over school desegregation in Milford, Delaware, in October 1954 he echoed Brady's obsession about interracial sex: "My daughters will never attend a school with Negroes so long as there is breath in my body and gunpowder will burn."[9]

The majority of leading white southern politicians took similarly rigid positions. Senator James Eastland of Mississippi, champion of resistance on Capitol Hill, was one of many who incited fears of radical subversion—strong in the Red Scare years of the early 1950s—in an effort to undermine the Court. Eastland professed to believe that blacks "did not themselves instigate the agitation against segregation. They were put up to it by radical busybodies who are intent upon overthrowing American institutions." Governor Herman Talmadge of Georgia was another champion of southern white resistance. Earlier he had announced that his state would never accept desegregated schools while he remained governor. "Desegregation," he added after hearing of *Brown*, would lead to intermarriage and "the mongrelization of the races."[10]

People like Eastland and Talmadge were especially crude and outspoken. Indeed, other southern foes of *Brown*, such as North Carolina Senator Sam Ervin, made "softer" defenses of segregation—defenses that put forward legalistic and constitutional claims. Ervin and his allies privately deplored the extremism of men like Talmadge, thinking it to be counterproductive. But the demagogues attracted a large audience in the South, where the vast majority of white people endorsed white supremacy. Almost without thinking, most white Southerners considered Negroes, as African Americans were called in those days, to be members of an inferior race, lazier and more stupid than white people. Because blacks were "oversexed," they had to be kept "in their place" lest they attack white women. Keeping blacks "in their place" would also preserve power relationships and ensure that whites could hold onto their jobs. Whites holding beliefs such as these professed that black people did not need—or desire—much education. One white Virginian told a reporter from the *Saturday Evening Post*, Negroes "want pool rooms and dance halls.

They're more interested in drinking and carousing than in reading. . . . That's what they've got—and they're happy with it. We have a saying around here: be a Negro on Saturday night and you'll never want to be a white man again."[11]

Southern whites who resisted northern intervention often disagreed over strategy, but in most important ways they put aside their differences in order to devise a host of ways to evade, indeed to nullify, the goals of *Brown*: until the late 1960s Jim Crow continued to flourish in southern schools. In so doing they frequently accused the North of hypocrisy, pointing out accurately that *Brown* took direct aim only at the South and at those border regions where segregation was *de jure*—sanctioned explicitly in laws. The decision did not challenge the North or threaten it with costs of any kind. It did not affect *de facto* racial segregation, which was widespread, especially in housing and schooling, in the North.

Much *de facto* segregation of schools reflected two central facts about America's public educational system. First, from the beginning the system had depended primarily on support from local property taxes, which varied considerably from town to town. It was therefore highly unequal: the wealthier the town, the better financed (in most cases) its schools. Second, class divisions in America normally replicated racial divisions. Parents who could pay higher taxes for better schools—mostly white parents—often moved to districts in wealthier towns. Many relocated primarily so that their children would not have to go to school with low-income black children. Blacks, far poorer, had to send their children to schools that were ill-financed and that often became increasingly segregated *de facto* over time. Small wonder that many black people, then and later, insisted that *de jure* and *de facto* segregation frequently amounted to pretty much the same thing in practice.

But *de facto* segregation of schools did not result only from private decisions, such as changing one's residence. It also rested on a raft of deliberate public policies—zoning, establishment of school bus routes, siting of new schools, and drawing of school district lines—that were implemented throughout the country by elected as well as nonelected officials so as to separate black and white children within districts. Much *de facto* segregation, in short, was as publicly sanctioned and as intentional as *de jure* segregation. Its ubiquity lent credence to an old saying: "In the South, white people don't mind how close a Negro gets to them as long as he doesn't rise too high [economically or socially], while in the North people don't mind how high a Negro gets as long as he doesn't get too close."

Thanks to a dramatic surge in civil rights activism in the early and mid-1960s, it seemed that blacks and their liberal white allies might succeed in demolishing Jim Crow. Boycotts, sit-ins, freedom rides, and demonstrations ultimately stirred Congress, which approved the historic Civil Rights Act of 1964 and the Voting Rights Act of 1965. Congress also passed the Elementary and Secondary Education Act in 1965, which featured a title authorizing cutoffs of federal aid to school systems practicing *de jure* racial segregation.

The civil rights movement was indeed heroic. Reflecting and accelerating more liberal attitudes toward race relations, it inspired even higher expectations than *Brown* had in 1954. Moreover, it had great and lasting consequences. The civil rights and education laws finally smashed Jim Crow in the South and promoted considerable desegregation of southern schools. The movement also sparked a wider rights-consciousness in the United States, leading a host of other activists—ethnic minorities, women, the elderly, the poor, the disabled, gay people—to protest and to demand their own rights. Deeply committed federal officials and judges, products of the liberal Kennedy-Johnson years, pitched in to help them and even—in time—to extend these rights. The movement transformed American society, politics, and culture in a host of ways that even survived the rise of political conservatism after 1968.

As it happened, however, many large expectations of the mid-1960s turned out to be too grand to achieve. The civil rights movement quickly lost force after 1965. Only five days after President Lyndon Johnson signed the Voting Rights Act in August 1965, race riots broke out in the Watts section of Los Angeles. Other, bloodier riots—notably in Newark and Detroit in 1967—convulsed cities in the next few years. At the same time, the civil rights movement split along racial lines, with some young militants demanding "black power." Many Americans were frightened and appalled by the riots. Others feared the rise of black power. Still others resisted the growth in the late 1960s of affirmative action and "forced busing" aimed at promoting "racial balance."

Indeed, progress in civil rights after 1965 ceased to be cost free for whites in the North. Fearful of blacks, increasing numbers of white people pulled out of the cities—"white flight," it was called—and moved into suburbs. White "backlash," much of it aimed against Johnson's liberal Great Society programs, helped conservatives to win office and to transform the partisan makeup of national politics. When Richard Nixon was elected president in 1968, he took advantage of four retirements from the Supreme Court (one of them Warren's, in 1969) in a determined quest to turn the Court toward the right. The economy then soured, arousing further fears and resentments, many of them directed against blacks. By the mid-1970s, advocates of civil rights feared for the worst.

Reflecting this more somber mood, which persisted in later years, various revisionist writers came to ask probing questions about the legacies of the *Brown* decision. Though conceding its symbolic uses for progressive change in race relations, they wondered if the decision did a great deal more. One scholar, Michael Klarman, argued that "political, economic, social, demographic, and intellectual forces" in the 1940s and 1950s were already liberalizing race relations in the United States, even in the South. These changes "would have undermined Jim Crow—perhaps with less white bitterness—regardless of Supreme Court intervention." Another scholar, Gerald Rosenberg, asked if *Brown* and subsequent judicial efforts accomplished very many things prior to the late 1960s: "Courts had virtually no effect on ending discrimination in the key fields of education, voting, transportation, accommodation and public places, and housing." *Brown*, he said, encouraged advocates of racial justice to depend too heavily on the courts and may if anything have delayed the spread of more effective direct action against racial discrimination.[12]

Some supporters of Warren's opinion also came to regret that he did not specifically echo in *Brown* the famous phrase of Supreme Court Justice John Marshall Harlan, a one-time Kentucky slaveowner who had issued a lone dissent in the precedent-setting case of <u>Plessy v. Ferguson</u> <u>(1896)</u>. This case had arisen when Homer Plessy, a mixed-race man who was officially classified as a Negro, challenged a Louisiana law requiring railway companies in the state to provide "equal but separate accommodations for the white, and colored race." All the justices but Harlan upheld the law, thereby enshrining the principle (soon extended by the Court to schools) that racially "separate-but-equal" facilities were constitutional. Harlan had disagreed. "Our Constitution," he wrote, "is color-blind, and neither knows nor tolerates classes among its citizens."[13]

But Warren and his colleagues did not say that. While their ruling

Kenneth and Mamie Clark. *(Library of Congress, Prints and Photographs Division, New York World-Telegram & Sun Collection, 1966 photo)*

in *Brown* superseded *Plessy*'s separate-but-equal principle—and had long-range consequences on American jurisprudence—it understandably focused on the issue to be decided: state-sponsored segregation in the schools. *Brown* therefore did not maintain that all racial classifications (as, for instance, laws against interracial marriage) were unreasonable and therefore impermissible. It did not proclaim that the Constitution was color-blind. Instead, Warren penned a brief and prosaic opinion that drew in part on evidence from the academic field of psychology. Some of this evidence relied on the scholarship of Kenneth and Mamie Clark, psychologists whose research concluded that racial segregation in the schools caused black children to be ashamed of themselves and therefore to prefer white-to brown-colored dolls. Racial segregation in education, Warren agreed, made black children in black schools feel inferior and undermined their motivation to learn. Critics of Warren's view lamented that he depended too heavily on suspect "social science," thereby affording conservative critics a convenient avenue of attack.[14]

The Court's argument, moreover, later led to very considerable problems of implementation. In *Brown*, Warren and his colleagues rejected state-sponsored school segregation, which they said violated the Fourteenth Amendment to the Constitution. Clearly, they opposed school districting based on prejudicial considerations of color. Yet in citing the Clarks and other authorities on the sociopsychological evils of segregation, the Court also indicated that it expected school administrators to embark on racial mixing in the schools. As it turned out, public officials ultimately had to engage in highly color-conscious policies. Subsequent quests for racial mixing led increasingly toward demands for racial balance, busing, affirmative action, and other strategies that few Americans, Marshall included, had anticipated in 1954.[15]

Black people in 1954 and later also reacted in varying ways to the decision. Most, of course, had long yearned for far better schools. They shared the white American romance with education as the source of advancement in life. "Get an education, boy," black grandmothers often said, " 'cause that's the one thing the whites can't take away from you." By the late 1940s some of these blacks had become angry enough to stand up as plaintiffs—first for equal schools, then after 1950 for the end of state-sponsored segregation—in cases that Thurgood Marshall, Robert Carter, and other attorneys, most of them African Americans, brought to the courts. Oliver Brown, a black welder, and others from Topeka were among the first of these plaintiffs to do so, in 1951.[16]

Blacks who volunteered as plaintiffs in these suits showed enormous courage, for whites were certain to retaliate. Many plaintiffs (and their kin) were fired from their jobs; others were denied credit by lenders. In Clarendon County, South Carolina, Levi Pearson, a black farmer who dared in 1948 to stand as a plaintiff on behalf of his three school-age children, discovered that he could no longer find a white farmer with a harvester to help him bring in his crops. He watched them rot in the fields. Angry whites later burned down the house and (then) the church of the Reverend Joseph Albert DeLaine, a black minister who led the move for desegregated schools in Clarendon County. When whites shot at DeLaine in the night, he fired back and fled, driving at eighty-five miles an hour over country roads to get across the state line. For a time he was an official fugitive from "justice."[17]

The words of two black people convey the intensity of feelings expressed by those engaged in these struggles. The first came in 1951 from the Reverend L. Francis Griffin, a militant spokesman for school desegregation in Farmville, Virginia. When some of his nervous, more conservative black parishioners sought to depose him as pastor, Griffin preached a fiery sermon:

> When I look and see healthy colored babies, I think how God has brought them into the world properly and how the rotten system of the Southland will twist them into warped personalities, cringing cowards, unable to cope with the society into which they were unwillingly thrown and which they have a God-given right to enjoy. . . . I would sacrifice my job, money, and any property for the principles of right. I offered my life for a decadent democracy [in World War II], and I'm willing to die rather than let these children down.

Inspired, Griffin's parishioners kept him on.[18]

The second speaker, Silas Hardrick Fleming, had joined Oliver Brown and others as a plaintiff in the struggle against segregation in Topeka. Fleming surprised his lawyers in 1951 by telling the judge he wished to make a statement. "You want to tell the court why you joined this lawsuit?" the judge asked. "That's right," Fleming replied. "All right," the judge said, "go ahead and tell it." Fleming did:

> Well, it wasn't for the sake of hot dogs. It wasn't to cast any insinuations that our teachers are not capable of teaching our children because they are supreme, extremely intelligent and are capable of teaching my kids or white or black kids. But my point was that not only I and my children are craving light, the entire colored race is craving light, and the only way to reach the light is to start our children together in their infancy and they come up together.[19]

Brave and eloquent though such protestors were, they were lonely voices in the 1940s and early 1950s. Most southern blacks at the time dared not speak out boldly against white racism. Although they were bitter about Jim Crow, they feared violent retaliation from whites. Many Negroes, moreover, were ambivalent about the quest for desegregated schools. A poll in November 1955—a year and a half after *Brown*—indicated that only 53 percent of blacks living in the South approved of the Court's historic ruling. Whether this poll was highly reliable may be questioned—it was surely difficult to quantify complex, changing attitudes such as these. Still, there was no doubting that many black people, especially in the Jim Crow South, were torn in mid-1950s. Some of those who said that they disapproved of *Brown* had no great wish to have their children mix with white people. Others suspected that desegregation would force them to assimilate into white culture. Still others, proud of their schools, worried about the impact of the decision on black educators. What would happen to black teachers and other employees in the existing schools? Teachers and principals were leaders of black communities and had often resisted Marshall's efforts to overturn the principle of separate-but-equal.[20]

The primary evil to be contested, many of these black people thought, was racial inequality, not segregation. Deeply suspicious of whites, they believed that efforts for racial integration—wherein people of different colors would come together in an increasingly respectful manner—were utopian. The National Association for the Advancement of Colored People (NAACP), they said, should continue to fight for educational equality and thereby force school boards to bring the black schools up to par with the white ones.

Still other black people wondered if desegregating schools would do much for racial justice. Oppressed by whites, they doubted that the ruling—which affected only *de jure* segregation in public schools—would really matter a great deal in so racist a country. Doubts of this sort, audible in 1954, grew louder after the mid-1960s, when race relations in America became ever more sour. Julius Chambers, a leading black lawyer, wrote, "*Brown* only served to siphon off conveniently and painlessly the discontent of minorities. . . . It gave blacks enough legal crumbs to satisfy them for a time, while the rest of America continued its feast."[21]

Zora Neale Hurston, a black folklorist-anthropologist-novelist (and a conservative Republican) expressed in 1955 other reservations about *Brown*—reservations that were very unfashionable (and uncommon) at the time, but that an articulate minority of black people was to echo in the years to come. What she disliked about the ruling was its insinuation that all-black institutions were second-rate. To argue, as *Brown* did, that racial segregation accentuated feelings of inferiority among blacks was to stigmatize their culture and to insult black teachers and administrators. Who could be sure, she exclaimed, that blacks would be better off in desegregated schools? She wrote:

> The whole matter revolves around the self-respect of my people. How much satisfaction can I get from a court order for somebody to associate with me who does not wish me near them? The American Indian has never been spoken of as a minority and chiefly because there is no whine in the Indian. Certainly he fought, and valiantly for his lands, and rightfully so, but it is inconceivable of an Indian to seek forcible association with anyone. His well-known pride and self-respect would save him from that. I take the Indian position.

It would help most, Hurston insisted, if authorities would strictly enforce compulsory education laws as they applied to black children. "The next 10 years would be better spent in appointing truant officers and looking after conditions in the homes from which the children come."[22]

Reactions of this kind indicate some of the many ways that *Brown v. Board of Education*, the most eagerly awaited and dramatic judicial decision of modern times, has aroused impassioned debate. This debate flourished not only in the 1950s, but also in later years. In the following pages I explore and evaluate these debates, which reveal much about race relations, America's most contested domestic issue since that time.

My goals are varied: to look into the controversies—legal, social, political, educational—that *Brown* has sparked from the late 1940s until the present. In so doing I listen to the voices of many actors, including some who are little known. I also explore a range of much debated questions. Were Thurgood Marshall and his fellow attorneys wise to target schools, which were especially sensitive institutions? Could the Court have done more than it did to demand compliance with its ruling? What can we say of the responses of America's political leaders, including President Dwight D. Eisenhower? What were the most important sources of the resistance to *Brown* that flared up in much of the South? How might this resistance have been more effectively countered?

As the story moves into the 1960s, other questions arise. Did the ruling in *Brown* deeply influence the civil rights movement, as some people claim, or did the power of the movement stem mainly from other sources? Why did the Court, having tolerated widespread evasion of *Brown* for more than a decade, move to enforce it in the late 1960s? Should we emphasize judicial action or legislative developments—notably the Civil Rights Act of 1964 and the Elementary and Secondary Education Act of 1965—in explaining the belated battering of Jim Crow after 1964? Addressing these questions can help to assess the various legacies of *Brown* and of the Supreme Court's role in the history of American race relations since the 1950s.

Later chapters carry the narrative to the present. These pages, too, pay attention to moves of the Court, which shifted gears again after 1973, this time to travel to the right. What can we say about the attempts of the Court (and of other institutions) to deal with *de facto* segregation, white flight to suburbs, and the "resegregation" that accompanied such movements of people? How useful for achieving racial balance was court-ordered busing? Under what circumstances can the courts play a major role in social change? Should they play such a role in a democratic society?

These chapters deal with other complex questions. One concerns the relationship between racial desegregation and academic achievement. To what extent and under what circumstances can desegregation of schools promote such achievement? Should reformers have battled more forcefully against other fundamental problems, such as family instability and socioeconomic inequalities in communities, instead of concentrating on fighting against segregation in schools?

How we judge Thurgood Marshall, Earl Warren, and many other actors in this long-running drama requires, finally, that we evaluate a range of later perspectives. A leading legal scholar, J. Harvie Wilkinson III, has asserted, "Very little could have been accomplished in mid-century America without the Supreme Court. . . . *Brown* may be the most important political, social, and legal event in America's twentieth-century history." Most scholars agree with Wilkinson that the decision—and other rulings that followed in its wake—dramatically improved the legal status of African Americans and in so doing greatly changed the nation for the better.[23]

Some people, however, are more reserved about the legacies of the decision. Kenneth Clark was one of many participants in the struggle who in time became pessimistic when looking back at *Brown*. He wrote in 1993: "I am forced to face the likely possibility that the United States will never rid itself of racism and reach true integration. I look back and shudder at how naive we all were in our belief in the steady progress racial minorities would make through programs of litigation and education." Clark concluded, "While I very much hope for the emergence of a revived civil rights movement with innovative programs and dedicated leaders, I am forced to recognize that my life has, in fact, been a series of glorious defeats."[24]

Viola Pearson, the widow of Levi, seemed to agree with this pessimistic assessment. Asked in 1994, forty years after *Brown*, if she thought their efforts had been worth it, she was quick to respond. "No way," she said. "We went through too much. I'm finished with that now." Summerton, South Carolina, where she lived, had an all-white town council and a virtually all-black high school in 1994.

The response of Summerton to *Brown* was hardly typical in the South. Virtually all southern communities, forced to desegregate in the late 1960s and early 1970s, accepted some forms of mixed-race schools well before 1994. And the majority of African Americans, refusing to despair, have remained committed to desegregation throughout the often contentious battles over schools in the post-*Brown* era. Viola Pearson's lament, therefore, is unduly glum about the legacy of *Brown*. Still, her pessimism reveals the disillusion that set in when many of the high expectations of the 1950s and 1960s did not come to pass. Her doubts also expose the persistence of doubts about the capacity of the courts to promote fundamental changes in race relations—and about the willingness of many people, northern as well as southern, to push for racial equality.

Let John Hope Franklin, dean of historians of African-American life, have a last word on these subjects for now. In 1993 he reminded readers of W. E. B. Du Bois's prescient warning ninety years earlier: "the problem of the twentieth century is the problem of the color line." Franklin, as if echoing the doubts of people like Clark in the 1990s, then added,

> The problem of the twenty-first century will be the problem of the color line. . . . By any standard of measurement or evaluation the problem has not been solved in the twentieth century and thus becomes a part of the legacy and burden of the next century.[25]

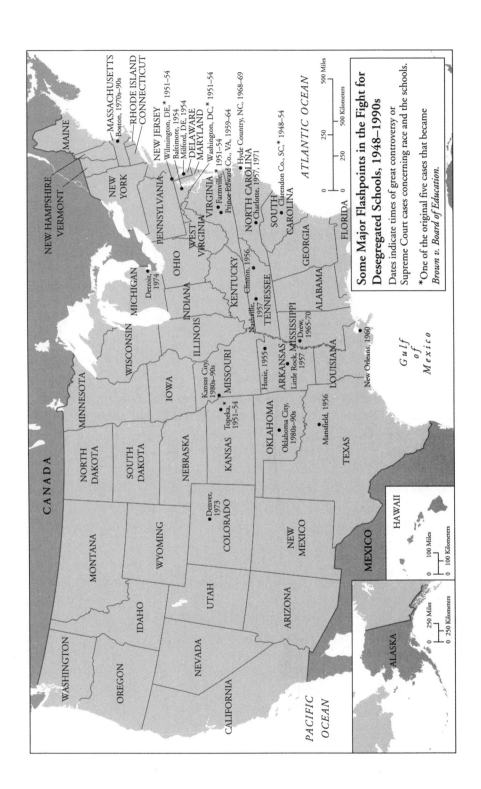

Some Major Flashpoints in the Fight for Desegregated Schools, 1948–1990s

Dates indicate times of great controversy or Supreme Court cases concerning race and the schools.

*One of the original five cases that became *Brown v. Board of Education.*

CANADA

WASHINGTON
OREGON
CALIFORNIA
NEVADA
IDAHO
MONTANA
UTAH
ARIZONA
WYOMING
COLORADO
• Denver, 1973
NEW MEXICO
NORTH DAKOTA
SOUTH DAKOTA
NEBRASKA
KANSAS
Topeka,* 1951–54
OKLAHOMA
Oklahoma City; 1980s–90s
TEXAS
MINNESOTA
IOWA
MISSOURI
Kansas City, 1980s–90s
ARKANSAS
Hoxie, 1955
Little Rock, 1957
LOUISIANA
New Orleans, 1960
WISCONSIN
ILLINOIS
INDIANA
MICHIGAN
Detroit, 1974
OHIO
KENTUCKY
TENNESSEE
Clinton, 1956
Nashville, 1957
MISSISSIPPI
Drew, 1965–70
Mansfield, 1956
ALABAMA
GEORGIA
FLORIDA
SOUTH CAROLINA
Clarendon Co. SC,* 1948–54
NORTH CAROLINA
Charlotte, 1957, 1971
Hyde County, NC, 1968–69
VIRGINIA
Farmville,* 1951–54
Prince Edward Co. VA, 1959–64
WEST VIRGINIA
PENNSYLVANIA
NEW YORK
MAINE
NEW HAMPSHIRE
VERMONT
MASSACHUSETTS
Boston, 1970s–90s
RHODE ISLAND
CONNECTICUT
NEW JERSEY
Wilmington, DE,* 1951–54
Baltimore, 1954
Milford, DE, 1954
DELAWARE
MARYLAND
Washington, DC,* 1951–54

MEXICO

Gulf of Mexico

PACIFIC OCEAN

ATLANTIC OCEAN

HAWAII

ALASKA

0   250   500 Miles
0   250   500 Kilometers

0   100 Miles
0   100 Kilometers

0   250 Miles
0   250 Kilometers

xxx

BROWN v. BOARD OF EDUCATION

I

RACE AND THE SCHOOLS
BEFORE *BROWN*

istening to black people who dared publicly to challenge racism—
and to optimistic white liberals—in the 1940s and early 1950s, we
can see how they imagined the approach of a new, more egalitarian
world of race relations in the United States:

A black American corporal, 1945: "I spent four years in the Army to free a
bunch of Dutchmen and Frenchmen, and I'm hanged if I'm going to let
the Alabama version of the Germans kick me around when I get home. No
sirreee-bob! I went into the Army a nigger; I'm comin' out a *man*."

Gunnar Myrdal, in his magisterial study of race relations in the United States,
An American Dilemma, 1944: "Not since Reconstruction *has there been more
reason to anticipate fundamental changes in American race relations, changes
which will involve a development toward American ideals.*" (italics his)

President Harry Truman, addressing the annual convention of the NAACP,
June 1947: "The extension of civil rights today means not protection of the
people *against* the government, but protection of the people *by* the government. . . . We must make the federal government a friendly, vigilant defender of the rights and equalities of all Americans. And again I mean all
Americans."

Thurgood Marshall, head of the NAACP's Legal Defense and Educational
Fund, envisioning in March 1954 the centennial in 1963 of the Emancipation
Proclamation: "Come hell or high water, we are going to be free in '63."[1]

These hopeful voices, like others in the late 1940s and early 1950s, articulated the three most powerful forces behind changes in American race
relations at the time—and later: rising militancy among blacks, including
some 900,000 young men who had fought in a war for freedom and
democracy, and many others who were streaming out of the Jim Crow
South for jobs in the North or West; increasingly vocal support from
white liberals like Myrdal and Truman; and the activism of Marshall
and others who led legal campaigns for civil rights.[2]

These three forces were indeed promoting reform of race relations,
which had been terrible before 1940. Support for racism based on "scientific" ideas plummeted after 1945 to near insignificance outside the
Deep South. Membership in the NAACP, by far the most important
civil rights organization until the 1960s, jumped from 50,000 in 1940 to
450,000 in 1946. The NAACP, with only 800 branches in 1939, expanded to 14,000 branches by 1948. Eleven states and twenty-eight cities
in the North enacted laws between 1945 and 1951 that established Fair
Employment Practices Commissions (FEPCs); eighteen states approved
legislation calling for the end of racial discrimination in public
accommodations.[3]

Blacks gained slowly in politics, too, winning elections as councilmen
in Richmond and Nashville in the late 1940s. Atlanta broke ground in
1948 by hiring its first black policemen. In the eleven states of the Old
Confederacy (the "South" in normal parlance), the percentage of eligible
black people who were registered to vote rose from 3 percent in 1940 to
20 percent twelve years later. That was one million black people in 1952.[4]

Truman's efforts especially encouraged advocates of more egalitarian
race relations. Although he moved cautiously at first—like Franklin Roosevelt, he was loath to antagonize powerful southerners in Congress and
in the Democratic party—he became bolder in 1947, in part because he
hoped to win northern black votes in 1948 and in part because he recognized that the United States, as leader of the Free World in the Cold
War, ought to practice what it preached. In 1948 he issued executive
orders calling for desegregation of the armed forces and for the end of
racial discrimination in federal hiring practices. He also asked Congress
to outlaw poll taxes, which prevented many blacks and other poor people
from voting; to establish a permanent FEPC at the national level; and
to make lynching a federal offense, thereby stripping racist white South-

erners of control over prosecution of that crime. Although Congress refused his legislative requests, liberals hoped for the future. Truman, after all, was the first American president since the Reconstruction era to concern himself much with extending the civil rights of blacks.[5]

The courts also gave liberals cause for high expectations. Endorsing Thurgood Marshall's efforts, the Supreme Court declared in 1944 that "white primaries" were unconstitutional. These primaries, widely used in the heavily Democratic southern states, had barred blacks from the all-important nominating process. In 1946 the Court ruled against state laws that had required segregated seating on interstate buses. In 1948 it decided that "restrictive housing covenants," private pacts used by whites to keep blacks (and other "undesirables") out of residential neighborhoods, were not enforceable in the courts. In 1950, the Court issued three notable rulings on the same day. Two of these attacked racial discrimination at the level of graduate education; the third struck down racially segregated dining facilities on interstate trains. These were heartening developments for foes of racial discrimination.[6]

Enjoying the supposed advantages of hindsight, some students of American race relations have looked at these developments and concluded that the Bad Old Days of racial discrimination, including segregation in the South, were slowly on their way out by 1954. Blacks were indeed restless, and they were making progress in politics, employment, and economic status.[7] But how strong was this progress, and how far might it have moved in the absence of something so dramatic as *Brown*? There is no sure answer to such questions. But we can wonder if the Myrdals of the world—who predicted ever-onward and upward progress until the United States approached what Myrdal called the "American Creed" of equality and justice for all—exaggerated the possibilities for rapid change. In retrospect it seems clear that hopeful liberals in the 1940s and early 1950s had overly optimistic expectations. They underestimated the staying power of racist ideas and practices in the United States, where not only blacks but also other groups such as Mexicans, Native Americans, and Jews still encountered widespread discrimination.

To appreciate the strength of such discrimination in the early postwar years we may begin by looking at the difficulties faced by militant blacks at the time. A few, especially returning veterans, courageously protested against oppression. Like the Alabama soldier who said he had gone to war a "nigger" and was returning a "man," a South Carolina veteran recalled how he had refused to accept third-class status in 1945. Urged by an official of the Veterans Administration to seek a job as a laborer, he retorted, "I was a staff sergeant in the Army . . . traveled all over England . . . sat fourteen days in the English Channel. I wasn't going to push a wheel barrow." Many of the black leaders of postwar civil rights activity in Mississippi—Amzie Moore, Aaron Henry, Medgar Evers— had also become militant while serving in the segregated armed services during the war. (Evers insisted on trying to vote, only to be driven away by whites wielding pistols.) Harry Briggs, who was later to become one of twenty plaintiffs in the South Carolina case against racial discrimination that Marshall carried to the courts in 1948, was a Navy veteran with five children.[8]

Anger at racist practices in the South also broke out here and there among black students. In 1946, the youth council of the NAACP in Lumberton, North Carolina, called a strike of students to protest against the inferior facilities in their schools. Black students in Hearne, Texas, staged a similar strike a year later. When these groups demanded quick action from the Legal Defense Fund, Thurgood Marshall grew testy, complaining about people who "want the lawyers to prepare the case, file it, have it decided and have everything straightened out in fifteen minutes." But he lent assistance nonetheless. The controversies abated when Lumberton and Hearne officials, feeling the pressure, improved their black schools.[9]

To say, however, that some black Americans in the postwar years, notably veterans and increasing numbers of young people, stood up to challenge white racism is not to conclude that they were able to accomplish great things. To be sure, many African Americans came to enjoy better lives in the postwar era. Masses of black people poured out of the southern countryside in these and later years, and found—at last—industrial work. Over time they spearheaded the rise of a substantial middle class in southern cities and in the North. But whites generally wanted no part of them in their neighborhoods, or in their schools. Long before the 1960s and 1970s, when battles over busing of children to schools erupted in violence, white people in these cities resorted to firebombings and other intimidating tactics.[10]

Federal housing policies in these years deliberately discriminated against blacks seeking low-cost, federally supported home mortgages. Racist to the core, they represented a massive affirmative action program for whites and a major form of *de jure* discrimination against blacks. Municipal and education officials in the North manipulated zoning regulations, gerrymandered school districts, and built schools next to all-black public housing projects so as to ensure maximum separation of the races in the classroom. They also discriminated against blacks who wished to teach in city schools. San Francisco had no black teachers between the 1870s and 1944. Philadelphia did not assign a black teacher to a predominantly white high school until 1947. Some 90 percent of Chicago's black teachers at the time were placed in schools that were 95 percent or more black.[11]

In the South, the masses of black people—most of them still scattered in rural areas—had trouble mobilizing effectively in the 1940s and early 1950s. Given the vast reach of Jim Crow, they also had formidable obstacles to overcome. While racial oppression varied in its power—the South was not a monolith—most white Southerners refused to loosen their grip. During the war, they often treated German prisoners of war better than their own people of color. As Senator Eastland of Mississippi put it, "What the people of this country must realize is that the white race is a superior race, and the Negro race is an inferior race." Even Myrdal conceded that white people in the South "do not see the handwriting on the wall. They do not study the impending changes; they live in the pathetic illusion that the matter is settled."[12]

Firm in their dedication to Jim Crow, white Southerners like Eastland resisted efforts for desegregation—or mixing, as they often called it. Violence, of course, was their ultimate weapon. Lynchings of blacks, while declining in number during the 1940s, remained an ever-present threat. There were sixteen such lynchings officially recorded between 1941 and 1945, and six more in 1946 alone—a sign, some thought, that southern whites proposed to stamp out all traces of postwar black militancy.[13] Most whites in the South feared that mixing would lead to a world in which black men might challenge white domination of life, including decent jobs. Worse, the blacks might socialize or have sex with white women. One white minister asked, "Do black birds intermingle with the blue birds? Does the redwing fly with the crows? Would it make sense to mix Black Angus cattle with . . . pure-bred Herefords?" An Alabama state senator exclaimed that the goal of desegregationists was "to open the bedroom doors of our white women to black men."[14]

The extremes to which such thinking had moved shook the Supreme Court in 1950, when it considered the case of Elmer Henderson, a black man who had brought suit in 1943 against segregated facilities in the Southern Railway's dining cars. At that time it was common practice in the South to draw a curtain across the dining car near the kitchen and set up a table behind it. Blacks who wished to eat would be served behind the curtain. If whites filled their (larger) portion of the car, the curtain would be pulled back, and they would be seated in the "black" section. Blacks who then arrived in the car had to wait until these white people had finished dining, at which point the curtain would be drawn again and they could sit down and eat. "It was as if you were a pig or some kind of animal," Henderson's attorney complained. The Court was unanimous in striking down this practice. Henceforth, it ordered, segregated dining facilities on interstate trains were not to be allowed; everyone who wished to eat in the diner must be free to sit wherever there was space.[15]

For many whites, the very idea of desegregated schools prompted the ugliest imaginable images of racial mixing. No one expressed this feeling more clearly than Herbert Ravenel Sass, a South Carolinian, in the *Atlantic Monthly* in 1956:

> To suppose that, proclaiming the virtual identity of the races, we can promote all other degrees of race mixing but stop short of interracial mating is—if I may use an overworked but vivid simile—like going over Niagara Falls in a barrel in the expectation of stopping three fourths of the way down. The South is now the great bulwark against intermarriage. A very few years of thoroughly integrated schools would produce larger numbers of indoctrinated young Southerners free from all "prejudice" against mixed matings.[16]

Confronted with such a wall of racism, activist blacks in the South— many of them members of militant local chapters of the NAACP— countered by staging voter registration drives and rallying against police brutality. Many (in the North as well as the South) concentrated in the late 1940s on uniting with whites in labor unions. This effort seemed especially promising at the time, because strong, interracial unions had the potential—or so it appeared—to promote an economic and political base for liberal racial policies. These and other assertive acts helped to nourish the roots of civil rights activity that blossomed into a mass movement in later years. But employers mounted strong drives against unions, often tarring them with the brush of communism. And white working-class Americans, like other whites, more often than not proved to be unreliable allies of blacks. After all, only the caste system of Jim Crow separated many poor whites from the masses of poor blacks. As so often in the history of American race relations, the race card trumped the card of class.[17]

For all these reasons, most blacks tended to act cautiously in the late 1940s. The vast majority of black soldiers (unlike Evers or Jackie Robinson, a well-educated officer who dared to protest against discrimination) had sullenly abided segregation in the military—there was little they could do about it. When black soldiers returned to the South in 1945, they knew that they would encounter the same unyielding system of race relations that they had endured prior to the war. Many, fearful of seeming "uppity" to whites, put on civilian dress before going back to their homes. The story is told of a black soldier about to be mustered out near his home town of Starkville, Mississippi. His father went to the army camp and told him to dress in civilian clothing. He warned his son that if he had any photos of white women in his wallet, he would be killed.[18]

Thus it was that a cadre of black leaders like Thurgood Marshall—not black masses—tended to dominate the strategies that were employed into the early 1950s to promote change in southern race relations. These leaders, too, acted carefully, relying primarily on legal campaigns that were unavoidably slow. By the late 1940s, Marshall was thinking seriously about confronting segregation head-on. But many other black leaders in local NAACP branches resisted such a move. Some of them could not imagine that the white-dominated courts would support any significant transformation in racial mores. Others fretfully wondered: what would desegregation of schools really mean in practice? And still others, notably teachers, worried that desegregation would destroy black institutions, including schools. The NAACP, they said, should contest inequality, not segregation. It should push to ensure the "equal" part of "separate-but-equal." Not until 1950, after much debate within the NAACP, did Marshall dare to demand the demolition of Jim Crow in the schools.[19]

Advocates such as Marshall also had difficulty arousing active backing from white Northerners. Public opinion polls, to be sure, seemed to reveal steadily increasing support among northern whites for liberal policies concerning race: in 1942, 40 percent of white people in the North believed that "white students and Negro students should go to the same schools"; by 1956, 61 percent thought so. (In the South, 2 percent of whites thought so in 1942, 15 percent in 1956.) But opinions were one thing, actions another. In fact, most white Northerners ignored widespread discrimination in their midst. Imagining that only the South had a "race problem," they concluded that Southerners, not the federal government, ought to deal with it. Periodic Gallup polls since 1935 had asked people what they considered to be the "most vital issue" of the day. Until 1956, no more than 4 percent ever answered race relations. Civil rights, Truman's initiatives notwithstanding, was not a central issue in American electoral politics until the 1960s.[20]

Blacks were quick to recognize and to resent such hypocrisy. Zora Neale Hurston wrote in 1943, "I laughed to myself watching northerners, after saying to Negro individuals how distressed they were about the awful conditions down South, trying to keep Negroes from too close a contact with themselves. . . . in some instances, the South is kinder than the North. Then the North adds the insult of insincerity to its coldness." In 1953 the novelist James Baldwin described the racism that he encountered in New Jersey and Manhattan in the 1940s as being like "some dread, chronic disease, the unfailing symptom of which is a kind of blind fever, a pounding in the skull and fire in the bowels." He added, "There is not a Negro alive who does not have rage in his blood."[21]

Outbursts such as these lead the historian to pose what may seem a heretical question: given the Negrophobia of many whites, and the rage of many blacks, why strive to mix the races, especially in the schools? Might it have been better for reformers instead to demand an end to racial inequality, rather than of segregation? Why not press the courts to enforce—à la *Plessy*—facilities for blacks that were truly equal? Several southern states, finally seeing a little of the handwriting on the wall, were in fact taking frightened steps to improve black schools during the early 1950s. They were far readier, it was clear, to move against educational inequality than they were to consider desegregation.

Hurston was not the only black person who worried about the wisdom of combating desegregation. W. E. B. Du Bois, who had long spoken against racism, also had harbored doubts, notably expressed in a controversial essay in 1935, "Does the Negro Need Separate Schools?" In answering his question, Du Bois admitted that "no general and inflexible rule can be laid down." "Theoretically the Negro needs neither segregated schools nor mixed schools. What he needs is Education." But Du Bois, a founder of the NAACP in 1909 and until the 1930s a forceful crusader for integration, had become disillusioned and edged on this issue toward black separatism. "Race prejudice in the United States," he wrote, "is such that most Negroes cannot receive proper education in white institutions." He added:

> A separate Negro school, where children are treated like human beings, trained by teachers of their own race, who know what it means to be black . . . is infinitely better than making our boys and girls doormats to be spit and trampled upon and lied to by ignorant social climbers, whose sole claim to superiority is ability to kick "niggers" when they are down.[22]

Neither in 1935 nor later did Du Bois's ideas about schools command majority support among black leaders. The NAACP stayed committed to a desegregated society. Later leaders such as the Reverend Martin Luther King, Jr., who was far and away the most revered black spokesman during his lifetime, not only demanded the end of Jim Crow; he also dared to dream of interracial harmony. Du Bois's essay nonetheless articulated a stubbornly persistent minority view, one that seemed especially attractive to many blacks during periods of rising interracial tension. They were sure that blacks in mixed schools dominated by whites would always be looked down on and made to feel inferior. Many children would be miserable.[23]

Advocates of desegregated schools, however, retorted—then and later—with formidable replies. Yes, they said, there were a number of very excellent, academically rigorous black schools—in Washington, among other places. They emphasize, however, that most black children living in the South and border states before 1954 did not have a *choice* between racially segregated and desegregated public schools. The children were required to attend all-black schools in parts of twenty-one states, and everywhere in the South.[24] The system, moreover, was not only segregated; it also featured glaring inequalities in spending per pupil, facilities, and the training of teachers—indeed, in every way. In part because of such inequality and in part because of widespread poverty among blacks, African-American parents were much more likely than white parents to pull their children out of school at a young age. As late as 1940 the median number of years of schooling for blacks age twenty-five or older in the segregating states and the District of Columbia was five, as opposed to 8.5 for whites.[25] Perhaps one-fourth of American blacks at the time were functionally illiterate. "Separate-but-*equal*" remained a far-off dream before 1954, especially in the Deep South.

Many liberal crusaders for change in the late 1940s, moreover, were losing interest in seeking separate-but-really-equal. Some concluded that equality was simply impossible to achieve so long as Jim Crow persisted. Others believed that racial mixing—especially in the schools and in the armed forces—promoted tolerance. Still others thought that bringing black children into classroom contact with white children from better educational backgrounds would improve the academic performance of the blacks, which was far below that of white students in a variety of ways. Reformers argued also that segregated schools cut blacks off from valuable networks that whites enjoyed, thereby worsening job discrimination and poverty.

Proponents of desegregated schools pressed many other points. Jim Crow in education, they emphasized, violated constitutional guarantees (in the Fourteenth Amendment) of equal protection under the law. It also deprived black parents of a basic right: to send their children to neighborhood schools, including schools that were predominantly white, if they so wished. Critics of Jim Crow further stressed that whites had erected a segregated and discriminatory system with the deliberate intent not only of preventing interracial contact but also of keeping black people in servile positions. "When they [blacks] learn to spell dog and cat," whites said, "they throw away the hoe."[26]

Schools for black people were especially bad—indeed primitive—in many rural regions. Sunflower County, Mississippi, a cotton plantation region (where Senator Eastland owned thousands of acres), had no high school for blacks. In the elementary grades of the county's black schools, many of the teachers worked primarily as cooks or domestics on the plantations. Most had no more than a fourth-grade education themselves. Mae Bertha Carter, who was to become a stubborn champion of integrated schools in the area during the 1960s, remembered growing up in the 1930s on one of these plantations, near Drew, Mississippi. A sharecropper's child, she was expected to tend to the cotton and was allowed to go to her elementary school only in the three winter months when there was relatively little for a child to do in the fields. Her fourth-grade teacher, who did not understand mathematical fractions, coped with forty to fifty children at a time. Mae Bertha left school after the fifth grade, scantily educated but with a lifelong passion to do better for her own children. Most southern whites, regarding education of blacks as a waste of time, had no interest in reforming this system. "A million years from now," they said, "a nigger will still be a nigger in the South."[27]

Many city schools for blacks in the South were little better. In Atlanta

Schools for black children were primitive in many parts of the segregated South. *(Library of Congress, Prints and Photographs Division, New York World-Telegram & Sun Collection)*

during the 1940s, overcrowding in black elementary schools led to double sessions that limited children to three hours per day. Many black children roved the streets during the rest of the time. In the 1948–49 school year, the average investment per pupil in Atlanta public school facilities was $228.05 for blacks, $570 for whites. In 1949–50 there was an average of 36.2 black children per classroom, compared to an average of 22.6 among whites. Only after 1950, when the NAACP brought suit against segregation, did worried city and school officials build new facilities so as to claim that they were meeting the constitutional principle of separate-but-truly-equal. Disgusted blacks called these hastily constructed buildings "Supreme Court schools."[28]

In these ways, school segregation was indeed a major component of a larger conspiracy of white supremacy that attempted to suppress a whole category of people. It stigmatized blacks, as Justice Harlan had said in *Plessy,* with a "badge of inferiority." The system of segregated schools, like the broader institution of Jim Crow that pervaded the South, made all white people complicit in a wickedness that was deliberate, and it fostered rising resentment and anger among black people.

Racial segregation—and the inequality that had long been associated with it—was an evil for people of all colors.[29]

The man who took the lead in litigating against this evil, Thurgood Marshall, turned forty-two in 1950, the year that he and his team of attorneys decided to challenge segregation head-on. Tall and sturdy— around six-feet-two and 200 pounds—he had thick, wavy black hair combed straight back and a narrow, triangular moustache. Some people mistook him for Representative Adam Clayton Powell, Jr., the light-skinned Negro politician who represented a Harlem district for many years in the postwar era.[30]

Marshall had grown up in West Baltimore, raised by proud and hard-working parents of mixed racial background. Some of his ancestors had been slaves. By the standards of black America, Marshall's family was middle class. His father had been a dining car waiter for the New York Central railroad and then served as head steward of an all-white yacht club on Chesapeake Bay; his mother was an elementary school teacher in an all-black school. Attending the Colored High and Training School, Marshall learned from experience what inequality meant. The school had no library, cafeteria, auditorium, or gym. A tiny brick-paved yard in the back served as a playground. Crowding was so great that the school had to run half-day sessions. Marshall did well as a student, and then went to Lincoln University in nearby Pennsylvania, which had a black student body and a white faculty. Resentfully giving up hope of attending the University of Maryland Law School—it excluded blacks— he went to Howard University Law School in Washington, D.C.

For Marshall, as well as for many other blacks who advanced in the practice of law after 1930, Howard provided an invaluable education. Led by Charles Houston, its passionate, demanding dean, the school maintained high educational standards. Marshall idolized Houston, who saw litigation as the key to better civil rights for black people. "It all started with Charlie," he said later. When he graduated as a star student in 1933, he went to work as counsel for the Baltimore branch of the NAACP. In 1936 he moved to New York as assistant to Houston, who was then national counsel for the NAACP. Two years later, when Houston returned to private practice, Marshall took over the top job. He was then only thirty years old. The next year he helped found the NAACP Legal Defense and Educational Fund. The LDF, or the "Inc. Fund," or

"Fund," as it was often called, shared office space with the NAACP in New York City but was largely autonomous after 1941. It formally separated from the NAACP in 1957. Under Marshall, the Fund led an increasingly focused attack on racial discrimination.[31]

Some of the more urbane black attorneys who worked under Marshall in these years considered him to be a bit earthy for their taste. Although he ordinarily talked with a gentle southern accent and in refined language, he could switch on a "Rastus" dialect at the drop of a hat. ("Axe" for "ask," "substantual" for "substantial," lots of double negatives and "deses" and "dats.") Other assistants, such as his impatient top aide, Robert Carter, urged him to move more rapidly against racial segregation. Franklin Williams, another assistant, remembered that Marshall "knew where cases had to move, which ones would and should move, and how to move them, but more often than not cases were undertaken reluctantly. Thurgood had to be convinced of victory beyond a reasonable doubt before he said yes."

Notwithstanding such differences over tactics, these and other assistants deeply admired Marshall and gave him the kind of loyalty needed in an organization like the shakily funded, thinly staffed Defense Fund. Appreciating the enormous, highly expensive task of challenging Jim Crow, they understood that they had to pick cases very carefully. Plaintiffs must be responsible, upright, steadfast local citizens, preferably people who had jobs (as Pullman porters, or federally protected mailmen, for instance) that shielded them a little from white retaliation. Marshall also stressed the importance of bringing suits in communities where there was substantial support among local blacks—and, if possible, where there were some home-grown black lawyers who might help the "outsiders" from the Fund in New York.

Marshall's fellow lawyers especially admired the skill that he displayed as a listener during preparatory meetings that fashioned courtroom strategies. Williams recalled, "He had great success in picking people's brains and manipulating them in the interests of a cause. He'd get a lot of outside lawyers together in a room, and he'd be talking and laughing and drinking along with the rest of them and getting everybody relaxed and open, and he'd seem to be having such a good time with them that you wouldn't think he was listening. But after they'd left, there it all was—he'd had the benefit of all their brains, which was his strategy in the first place."

Marshall was particularly skilled at maintaining morale among his co-workers—not an easy task given the obstacles they faced. "I never had so much fun in my life," one top-level attorney remembered of the long and otherwise exhausting strategy sessions that Marshall conducted in preparing for *Brown*. A gifted raconteur, Marshall enjoyed engaging in repartee with his fellow lawyers, who had fun calling him "No good" and "Turkie." He often relied on humor, some of it calculated to shock white lawyers. When leading a discussion of the Supreme Court's power to rule in the segregation cases, he leaned forward and acted as if he were addressing the judges in court: "White bosses, you can do *any*thing you want 'cause you got de power." On another occasion he jolted Alfred Kelly, a white professor of history, by playfully turning to a secretary at the Fund and asking if she had forgotten who "de H.N." was around there. "H.N.," Kelly learned in surprise, stood for "Head Nigger."[32]

While use of the word "nigger" bothered some of the attorneys with the Fund, they also understood that this was Marshall's manner—a way, perhaps, of relieving tensions. Moreover, he had a common touch that endeared him to people, especially the southern blacks who endangered their livelihoods and sometimes their lives to sign on as plaintiffs against racist practices. These were the people to whom Marshall often spoke in black dialect. They knew also that Marshall himself was risking his life. By the late 1940s he was traveling thousands of miles a year in the South, where he was careful not to violate Jim Crow practices. "I've got back trouble, you know," he said. "A big yellow stripe down the middle."[33] His courage, his legal expertise, and his common touch made him known as "Mr. Civil Rights" by 1950. *marshall*

Marshall and others undertook many kinds of cases between 1939, when the Fund was founded, and the early 1950s. At the end of 1951, for instance, they were involved in twenty elementary and high school segregation cases, a dozen higher education cases, five in housing, five against white-run railway and bus companies, a half dozen in recreation (mainly against segregated golf courses), one voting case, two battles over discriminatory teachers' salaries, a huge number of courts martial, and eleven major criminal cases. Jack Greenberg, a young attorney with the Fund, said later of these criminal matters, "Those with a sex factor loomed large, partly because of the death penalty for rape. Southern irrationality about interracial sex made all such charges suspect."[34]

Suits involving public education held center stage at Fund headquarters. As early as 1931, the NAACP had decided to concentrate on such cases, with the hope of piling up precedents that would ultimately better the lot of black students in the segregating states. Several considerations prompted adoption of this key decision, which many years later meant that high profile *school* segregation cases were among the first to reach the level of the Supreme Court. First, it made sense to aim at discrimination in public, not private facilities, which thanks to constitutional precedents were presumed to be safer from legal attack. The Fourteenth Amendment to the Constitution, ratified in 1868 during the era of Reconstruction, stipulated that states—public bodies—should not make or enforce laws abridging the "privileges or immunities" of United States citizens. Further, a state must not deprive any person of "life, liberty, or property, without due process of law; nor deny to any person within its jurisdiction the equal protection of the laws."

Relying heavily on the Fourteenth Amendment, the NAACP—and later the Fund—aimed first at racist practices in publicly supported graduate and professional schools. Here the discrimination was especially glaring. Other than Howard's, there was only one accredited medical school for blacks in the South—Meharry in Nashville—as opposed to twenty-nine for whites, and only one provisionally accredited law school, as opposed to forty for whites. Nowhere in the South could a black person study for a doctorate. Racially discriminatory law schools, NAACP leaders thought, were especially promising targets, mainly because white judges knew from their personal experience as students what a good law school had to have in the way of facilities and professors. Marshall especially hoped that southern states, if forced in time to set up separate-but-truly-equal black law and professional schools, might balk at the high cost of well-supported dual institutions and consolidate instead.[35]

In the 1930s and 1940s Marshall and his allies did not challenge the "separate" part of the separate-but-equal test established by *Plessy* in 1896. Such a strategy, of course, would have targeted segregation itself—an institutionalized system so well entrenched as to seem impregnable at that time. Instead, the NAACP tried to make segregating states live up to the "equal" part of separate-but-equal.

In quest of such equality, the NAACP concentrated its efforts between 1936 and 1938 in support of Lloyd Gaines, a graduate in 1935 of Missouri's state-supported black college, Lincoln University, who then applied for admission to the University of Missouri Law School. The university refused, rejecting him solely on the grounds of his race. It offered instead to set up a separate "law school" for him at Lincoln or to pay any tuition in excess of what he would have been charged if he had enrolled at the University of Missouri, so that he might attend a law school in an adjacent state that would take him. At the time, law schools in Kansas, Nebraska, Iowa, and Illinois accepted out-of-state black graduates. Refusing to tolerate such an arrangement, Gaines sued to compel the University of Missouri to admit him.[36]

The *Gaines* case, like many that the NAACP handled, was expensive, time-consuming, and frustrating. Lower courts supported Missouri's discriminatory actions. In December 1938, however, the Supreme Court decided, six to two, in Gaines's favor. Writing for the majority, Chief Justice Charles Evans Hughes said that "a privilege has been created for white students which is denied to Negroes by reason of their race." Gaines, he added, "was entitled to the equal protection of the laws, and the State was bound to furnish him within its borders facilities for legal education" that were equal to those offered to whites.

This was an encouraging victory for the principle of separate-but-truly-equal—one that foes of discrimination frequently cited in later lawsuits. But Missouri then began to set up what was plainly an ill-funded, inferior law school for blacks, thereby forcing the NAACP to resume the fight. At this point, early in 1939, Gaines simply disappeared from view, never to surface again. No one knew then—or later—what happened to him. Some thought that he had been murdered, others that he had become miffed at the NAACP and accepted a bribe to disappear. Whatever the truth, the NAACP no longer had a plaintiff and had to drop its efforts. This was a sad ending to several years of expensive litigation. It was also testimony to the formidable difficulties that stood in the way of legal strategies against Jim Crow.

Marshall and his colleagues nonetheless kept trying, and they were finally rewarded in June 1950—twelve years after *Gaines*—when the Supreme Court again ruled in their favor in two more higher education cases.[37] The first backed the efforts of Heman Sweatt, a Houston mail carrier who had been rejected on racial grounds in 1946 when he sought admission to the state's all-white law school. Instead, the state set up a poorly supported "law school" for blacks in a basement. Sweatt fought back, not only against the state of Texas but also, over time, against briefs filed in support of Texas by eleven southern and border states. After litigation in four different courts, Marshall pleaded Sweatt's case before a packed Supreme Court chamber in April 1950. In June the

Heman Sweatt, the Negro mail carrier who brought suit in the 1940s against segregated law school education in Texas. *(Library of Congress, Prints and Photographs
Division, New York World-Telegram & Sun Collection, 1950 photo)*

Supreme Court held unanimously that it could not "find substantial
equality in the educational facilities offered white and Negro law students by the state." Because Sweatt had no chance of an equal legal
education in the state's pathetically inadequate law school for blacks, he
was ordered admitted to the University of Texas Law School. This was
the first time that the Court had told a state to admit a black person to
an all-white educational institution.

On the same day the Court also supported the quest of George
McLaurin, a sixty-eight-year-old black teacher who had applied in 1948
to get a doctorate in education at the all-white University of Oklahoma.
The state reluctantly admitted him in 1949 but forced him to remain in
an anteroom off the regular classrooms where course work was given. In
the library he was made to sit at a segregated desk behind a pile of
newspapers in the mezzanine. In the cafeteria he had to eat in a dingy
alcove by himself and at a different hour from the whites. McLaurin
testified that it was "quite strange and humiliating to be placed out in

that position, and it handicaps me in doing effective work." The Court agreed. It decided unanimously that Oklahoma's actions "impair and inhibit [McLaurin's] ability to study, to engage in discussion and exchange views with other students, and, in general, to learn his profession."[38]

For the Fund these were heartening decisions, the more so because the Court also ruled on that day, in the *Henderson* case, against segregated dining on interstate trains. Moreover, the Truman administration's solicitor general, Philip Pearlman, had backed the Fund by filing a brief as a "friend of the court" in these cases. The way now seemed clear for the Fund to fight against racial discrimination not only in graduate and professional schools but also across the board. Even more encouraging to Marshall was the Court's reasoning, especially in *Sweatt*. In defending their exclusion of Sweatt from the white law school, Texas officials maintained that its new black law school had equal facilities. It had comparable floor space, and it gave blacks access to the state law library. The Court, however, rejected this narrow approach to "facilities" and "equality" and listed a number of other assets, some of them intangible, that the black school lacked. Black students, for instance, were denied contact with white law students and professors; they had no well-established alumni to turn to for placement; they would earn a law degree far less prestigious than whites received at their school. With reasoning such as this the Court was all but saying that racially separate law schools within a state *could not be* equal. Recognizing this thrust, Marshall wrote a friend, "All three of the decisions are replete with road markings telling us where to go next."[39]

But Marshall moved cautiously. After all, the cases had taken years— since 1943 in the *Henderson* case. During Sweatt's four-year battle for admission to the UT Law School he had no choice but to continue working as a mailman. McLaurin, a dignified, experienced educator, had been humiliated. More important, Chief Justice Fred Vinson, a Kentucky moderate, and his colleagues on the Court were well aware of the political implications of what they were doing. Vinson couched the opinions in careful language chosen so as to call for truly equal education only at the graduate level and so as not to offend southern sensibilities. Indeed, the decisions sustained *Plessy v. Ferguson*, which had established the constitutionality of separate-but-equal racial segregation.

The *Sweatt* and *McLaurin* decisions, moreover, did not have a large impact. Texas admitted Sweatt, who had to deal with intimidation from

George McLaurin, a black graduate student in education, sits in a segregated anteroom at the University of Oklahoma, 1948. *(Library of Congress, Prints and Photographs Division, New York World-Telegram & Sun Collection)*

whites. A cross was burned next to his car, and his tires were slashed. He became ill and flunked out. The school took in only a handful of black students later in the 1950s. And the decisions did not change much else, for the segregating states maintained their barriers. Undergraduate education was unaffected. While several southern states, notably South Carolina, embarked on crash programs to improve black public schools, none even considered plans for gradual desegregation. If Marshall expected to ensure full equality under such segregated circumstances, he faced the task of arguing case after case in state after state. This could take forever and bankrupt the Fund.

Considering this gloomy prospect, Marshall and others understandably considered sailing off on a different tack: litigating to overturn segregation itself. In many ways, of course, this was an alluring course, especially because true equality within a Jim Crow system was impossible. But targeting segregation continued to be frightening as well, especially for the black principals, teachers, coaches, and other school employees who might lose their jobs if Jim Crow in education were to be abolished. (Contending with blacks of this persuasion, Marshall observed, "the easy part of the job is fighting the white folks.") It also seemed likely that a challenge against segregation would take years before being heard or decided by the High Court. And what if the challenge were to fail? The Court, badly divided on many issues in 1950, might reject his arguments, thereby reaffirming *Plessy* and further solidifying the constitutionality of segregated facilities. For Marshall and his fellow advocates in 1950, a fateful choice lay ahead.[40]

2

THE GRASS ROOTS AND
STRUGGLING LAWYERS

Marshall did not in fact wait long after *Sweatt* and *McLaurin* to make up his mind to fight segregation. Following debates with lawyers and NAACP state branch presidents in June 1950, he took the fateful step: to challenge the constitutionality of racially segregated public schools. In October the board of the NAACP dropped its emphasis on achieving equality within segregated education and supported Marshall. Henceforth, "pleading in all education cases . . . should be aimed at obtaining education on a non-segregated basis and . . . no relief other than that will be acceptable." The die had been cast that led to *Brown* in May 1954.[1]

What else besides the determination of Marshall and his board accounts for such a historic shift in strategy?

We cannot look to pressure from the majority of white people for an answer. Many in the North, to be sure, opposed Jim Crow in the South. But most white Americans in 1950, as in the past, did not much bestir themselves to better the plight of blacks. Liberal politicians, too, had other priorities. At the very time that Marshall was meeting with the branch presidents, North Korean soldiers were pouring across the thirty-eighth parallel and threatening to overrun South Korea. Soon the Truman administration committed American soldiers to desperate fighting on that far-off peninsula. At the same time, Truman struggled to combat ever-escalating charges by Senator Joseph McCarthy and others that he was sheltering communists in government. Korea and "McCarthyism" pushed the Cold War into an ever more frigid stage and dominated

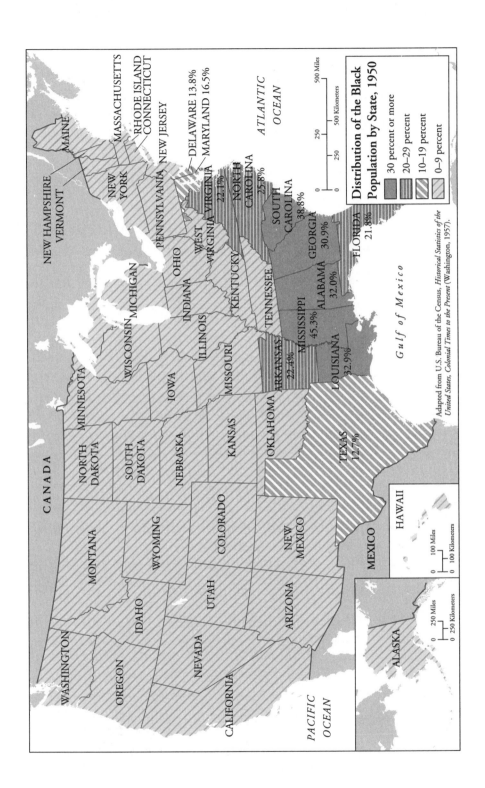

Distribution of the Black Population by State, 1950

30 percent or more
20–29 percent
10–19 percent
0–9 percent

Adapted from U.S. Bureau of the Census, *Historical Statistics of the United States, Colonial Times to the Present* (Washington, 1957).

CANADA

NEW HAMPSHIRE
VERMONT
MAINE
MASSACHUSETTS
RHODE ISLAND
CONNECTICUT
NEW JERSEY
NEW YORK
PENNSYLVANIA
DELAWARE 13.8%
MARYLAND 16.5%
VIRGINIA 22.1%
NORTH CAROLINA 25.8%
SOUTH CAROLINA 38.8%
GEORGIA 30.9%
FLORIDA 21.8%
ALABAMA 32.0%
MISSISSIPPI 45.3%
TENNESSEE
KENTUCKY
WEST VIRGINIA
OHIO
INDIANA
ILLINOIS
MICHIGAN
WISCONSIN
MINNESOTA
NORTH DAKOTA
SOUTH DAKOTA
NEBRASKA
IOWA
MISSOURI
KANSAS
ARKANSAS 22.4%
LOUISIANA 32.9%
OKLAHOMA
TEXAS 12.7%
COLORADO
WYOMING
MONTANA
NEW MEXICO
ARIZONA
UTAH
NEVADA
IDAHO
WASHINGTON
OREGON
CALIFORNIA

ATLANTIC OCEAN
Gulf of Mexico
PACIFIC OCEAN
MEXICO

HAWAII
ALASKA

500 Miles
250
0
500 Kilometers
250
0

100 Miles
0
100 Kilometers
0

250 Miles
0
250 Kilometers
0

domestic politics for many years. Civil rights could not easily compete with the Cold War.

We can look instead to the evolution by 1950 of lawsuits concerning schools that Marshall and his colleagues had earlier initiated. Most of the black plaintiffs in these suits were badly educated and desperately poor. Scattered, they were some years away from mobilizing into anything like a movement. What most of them wanted in the late 1940s was not integration, but equality of opportunity.[2] Here and there they had been agitating openly to get better schools for their children. "Without the schools," one parent said, "there was no way to break out." Having encouraged such efforts, Marshall was in a position by 1950 to transform litigation against inequality into suits attacking segregation.[3]

No case loomed larger than the one that the Reverend Albert Joseph DeLaine and other black people in Clarendon County, South Carolina, had been urging since 1947. DeLaine, the eighth of fourteen children, had grown up in the area, where as a boy he had had to walk ten miles round-trip to school. By 1947 he and his wife, both schoolteachers, lived in the small community of Summerton, near the southern end of the county, where their three children attended the local black schools. Like other black children, they still had no school buses. Most black children in the area, sons and daughters of poor farmers, left school by the fifth or sixth grades. A survey in 1938—the last time one had been done—revealed that 35 percent of blacks over ten years of age in the county were illiterate.[4]

As a preacher, a teacher, and a parent, Delaine had long been angered by racism. In March 1948 he persuaded Levi Pearson, a farmer and a parent with three children in the local black schools, to bring a suit that asked local authorities for relatively little: buses to carry their children to school. The brief, developed by Marshall and others, targeted racial inequality, not segregation. It demanded that the court issue a permanent injunction "forever restraining and enjoining the defendants . . . from making a distinction on account of race or color" in providing free bus transportation for white children while denying it to blacks.

Pearson got nowhere in 1948. When it was discovered that he lived just across the district line from the jurisdiction where he had entered the suit, his case was thrown out. One white observer snickered, "Our niggers don't even know where they live." It was then that Pearson could not find a white farmer who would lend him a harvester to bring in his

The Rev. Joseph DeLaine and his wife, Mattie. *(Library of Congress, Prints and Photographs Division, New York World-Telegram & Sun Collection, 1966 photo)*

crop. He was helpless as his beans and oats and wheat rotted in the fields.

DeLaine, Pearson, and others did not give up. Working with Marshall, who went south to help them, they agreed in 1949 on a bolder strategy. This involved getting twenty plaintiffs—evidence of significant local solidarity—to support a suit that went well beyond buses. It demanded equal treatment across the board: in transportation, buildings, teachers' salaries, and educational materials. The discrepancies between white and black schools, the plaintiffs asserted, were in patent violation of the Fourteenth Amendment to the Constitution. It was difficult at first to find people who would sign on—retaliation from whites was sure to be swift. But some came forward. "We ain't asking for anything that belongs to these white folks," one parent explained. "I just mean to get for that little black boy of mine everything that every other white boy in South Carolina gets—I don't care if he's as white as the drippings of snow." By November 1949, DeLaine and his allies had the twenty names. Their suit was called *Briggs v. Elliott*—after Harry Briggs, the plaintiff whose name topped the twenty in alphabetical order, and Roderick Elliott, the white chairman of the local school district. Revised in 1951 to challenge segregation, it later became one of the five suits known collectively as *Brown v. Board of Education.*

The petitioners adduced compelling evidence. During the school year 1949–50, Clarendon County spent $149 per white child in the public schools, as opposed to $43 for each black child. The total value of the sixty-one black schools, attended by 6,531 students, was listed officially as $194,575; the value of the twelve white schools, accommodating 2,375 students, was placed at $673,850. The schools for whites were generally built of brick or stucco and enjoyed abundant teaching supplies. More than half of those for blacks were ramshackle shanties in which one or two teachers had only the most rudimentary instructional materials.

Early in 1951, when the *Briggs* case finally reached the level of federal district court, Matthew Whitehead, a Howard University professor of education, inspected the schools in District No. 22 of the county. His report to the Legal Defense and Educational Fund captured these inequities in greater detail. Class sizes were significantly larger in the district's three schools for blacks (which accommodated 808 students) than in the two for whites (with 276 children). At the white elementary school, teachers handled an average of twenty-eight students per class; at the two elementary schools for blacks, they dealt with an average of forty-seven. In addition to the courses offered at both high schools, the curriculum at the high school for whites included biology, typing, and bookkeeping; the black high school offered as extras only agriculture and home economics.

One of the two "colored" grade schools lacked running water; the other had no electricity. Both white schools had flush toilets, but the three black schools had none—only outhouses. The black schools had no janitorial services—cleanup was a chore for black teachers and the children. Pupils at these schools got their drinking water not from fountains, as in the white schools, but from dippers in open buckets. The black schools did without auditoria, gymnasia, and instruction in the arts. One of them lacked desks. And the black children still had no school buses. Whitehead discovered that two six-year-old first-graders walked a round-trip of ten miles each day to get to school.[5]

Well before 1951, when Whitehead wrote his report, most of the petitioners suffered for their daring. Briggs was fired from his job of fourteen years as a gas station attendant. "After the petition was signed," Briggs remembered, "I knew it was different. The white folks got kind of sour. They asked me to take my name off the petition. My boss, he said did I know what I was doin' and I said, 'I'm doin' it for the benefit of my children.' He didn't say nothin' back. But then later—it was the day before Christmas—he gave me a carton of cigarettes and then he let me go. He said, 'Harry, I want me a *boy*—and I can pay him less than you.'"[6]

Many of the other petitioners also paid a price for their boldness. Briggs's wife Liza (who had not signed) was given a week's notice and dropped from her job as a chambermaid at a nearby motel. She had been employed there for six years. DeLaine's wife and nieces lost their teaching jobs. Others on the list of twenty were fired, denied credit, told to pay up debts at once or be foreclosed. DeLaine received threatening letters from people signing themselves "the Ku Klux Klan." In the end, his home was burned down, and he had to flee the state.

The other plaintiffs generally tried to stay in the area—it was where they had roots. The Briggses hung on in the county for four years, struggling to farm twenty acres of rented land while the lawsuits moved slowly toward Washington. After whites cut off his credit at the bank, Briggs had to move twenty-three miles north to get a loan. When the whites there found out who he was, they, too, called in his loan. His experience, like that of others, exposed the uncompromising hostility that many whites in the Deep South displayed when they faced challenges to racial mores.

Briggs's experience also revealed the courage and toughness of black people in places like Clarendon County, which was 70 percent African American in population. In those communities where blacks were in the majority, they could and sometimes did come together and stay together. When the *Briggs* case reached federal district court in Charleston in May 1951, more than 500 blacks from the county packed into cars for the two-hour drive to the city. They crowded into the courtroom, where many of them stood throughout the trial, for they were eager to see for themselves what sort of justice they would get.

Solidarity such as this was one of the unintended results of segregation: blacks often drew special strength from being forced into all-black communities and institutions. As the historian C. Vann Woodward has written of the budding civil rights movement, "the inspiration, the energy, the power, the recruits, and the leaders of the mighty movement against segregation came out of the tightly segregated black communities of the South. The whole thing is inconceivable without these all-black churches, colleges, and schools."[7]

So it was that many black people of Clarendon County refused to bend, and in so refusing helped Marshall and others to litigate. Having waited so long for justice, they became steadily more militant between 1947, when DeLaine first agitated for buses, and 1950. By then they were demanding equality in all aspects of education. More important, they then agreed to fight for desegregated schools, without which, they had come to think, equality was impossible. This was what Marshall, moving along the same path, called for at the trial in Charleston.[8]

The *Briggs* case, while the first to be heard by a federal district court, was just one of five that the Supreme Court decided on May 17, 1954. The other four, concerning Prince Edward County, Virginia; the District of Columbia; Wilmington, Delaware; and Topeka, Kansas, also featured determined black plaintiffs, unyielding opposition from defenders of racial segregation, and prolonged litigation.

Much of the inspiration for the fight against segregation in Virginia came from black high school students at Robert R. Moton High School in Farmville. This was a predominantly rural area in the "Southside" of the state, at the northern end of the great black belt that swept into the Deep South. Moton High, built in 1939, was badly overcrowded. Unlike Farmville High School for whites, it had no gymnasium or cafeteria. There were no locker rooms or showers—or late afternoon buses for those who wanted to play sports or engage in after-school activities. To cope with the crowding, white authorities had attached a few wooden, tarpaper shacks to the main building. These leaked in the rain, and were heated by wood stoves that a black teacher, doubling as a bus driver, set and lighted in the winter months. Nonetheless chilled, the students wore coats indoors on many of the coldest days. The highest paid teacher at Moton received a lower salary than the most poorly paid teacher at Farmville High.[9]

Blacks in the area had long been pressing white authorities to build a new school for blacks. Among them was the Reverend L. Francis Griffin, a four-year Army veteran of World War II (he had served with General George Patton's Negro tank corps). Griffin returned from the war and helped to organize a local branch of the NAACP. Thirty-three years old in 1950, he emerged as a dynamic leader in the struggles over unequal schools that escalated during the 1950–51 school year.

Black high school students took the lead in these struggles, commanded by Barbara Johns, a sixteen-year-old junior at Moton High in 1950. Johns was a member of the chorus, the drama group, the New Homemakers of America, and the student council, all of which had enabled her to see a bit of the world outside Farmville. Her uncle, the Reverend Vernon Johns was pastor of Dexter Avenue Baptist Church in Montgomery, Alabama. He had also helped her widen her intellectual horizons. The Reverend Johns was a learned, irascible, thunderingly eloquent foe of white racist practices in the South.

During the school year, Barbara Johns grew increasingly impatient with the foot-dragging of white authorities, who somehow never seemed to get around to building a better school for blacks, and with the caution of black leaders loath to antagonize whites. Working quietly but effectively with fellow students, she electrified the community on April 23, 1951, by leading 450 students in a strike. While many of the students still hoped for a new school, Johns quickly made it clear that her goal was desegregation. The local branch of the NAACP, which feared the retaliation of whites, was at first reluctant to back the students. But the Reverend Griffin stood passionately by their side, and Johns, a poised and remarkably level-headed teenager, kept the students on their course. The strike lasted two weeks, by which time two lawyers from the Fund had agreed to come to their aid. They were Oliver Hill and Spottswood Robinson III, black graduates of Howard Law School. Hill, who had finished second in his class at Howard in 1933 (Marshall had been first), had led many fights for the NAACP in Virginia, his native state, and became the first black person to serve on the city council of Richmond. Robinson, soft-spoken and light-skinned, was thirty-four years old in 1951 but was already a well-regarded black attorney in Virginia. He was later to become a dean at Howard Law School and then a federal judge.

As in South Carolina, local whites fought back. The black principal of Johns's school, who had had nothing to do with the strike, was fired on the grounds that he had not squelched it. Worried by the threat of litigation, the local school board applied for and received $600,000 from the state to build a new high school for blacks. It was slated to open (and did) in September 1953. But this decision was too little and too late for the students and for Griffin, who gave a rousing speech demanding desegregation. On May 23, a month after Johns had called the strike, Robinson and Hill brought suit. For her own safety, Johns was then sent away by her fearful family to school in Montgomery, Alabama, where she stayed at the home of her uncle, the Reverend Johns.[10]

A driving force behind change in Washington, D.C., was Gardner Bishop, a poorly educated black barber who had grown up in North Carolina before migrating to the big city in 1930. In Washington, the segregated education system supported white schools at a cost of $160 per pupil and black schools at a rate of $121. Save for segregation, Bishop's daughter could have gone to a nearby white junior high school that had hundreds of openings (whites were fleeing to suburbs). Instead, she had to attend an overcrowded black school farther from her home. Black parents in the area grew so angry by 1948 that they supported a strike demanding equal facilities for black children.[11]

Bishop was a tough, class-conscious black man. He resented black elites, whom he found cautious as well as condescending, almost as much as he disliked segregationists. But during the course of the strike he met

Jack Greenberg, a leading lawyer for the Legal Defense and Educational Fund. *(Library of Congress, Prints and Photographs Division, New York World-Telegram & Sun Collection, 1963 photo)*

Charles Houston, Marshall's old mentor, who treated him with respect and brought suit on his behalf for equal facilities. When Houston died in 1950, James Nabrit, Jr., a law professor at Howard, took his place. A native of Atlanta and the top-ranked graduate in his class at Northwestern University Law School, Nabrit was an outspokenly militant member of the Fund's inner circle of advisers. (In the 1960s he became president of Howard.) In early 1951 he filed a new suit in the District of Columbia, carrying the name of *Bolling v. Sharpe*, on behalf of Spottswood Bolling, Jr., and other plaintiffs. Bolling, a twelve-year-old student, had been turned away from a modern school for whites with empty classrooms. Instead, he went to a dingy school for blacks, whose science lab consisted of one Bunsen burner and a bowl of goldfish. The suit said nothing about equalizing schools. Reflecting the new strategy of the NAACP, it challenged segregation itself.[12]

The struggle in Delaware, a border state where Jim Crow was widespread, also owed much to the resolve of black parents. Claymont, nine miles north of the city of Wilmington, barred black students from attending the town's attractive, well-equipped local school. Instead, the children were bused to an old school in Wilmington. Hockessin, a rural village west of the city, provided school buses for white students but not for blacks in its segregated system. This inequality upset Sarah Bulah, a black parent whose daughter Shirley Barbara was not allowed to board a school bus that ran right in front of her house. Sarah Bulah had to drive her daughter two miles each day to and from a one-room schoolhouse that served blacks.[13]

As in South Carolina, Virginia, and Washington, these and other parents turned to lawyers for help. One was Louis Redding, who had graduated in 1923 from Brown University, where he did well enough to be a speaker at his commencement. He earned a scholarship to the Harvard Law School and then broke the color line by being admitted in 1929 as the first black member of the Delaware bar. A short, dignified man, Redding took the lead in legal struggles on behalf of blacks in Delaware during the ensuing twenty years. Joining him in 1949 was a much younger white attorney, Jack Greenberg, who finished law school at Columbia University and went to work for Marshall that year. Greenberg was a determined, no-nonsense, hard-working man who was entirely comfortable among his black colleagues at Fund offices. Only twenty-five years old in 1949, Greenberg stayed with the Fund throughout the 1950s and succeeded Thurgood Marshall as head of it when Marshall became a federal judge in 1962.

In 1950 the team of Redding and Greenberg had already fought and won a case that called on Delaware to desegregate its university system. That was the first time that any white state institution of higher education in the United States—the University of Delaware—had been required by a court order to open its doors to black undergraduates. Early in 1951, five downtown Wilmington movie theaters, bowing to local pressures, also admitted black people for the first time.

By then it seemed possible, in a border state like Delaware, that the public schools, too, might desegregate under legal pressure. Sarah Bulah was ready to fight, but she received little sympathy from other black parents, who did not want trouble, or from her minister, who recalled, "I was for segregation. These folks around here would rather have a colored teacher. They don't want to be mixed up with no white folks." Attitudes such as these—which militants like Griffin, Johns, and Bishop had also encountered—exposed an important reality about American race relations in mid-century America: for a variety of reasons, many black people were cautious about challenging segregation.

Redding and Greenberg eagerly took the cases. Like Marshall in South Carolina, Hill and Robinson in Virginia, and Nabrit in Washington, they did not demand equality across separate systems. Instead, they attacked segregation itself, and in April 1952 they succeeded when Judge Collins Seitz, presiding over Delaware's Chancery Court, decided in their favor. Seitz, only thirty-eight years old, was a Wilmington native who had earlier demanded the desegregation of his alma mater, the University of Delaware. In 1952 he ruled that Shirley Barbara Bulah and ten other black children were entitled to immediate admission to the white schools in their communities. The ruling did not go so far as to say that racial segregation was itself unconstitutional—*Plessy*, after all, was still the law of the land. But the court did maintain that segregation was illegal as practiced, because it failed to provide equality to blacks. The opinion heartened lawyers for the Legal Defense Fund: it was the first time that a court had ordered a segregated white public school to admit black children.

Finally, there was the battle in Topeka. There, race relations were considerably different from those that had given rise to the other four cases. Kansas law permitted cities with populations of 15,000 or more to segregate their elementary schools. Topeka, a city of approximately 100,000 people (7.5 percent of whom were black), still did so in 1951: all twenty-two of its schools (eighteen white, four black) at the elementary level were segregated. Otherwise, Jim Crow had a little less strength than it did in the South. Topeka did not impose a color line in the waiting rooms of its bus and train stations or on its buses. Yet five of its seven movie houses barred black people, a sixth was for blacks, and the seventh admitted blacks to its balcony—"Nigger Heaven," it was called. The park swimming pool was closed to blacks except for one day in the year. A restaurant regularly patronized by the white lawyer who was to handle the *Brown* case on behalf of Topeka featured a sign, "Colored and Mexicans served in sacks only." The nonsegregated high school had racially separate basketball, swimming, wrestling, golf, and tennis teams, as well as separate cheerleading squads and pep clubs. Black students there were discouraged from taking courses in typing and stenography because, they were told, there would be very few jobs for them in such fields when they graduated.[14]

The segregated elementary schools were by almost all accounts equal in facilities. The city, indeed, offered bus transportation to black children, but not to whites, who generally attended schools within walking distance of their homes. For a few white children, this meant paying for public transportation, being driven to school, or walking thirty or more blocks. Linda Brown, the seven-year-old third-grader who became famous as the eldest child of the first-listed plaintiff in *Brown*, her father Oliver Brown, walked six blocks to catch the school bus that drove her to school a mile from her home.

The local people who opposed the city's segregated school system— mostly white and black leaders of the NAACP—agreed that school facilities were not the central issue. They did argue, however, that the system deprived some black children—those who lived (as Linda Brown did) in racially mixed neighborhoods—of access to schools near their homes. Linda, for instance, had to leave home at 7:40 in the morning, walk through dangerous railroad switching yards, and cross Topeka's busiest commercial street to board a bus that took her to school that opened at 9:00. If the city had used a nonsegregated neighborhood-districting system, she might well have attended Sumner School, seven blocks from her home.[15]

When local activists in the NAACP sought people to serve as plaintiffs in a case against this system, they turned to Oliver Brown and other

Linda Brown, in the yard of the all-black Monroe School in Topeka, 1953, when she was ten. *(Carl Iwasaki, Life/Timepix)*

black parents. A quiet, somewhat withdrawn man, Brown was hardly a militant. At first he seemed diffident about the issue. But for NAACP leaders he was a promising plaintiff. Thirty-two years old in 1951, he was a lifelong resident of Topeka and a World War II veteran. He worked as a welder in the shops of the Santa Fe Railroad and served as an assistant pastor and sexton of a local Methodist church. Although he had not taken part in NAACP activities, he came to believe that God approved of his engagement in the case. There was no way that segregationists could paint Oliver Brown as a dangerous radical.

Having secured the involvement of Brown and twelve other plaintiffs, the local NAACP filed suit in federal district court on February 28, 1951.[16] Its action did not arouse great excitement in the city, even among black people. Indeed, when the case was heard in June, many seats remained unoccupied in the courtroom. The passionate engagement of local black people that was so striking in predominantly black Clarendon County was lacking in the different, less thoroughly segregated world of Topeka.

Well before the case was filed, the activists in Topeka had been in close touch with Marshall and others at the Fund, who had high hopes of winning in a border state where race relations were less contentious than in the Deep South. It was not long before Robert Carter, Marshall's right-hand man, Greenberg, and others were on the scene and pressing hard for victory. Carter, a Northerner, a graduate of Lincoln University (Marshall's alma mater) and of Howard Law School, and a veteran of the segregated Army Air Force during World War II, was among the most militant of the top attorneys around Marshall. In 1951 he was eager to make a headlong assault on segregation.

In developing the case during the next few months Carter and others did not rely mainly on utilitarian arguments concerning the length of time that it took children to get to school. They did not even emphasize that racially separate schools, if freely chosen, were necessarily all bad—after all, the facilities in Topeka were not unequal. What was intolerable, they asserted, was that the system of segregation in Topeka was legally required, and that it was enforced. Children who were part of such an officially sanctioned system, they said, were made to feel inferior. And children who felt inferior would necessarily lose motivation to learn.

This argument, drawn from psychological research, was at the core of the Fund's case in Topeka. The court, moreover, accepted it. In June 1951, speaking for a unanimous three-judge court, presiding Judge Walter

Huxman found no violation of *Plessy*. Huxman, a conservative Democrat, had served a term as governor of Kansas in the 1930s. Flinty, impatient with long-winded lawyers in his court, Huxman decided that the black and white schools in Topeka had essentially equal facilities. The principle of separate-but-equal would therefore stand in Topeka's public schools until the High Court overruled itself. But the court attached nine "Findings of Fact" to its opinion. One of these endorsed the psychological theories:

> Segregation of white and colored children in public schools has a detrimental effect upon the colored children. The impact is greater when it has the sanction of the law; for the policy of separating the races is usually interpreted as denoting the inferiority of the Negro group. A sense of inferiority affects the motivation of a child to learn. Segregation with the sanction of law, therefore, has a tendency to retard the educational and mental development of Negro children and to deprive them of some of the benefits they would receive in a racially integrated school system.

Greenberg was certain that Judge Huxman sympathized with his case. "Judge Huxman's decision," he wrote a few days later, "puts the Supreme Court on the spot, and it seems to me that it was purposely written with that end in view." He was correct on both counts. The psychological argument resonated not only with Huxman but also, three years later, with the Supreme Court. For that reason alone, the struggle in Topeka may have merited the top billing that it was ultimately to receive.[17]

These, then, were some of the major players in the drama that culminated in one of the most visible Supreme Court decisions in modern American history. We can generalize a bit about these players and about the ideas that they highlighted in the course of their engagement.

Many of those who stood up to be counted, either as plaintiffs or as agitators for change, had personally experienced the evils of racial segregation and dared to promote collective, legal actions that promised to help others as well as themselves. They included courageous parents, like DeLaine, Pearson, Bishop, Bulah, and Brown, and high school students, like Barbara Johns and her classmates. A few, like DeLaine, Bishop, and Vernon Johns, embraced militant attitudes dating to the mid-1940s. Several—not only DeLaine and Vernon Johns but also L. Francis Griffin—

were motivated as well by religious faith. Their positions as pastors endowed them with an authority that helped them to reach devout black people in the South.

Facing the hostility of white neighbors, most of these plaintiffs were not anxious to become martyrs for a cause. Their demands, such as buses for black children in Clarendon County, South Carolina, or Hockessin, Delaware, were moderate in the beginning. They did not often talk about "civil rights," let alone imagine that they could smack a huge hole in the larger edifice of Jim Crow in the South.

What these and other parents yearned for above all was part of the American Dream: equal opportunities for their children. That is why schools, which as later events indicated were among the toughest of all institutions to desegregate, became some of the fiercest battlegrounds in conflicts between the races in postwar America. Like many white people, the parents and students who engaged in these struggles believed in a central creed of Americans: schools offered the ticket to advancement in life. It was a creed that forced schools to the center of racial turmoil for the remainder of the century.

Until 1950 these parents and their allies most often demanded educational equality, not desegregation: a separate-but-equal system of schools was tolerable if it was truly equal. It was only when they became convinced that whites would never grant equality that they began to call for the dismantling of Jim Crow in the schools. This important strategic shift accelerated with remarkable speed between late 1950, when the NAACP supported such a stand, and mid-1951. All five cases leading to *Brown* were filed within that brief period.

In waging this war, these people knew that they could not triumph by themselves. The changes that they drove from the bottom up had to have help from the top down. Those at the grass roots consistently turned to the only significant organization—one that had ties in many southern communities—that was in a position to help. This was of course the NAACP, and its autonomous arm, the Legal Defense and Educational Fund. The Fund, in turn, had its deepest roots in Howard University Law School, where Charles Houston had set a high standard many years earlier. Marshall, Carter, Hill, Robinson, and many others who litigated the cases had studied there. Nabrit was a professor at the school.

Those who challenged Jim Crow in the schools deserve to be remembered. They were in the vanguard of the most powerful and inspiring social movement of modern American history. It does not take away from their courage, however, to recognize that their cause benefited from one final circumstance: the rigidity of southern opponents in the 1940s and 1950s. If white segregationists had given more ground, some of the blacks who called for change might have accepted, at least for a time, various degrees of accommodation short of total desegregation. Many blacks indeed indicated—even after 1950—that they could manage all right in a world in which separate-but-equal really meant equal. (They did not yearn to mix with whites.) But most southern whites fought back, sometimes violently. Their refusal to compromise revealed that they were oppressive and that they did not care about education for black people. Their unreasonableness highlighted the justice as well as the courage of blacks who dared to oppose them. Their unfairness was central, not only to the chain of events leading to *Brown v. Board of Education*, but also to the more militant civil rights movement of later years.

With the law suits filed in 1951, the local people had done what they could. They relied now on the lawyers, and on the federal district courts, where the cases were soon to be heard. While the attorneys achieved heartening results in Delaware, they suffered defeats in South Carolina, Virginia, the District of Columbia, and Kansas. In none of the five cases, moreover, did the district courts dare to reverse *Plessy*. Separate schools, if equal, remained constitutional. The cases moved up on appeal to the Supreme Court, which scheduled them for oral argument in December 1952.

Led by Marshall, the struggling lawyers gathered for a number of drawn-out, smoke-filled, and often contentious meetings in late 1951 and 1952. At some of these—mostly in the New York City offices of the Fund—fifty-odd people crowded together, a few sitting on tables amid piles of scattered law books. They labored to deal with a range of complex questions that were sure to trouble the Supreme Court. Some of these issues affect race relations a half century later.

One of these concerned the mind and mood of whites in the South. Black leaders at these sessions, having made the choice to challenge segregation itself, hoped that many white Northerners shared their detestation of Jim Crow and that all but the most reactionary of white Southerners would surrender to the inevitable. But was this likely to happen? Harry Ashmore, a liberal journalist with the *Arkansas Gazette* who was invited to some of the meetings, warned them that it was not. Conservatives, he said, were dominant in the South, and they were "a long way from being resigned to the abandonment of segregation in the public schools." Some southern leaders, such as Governor James Byrnes of South Carolina, had already announced that they would move to lessen racial inequality in education by improving black schools. This they did: spending for these schools rose greatly between 1950 and 1954. But Byrnes had also exclaimed that he would sooner close down the state's public schools than accept the mixing of blacks and whites. The Supreme Court, Ashmore insisted, was extraordinarily sensitive to such white feelings. Anticipating unbending white resistance, it was likely to move with great caution rather than deliver a decision that it could not enforce.[18]

In response to such warnings, a few among the lawyers reconsidered their key decision, made in October 1950, to challenge segregation head-on. It might be wiser, they said, to pursue the strategy that had led to the triumphs of *Sweatt* and *McLaurin*. Nabrit, however, helped to squelch such an effort. Citing the legal theorist Roscoe Pound, he stated, "Law makes habits, it does not wait for them to grow." What good, he asked, had caution done in the past? What good would it do in the future, especially if the Supreme Court—then consisting of men named by Roosevelt and Truman—were to become dominated by more conservative justices? Arguments such as these easily carried the day: segregation remained the target.[19]

Given the rising expectations of the lawyers since 1950, it was hardly surprising that Ashmore's warnings fell on deaf ears. Still, he was correct in sensing that NAACP and Fund leaders underestimated the depth of racist attitudes in the United States. Indeed, his concerns were prophetic. District court judges, some of whom were later to brave extraordinary abuse—indeed ostracism—from friends and neighbors who clung to Jim Crow, worried deeply about angry reactions to any decision they might make that would challenge the system of segregated schools in the South. When the Supreme Court first considered the cases in December 1952, it, too, procrastinated, calling instead for a rehearing. This did not occur until a year later. Even then the Court hesitated, issuing its opinion only in May 1954 and postponing its guidelines for implementation until May 1955.

Marshall and his team also struggled to develop convincing arguments concerning the constitutional history of Jim Crow in the schools. This effort called on them to make sense of the intent of the framers of the Civil Rights Act of 1866 and of the Fourteenth Amendment, ratified in 1868. Did these framers, who were advocates of greater racial equality, have schools in mind when they devised the language of the amendment that barred states from abridging citizens of "privileges or immunities?" Were they thinking of schools when they added to the amendment the crucial phrase: "nor shall any State deprive any person of life, liberty, or property, without due process of law; nor deny to any person within its jurisdiction the equal protection of the laws"?[20]

To many hopeful advocates of racial justice in the 1950s, the answer to questions such as these had to be yes: of course the framers had opposed racially segregated schools. Marshall and his fellow lawyers, however, knew that the historical record was more obscure. The framers had preferred to talk in broad generalities and had said almost nothing about schools. Their silence on that subject was hardly surprising, for public education in the United States in the 1860s had been at a rudimentary stage. No southern state at that time had what could be called a public school system. Worse yet for Marshall and his colleagues, the very Congress that designed the Fourteenth Amendment passed legislation supporting segregated schools already in place in the District of Columbia. The same Congress also supported racially separate schools operated by the Freedmen's Bureau, a federal agency concerned with race relations in the South.

Although discouraging, historical findings such as these did not deter Marshall's legal team from producing counterarguments. These took varying forms over time, but emphasized that the framers in the 1860s had intended to stop all forms of state-imposed racial discrimination. The efforts of the framers, they added, had been sabotaged by subsequent developments, including the enactment of segregated school systems in some thirty states by the mid-1890s. Court decisions such as *Plessy* in 1896, the lawyers said, reflected feelings that had arisen in the different, much more racist era of the late nineteenth century. Moreover, the framers surely had not foreclosed future generations from overturning segregation, either by congressional action or by judicial review.

Armed with such arguments, Marshall and his friends hoped that the Supreme Court would agree with them. Later—when the Court asked for more evidence on the matter—they embarked on major research into the political history of the Reconstruction era, enlisting such prominent historians as John Hope Franklin and C. Vann Woodward to support their efforts. When the Court finally reheard the cases in December 1953, however, the controversy over historical intent continued to concern the lawyers. It was even then not clear how damaging the historical evidence might be to Marshall's position.

Top leaders of the Fund had to worry a great deal, of course, about precedents established by the Court. *Plessy* was the most notable of these, for the Court had upheld the Louisiana statute requiring separate-but-equal cars on railways within the state. But there were other cases, too. As early as 1850 the Supreme Court of Massachusetts had rejected the efforts of black parents who challenged racially separate public schools in Boston. Six years later the state legislature passed a law against such segregation, effectively nullifying the court's decision. But Supreme Court justices later cited the state court's opinion, *Roberts v. the City of Boston*, as a precedent—for *Plessy*, among other cases. The controversy in Boston said much about northern white attitudes in the antebellum era. Then, as later, white Southerners had no monopoly on racist attitudes.[21]

Three years following *Plessy*, in 1899, the Court unanimously issued an opinion in *Cumming v. Richmond (Ga.) County Board of Education* that upheld a decision of white officials to close down the only high school in the county for blacks. In doing so, the authorities claimed that they needed the space for black elementary schools. (Among the many problematic aspects of school segregation in the Jim Crow era was the extra cost of maintaining dual systems.) Black litigants demanded that the Court grant an injunction that would have prevented the use of taxes for operation of the white high schools (there was one for boys and one for girls) until the county reestablished the black school.[22]

Justice John Marshall Harlan—who had issued a lonely dissent in *Plessy*—refused to grant the injunction. The county's action, he emphasized, "was in the interest of the greater number of colored children." This decision gave a green light to school officials to discriminate, and it discouraged other blacks who might have litigated. So much for the notion that separate-but-equal guaranteed racial equality in the South.

Yet another precedent that worried Marshall and his fellow lawyers was *Gong Lum v. Rice*, announced on behalf of a unanimous Supreme Court by Chief Justice William Howard Taft in 1927. The case had arisen in 1924 when Gong Lum, a Chinese merchant who lived in Mississippi, sent his daughter Martha to a white school. To his surprise, she was sent home—she was not "white." Her father did not challenge racial segregation, arguing instead that Martha should not be categorized as colored. When the case reached the Supreme Court, Taft refused to reverse what the school officials had done. Citing *Cumming*, he said that the question raised "has been many times decided to be within the constitutional power of the state legislature to settle without intervention of the federal courts under the Federal Constitution." Twenty-five years later *Gong Lum* understandably concerned Marshall's team. The Supreme Court, they feared, might use the precedent as a means of avoiding a decision on *Brown*.[23]

As later events were to demonstrate, the constitutional support that these cases offered for segregation was not impregnable. The *Roberts* decision predated the Fourteenth Amendment and was invalidly cited in many subsequent state cases that Taft invoked in 1927. *Plessy* concerned passenger trains, not schools. Neither of these rulings, nor *Cumming*, directly addressed the central constitutional question: whether state-sponsored school segregation denied black children equal protection of the laws. Marshall, Carter, and others made all these points in the district court cases. But they did not prevail. The constitutional barriers to an assault on segregation still seemed formidable when the cases first reached the Supreme Court in 1952.[24]

Marshall and the others battling against segregation had to consider yet another difficult issue: if desegregation were ordered, what implementation did they have in mind? Would they demand some form of "racial balance" in schools and classrooms? Challenged during the South Carolina trial to offer a formula that could be used to desegregate the system there, Marshall at first hedged, but then proposed that the district lines be shifted, thereby mixing the children or "sharing the schools equally."

It was clear, however, that neither Marshall nor others on his team had thought deeply about this question, which was later to prove so painful to answer. They yearned mainly to end state-sponsored racial segregation of the public schools. "If the lines are drawn on a natural basis, without regard to race or color," Marshall explained, "then I think that nobody would have any complaint." Although he did not elaborate on this idea, it seems clear that he was prepared to accept districting, especially in highly segregated neighborhoods, that would have resulted in highly segregated schools. As Carter said later, "we really had the feeling then that segregation itself was the evil—and not a symptom of the deeper evil of racism." For that reason, he added, "we attached no importance then to the ratio of blacks to whites in the Clarendon schools. It wasn't our concern to figure out how integration would work. . . . The box we thought we were in was segregation itself, and most of the nation saw it that way, too."[25]

Confronted with the formidable task of abolishing state-sponsored segregation in schools, Marshall, Carter, and others could be excused for their inattention to districting formulas in 1951–52. But the issue was to plague advocates of desegregation in the future, forcing courts and school districts to wrangle over redistricting plans, court-ordered busing, and ways of achieving what became known as racial balance. How inflammable these questions were to become was obvious in the Summerton, South Carolina, case at the time. There, the ratio of black to white school children was nine to one. Whites at this trial could scarcely believe that Marshall and his colleagues expected white parents in Summerton to send their children to desegregated schools where the children would be outnumbered by such a margin.

Another tough question that advisers threw at Marshall and his team involved the effect of segregation on individuals. Herbert Wechsler, a Columbia law professor, raised the issue most insistently at a strategy session in late 1951. Wechsler noted that the key to the Fund's case was the claim that *de jure* segregation was on its face discriminatory and therefore denied blacks equal protection under the Fourteenth Amendment. But did segregation necessarily do that, he asked? After all, segregation isolated whites as well as blacks. Why, therefore, was segregation per se more discriminatory against blacks than against whites?

Wechsler posed a related question—one that echoed in some ways the worry of W. E. B. Du Bois in 1935: was a black child in a segregated school necessarily worse off than a black child in a nonsegregated school where he or she was not wanted? As Wechsler later wrote, "denial by the state of freedom to associate . . . impinges in the same way on any groups or races that may be involved. . . . But if the freedom of association is denied by segregation, integration forces an association upon those for whom it is unpleasant or repugnant."[26]

Lawyers for the Fund had ready replies to such arguments. Carter insisted that segregation affected blacks differently from whites. Marshall added that blacks had not chosen segregation—it had been imposed on them. Kenneth Clark, a psychologist who took a major role in the discussions, was certain that segregation aroused feelings of inferiority that damaged black people. "Segregated school is a sort of fatality," he exclaimed. These were predictable answers—so obvious to the lawyers that they dismissed Wechsler's concerns. They were not so obvious later on, however—either to supporters of segregation or to black people like Zora Neale Hurston who took pride in all-black institutions.

The presence of Clark at many of these meetings indicated the importance that Marshall was giving to the argument that segregated schools damaged the psyches of black children and their motivation to learn. This argument had hardly originated with Clark. Du Bois had called segregation a "monstrous imposition on the psyches of black folk." Similar views had gathered strength in the early postwar years among leading social scientists, black as well as white, who relied ever more heavily on the growing prestige of psychology in American thought. Racial liberals, too, were attracted to the idea, which added another weapon to their arsenal against racial discrimination. President Truman's Commission on Civil Rights had deplored segregation, perceiving it as the source among minority people of "damaged, thwarted personalities."[27]

It was Clark, however, who had the ear of the lawyers. Born in the Panama Canal Zone, he had been taken by his mother to Harlem when he was five, where he attended nonsegregated schools. He then studied at Howard University before going to Columbia and receiving a PhD in experimental psychology in 1940. Like many other social scientists in the early 1940s, Clark assisted Gunnar Myrdal in research for *An American Dilemma*, published in 1944. From 1942 on he taught at the College of the City of New York. With his wife Mamie, a collaborator in many research projects, he founded in Manhattan a center that treated children with personality disturbances. By 1950 Kenneth and Mamie Clark were fairly well known in academic circles for their research in that field.

Most useful for attorneys with the Fund was research by the Clarks concerning the effects of segregation on school children. Testing for these effects, they showed young black children brown as well as white dolls, and asked them which ones they liked better. They asked questions of black children in both segregated and nonsegregated schools, in the South and in Springfield, Massachusetts. Before testifying at the district court case in Charleston, Clark tested again, this time showing drawings of brown and white dolls to sixteen Clarendon County black children between the ages of six and nine. Black children, all these experiments showed, were more likely to say that the white dolls were "good" or "nice." Ten of the sixteen in Clarendon County preferred the drawings of white dolls. Eleven said the brown dolls looked "bad." From studies such as these Clark concluded that the "Negro child accepts as early as six, seven, or eight the negative stereotypes about his own group." The black children in Clarendon County had been "definitely harmed in the development of their personalities."[28]

Some of the people around Marshall wondered about such research. Both Greenberg and Spottswood Robinson were skeptical. Another top lawyer, William Coleman, pounded the table in opposition to use of the research. He said later, "Jesus Christ. Those damned dolls! I thought it was a joke." Carter, however, was impressed by the research, and Marshall finally decided to use it in the district courts. Clark testified in South Carolina and Delaware. Findings such as his, alleging that legally imposed school segregation caused blacks to feel inferior, ultimately did much to impress Huxton and his fellow judges in Kansas. Marshall continued to rely on the Clarks' researches in his appeals to the Supreme Court.[29]

It was hardly surprising that he found this research attractive. Many lawyers who wished to use it in 1951–52 believed that it lent scholarly substance to what they already accepted as common sense: racial segregation stigmatized and damaged blacks. As early as 1952, however, scholars poked holes in Clark's methods. His terms were fuzzy: what were young children supposed to mean by "nice?" Why didn't Clark use dolls, instead of drawings of dolls, in South Carolina? Could tests on a mere sixteen children prove that segregation harmed all black children?[30]

Critics correctly questioned Clark's findings as well as his methodology. Was it fair to conclude from such tests, they asked, that school segregation per se caused children to choose dolls as they did? After all, the children had not been in school for long. Why not conclude that poverty or discrimination, not school segregation, generated whatever self-doubts blacks may have felt? Finally, Clark's own studies had shown that black children in the nonsegregated schools of Massachusetts were even more likely than the black children in segregated schools to prefer the white dolls. One might well have employed Clark's findings to support the preservation of all-black schools, where black children did not face academic competition from whites.

Later, as developments such as the quest for "black power" in the 1960s raised the pride of black people in their history and their institutions, arguments such as Clark's fell even further from favor. Why should we assume, some asked, that black people who admire white dolls (or other white images) necessarily have low self-esteem or succumb to self-hate? (Black civil rights leaders, most of them educated in segregated schools, did not seem to have such hang-ups.) Where were the solid studies of the personalities of black children that might firmly establish the social science of the doll studies? (The answer is: there were none). Studies such as Clark's, these critics declared, aimed to demonstrate the nasty consequences of white racism in American society but had the unintended effect of demeaning black people.

If Joseph DeLaine and others like him at the grass roots had been asked to resolve issues such as those the lawyers debated in 1951–52, they might have had reason to smile. For them, the issues were simple. Whites had used the constitutional principle of separate-but-equal to deprive blacks of equal schools. State-sponsored school segregation, therefore, had to be abandoned, replaced by a new system that guaranteed equality of educational opportunity.

Whether such a new system could come into being, however, remained unclear as of late 1952, when the district court battles ended. The cases then went to the Supreme Court of the United States, which had the motto "Equal Justice Under Law" inscribed under the pediment of its cold and imposing marble building in the Jim Crow city of Washington. It would be up to the High Court to decide.

3

THE COURT DECIDES

A great many Americans in the years before 1952—at least, white Americans—held the Supreme Court in high esteem. When President Franklin Roosevelt tried to pack it with justices of his own political persuasion in 1937, he aroused a storm of opposition. The Court, his foes thought, stood for impartial justice. Its members served for life, protected from the vicissitudes of political partisanship. Photographs commonly showed the justices wearing gowns that dramatized their eminence as defenders of a revered and unchanging Constitution.

Some people knew better. Throughout its history the Court had been caught up in major political controversies. Chief Justice Roger Taney, a southern sympathizer, had handed down a decision concerning Dred Scott, a slave, that had helped to incite the Civil War. Blacks, he wrote, were "so far inferior that they had no rights which the white man was bound to respect." In decisions such as *Plessy*, the Court imposed its own racist interpretations of the Fourteenth Amendment. The justices in Roosevelt's time, dominated by a politically conservative bloc, had threatened to destroy the New Deal.

The Court before which Marshall, Carter, and others appeared in December 1952 offered no exception to this historical pattern of political engagement. By that time, the justices—all of them political liberals or moderates appointed by Roosevelt or Truman—had jettisoned conservative notions about the virtues of laissez-faire. Since the late 1930s, the Court had consistently upheld laws that expanded the role of government, such as the Social Security Act, the National Labor Relations Act,

46

and the Fair Labor Standards Act. After 1952 it continued to support governmental intervention into economic life. Just as liberals had railed against the conservative Court of the Roosevelt era, so did many critics on the Right denounce the justices after 1937.

But the Court of the late 1940s and early 1950s—before the arrival of Earl Warren as Chief Justice in late 1953—suffered from deep internal divisions. By the third term of Chief Justice Fred Vinson, who was appointed in 1946, the Court managed to reach unanimity on only 26 percent of its decisions, compared to 85 percent in most years prior to 1935. Justice Robert Jackson, no admirer of Vinson, remarked in 1953, "This Court no longer respects impersonal rules of law but is guided in these matters by personal impressions which from time to time may be shared by a majority of the Justices."[1]

The Supreme Court visits President Eisenhower at the White House, February 1953. First row (*l. to r.*), justices William Douglas and Stanley Reed, Chief Justice Fred Vinson, President Eisenhower, and justices Hugo Black and Felix Frankfurter. Back row (*l. to r.*), Sherman Adams (Assistant to the President), Attorney General Herbert Brownell, and justices Sherman Minton, Tom Clark, Robert Jackson, and Harold Burton. (*Library of Congress, Prints and Photographs Division, New York World-Telegram & Sun Collection*)

Philosophical differences among the justices had done much to provoke these divisions. A majority of the Court, led by Jackson and Felix
Frankfurter, normally stressed the virtues of "judicial restraint." The
Court, they said, should restrain itself from striking down state or federal
laws passed by democratically elected legislators; it should expect that
the democratic political process would do the right thing in the long
run. To impose the Court's views on the country, they feared, was to
invite political attacks such as Roosevelt's in 1937. Other justices who
normally adhered to this philosophical position included Stanley Reed,
like Jackson and Frankfurter a Roosevelt appointee, and four relative
newcomers, all named by Truman between 1945 and 1949: Harold
Burton, a moderate former Republican senator from Ohio; Sherman
Minton, a Truman loyalist who had been a senator from Indiana; Tom
Clark, a Texan who had been Truman's attorney general; and Vinson
himself.

The other two justices, Hugo Black and William Douglas, had served
on the Court since the late 1930s. Liberals in their politics, they, too,
followed the path of judicial restraint concerning socioeconomic legislation in the 1940s. With the onset of the Cold War, however, growing
numbers of civil liberties cases, many of them featuring defendants opposed to Truman's tough foreign and domestic security policies, began
to arrive at the door of the Court. To the major contenders in these
cases the issues were profoundly important, involving the meaning of
the Bill of Rights and the role of the Court. Frankfurter and Jackson,
though well aware of the need to protect civil liberties, tended in many
of these cases to hold to the principle of judicial restraint, thereby up-
holding restrictions that curbed dissent. Eager supporters of America's
Cold War policies, Vinson, Minton, Reed, and Burton consistently upheld these laws.

Black, however, insisted on full recognition of rights guaranteed in
the Constitution, a dog-eared copy of which he always carried in his
jacket pocket. He argued that the freedoms enumerated in the Bill of
Rights and the Fourteenth Amendment, which covered state laws, were
absolute and should not be qualified. "I am for the First Amendment
from the first word to the last," he said. "I believe it means what it
says." For this reason Black and Douglas normally supported judicial
activism, not restraint, in civil liberties cases. They argued that the Court
must not abdicate its responsibility, as they saw it, to protect people
whose rights were threatened by state or federal laws. The Court, Black

wrote later, should "not depend at all . . . upon 'deference' to the Congress but on the Court's honest judgment as to whether the law was within the competence of the Congress."[2]

Personal animosities sharpened these philosophical divisions, so much so that the justices could barely bring themselves to maintain a prescribed ritual, shaking hands at the start of conferences. Some of these differences were relatively minor. Burton, a teetotaler and nonsmoker, was offended by Minton, who chewed tobacco and spattered him when he aimed at his spittoon. Other divisions were more serious. Some of the justices found it difficult to work with Douglas, a former law professor at Yale who was formidably knowledgeable, but was also a loner and a curmudgeon. "I have only one soul to save," he said, "and that's my own." Potter Stewart, later named to the Court, commented that "Bill Douglas seems positively embarrassed if anyone agrees with him." Although greatly admired by civil libertarians, Douglas did not shine as a craftsman, and he made no effort to assume a role of leadership on the Court. Frankfurter, an intensely serious and critical man, thought that Douglas was indolent. On another occasion, Frankfurter wrote that Douglas was "one of the two completely evil men" he had ever known.[3]

Black, too, had his foes on the Court. Roosevelt's first appointee, in 1937, he had been an aggressive supporter of New Deal policies while a senator from Alabama. By 1947 he was the senior justice. He had a pleasing Alabama drawl and—much of the time—a courtly manner. But he was also combative, playing highly competitive tennis every day on his home court in Alexandria. Associates knew that in conference, as at tennis, Black could be caustic and that he yearned to win. Douglas said, "You can't just disagree with him. You must go to war with him if you disagree." Frankfurter had harsher words than Douglas. "Oh, Democracy, what flapdoodle is delivered in thy name," he wrote in his diary after one of his many jousts with Black. "Not the less so because it was all said in Black's irascible and snarling tone of voice."[4]

Jackson, Frankfurter's closest ally on the Court, was especially estranged from Black. Jackson had served as Roosevelt's attorney general before being named to the Court in 1941. In 1946 he took a brief leave to become chief prosecutor for the United States at the trial of Axis war criminals in Nuremberg, Germany. An ambitious man, he became upset when Truman passed him over to name Vinson as Chief Justice in 1946. Blaming Black (unfairly) for working behind the scenes against him, Jackson sent a blistering 1,500-word cable to Truman, in which he as-

Justice Hugo Black. *(Library of Congress, Prints and Photographs Division, New York World-Telegram & Sun Collection, 1957 photo)*

sailed Black. He then went so far as to write the Senate and House judiciary committees in order to give them his side of intracourt feuding. This was an extraordinary act by a justice.[5]

Frankfurter was a special trial to many of his colleagues. A professor at the Harvard Law School before his arrival on the Court in 1939, he was a peppery, extraordinarily energetic presence on the Court until his retirement in 1962. Possessed of great intellectual curiosity, he was also learned about American constitutional history. But he could be infuriatingly disputatious and professorial. On the bench he relished asking complicated, unanticipated questions as he restlessly swiveled about in his chair above the attorneys before him. Lawyers, including Marshall and his entourage, spent many worried hours in dry runs so as to prepare themselves for the onslaught of queries that they expected from him. In conference with fellow justices, Frankfurter was known to rise and pace about, snatching books off shelves as references and delivering interminable monologues to his colleagues. (Douglas, it is said, once threatened to walk out, vowing to return only when Frankfurter had finished his

Justice Felix Frankfurter, a frequent foe of Black. *(Library of Congress, Prints and Photographs Division, New York World-Telegram & Sun Collection, 1957 photo)*

professorial perorations.) Such was the Court that the new Chief Justice was appointed to lead. [6]

When Truman named Vinson to manage these badly divided justices, he had reason to think that he had chosen a smooth and capable mediator. That was indeed Vinson's reputation. As a popular congressman from Kentucky until 1938, he had distinguished himself as the floor leader for the Social Security Act and as a patient, conciliatory manager of complicated tax legislation. Following a stint as a judge on the District of Columbia Court of Appeals, he accepted Roosevelt's request in 1943 that he serve as director of the Office of Economic Stabilization, a job that made him a "czar" of sorts over wartime economic policies. Truman, who had become Vinson's good friend and fellow poker player during their days together on Capitol Hill, named him Secretary of the Treasury before nominating him to the Court. In this capacity Vinson became the president's confidant. Vinson and his family joined the Trumans at the White House for Thanksgiving dinners. The two friends used bedside phones to talk at night.

Vinson, however, proved unable to bring unity to the badly fractured Court. On the contrary, his closeness to Truman—and to Truman's Cold War policies—quickly alienated Black and Douglas. Frankfurter and Jackson, too, worried about Vinson's often zealous defense of the governmental line. All four of these justices had stronger intellects than Vinson, and they found it hard to disguise their negative opinions of him. Some of them were so contemptuous of Vinson that they discussed even in his presence the idea of annually rotating the job of Chief. Well before December 1952, when the segregation cases were set for argument before the Court, Vinson—a long-faced man with bushy brows and deep pouches under the eyes—was an embattled and widely caricatured figure. His tired, doleful demeanor symbolized the mood of the Court.

In December 1952, when the Vinson Court met to hear the five desegregation cases, crowds descended on the Supreme Court building. Some 300 people packed the hearing room, with 400 more lining the corridors in hopes of being let in. About half the people were blacks. The Reverend Albert Joseph DeLaine of South Carolina, who had risked all to challenge racism in Summerton, was among them.

Like many other Americans, the spectators at these hearings, which took three days, understood the profound issues under debate. Thurgood Marshall, Robert Carter, James Nabrit, Spottswood Robinson, Louis Redding, Jack Greenberg, and others backing the defendants, having prepared far into the nights during the preceding months, were eager to be heard at last. They took turns arguing before the Court, an hour per case, beginning with Carter, who spoke for Oliver Brown and his fellow plaintiffs from Topeka. Marshall argued for plaintiffs in *Briggs v. Elliott*, which DeLaine and other black people had formally initiated more than three years earlier.

Opposing Marshall, as counsel for South Carolina and as overall leader of the defense team, was a man of exceptional standing, John W. Davis. The list of Davis's accomplishments over a long life—he was seventy-nine years old in December 1952—was extraordinary: congressman from West Virginia, solicitor general for the Wilson administration, ambassador to Great Britain, and Democratic presidential nominee in 1924. A native of West Virginia, Davis had gone to college and law school at Washington and Lee University in Virginia, and had long been

Eisenhower with John W. Davis, chief counsel opposing Thurgood Marshall, October 1952. *(Library of Congress, Prints and Photographs Division, New York World-Telegram & Sun Collection)*

a leader of the bar in New York City. By 1952 he had participated—often as chief counsel—in 250 Supreme Court cases, more than anyone else in twentieth-century United States history. He was a superb courtroom attorney—poised, articulate, and commanding. He was firmly, indeed emotionally committed to the position of South Carolina, where he regularly took vacations. When Governor Byrnes, a personal friend, asked for help, Davis quickly agreed, accepting no fees for his services. Davis's presence highlighted the importance that the pro-segregation forces attached to the case. Marshall understood that he faced formidable opposition.[7]

Marshall and his colleagues argued well, stressing in their attack on *Plessy* that state-imposed segregation was inherently discriminatory and therefore a denial of the equal protection clause of the Fourteenth Amendment. As in the lower court cases, they used the doll researches of the Clarks to maintain that segregation accentuated feelings of inferiority among black children. They also understood, however, that their arguments were already familiar to the justices. It was up to the nine, black-robed jurists looking down from the bench to resolve in their own minds where they stood on an issue—segregated public schools—that was as much political as it was judicial in nature.

Like others who engaged in guesswork about the Court at the time, Marshall was fairly sure that four of the justices were ready to support his argument and declare that *Plessy* be reversed. Subsequent evidence from archives, notably a diary kept by Burton and notes jotted down by Jackson, confirm his speculation. These four included Truman's midwestern appointees, Harold Burton and Sherman Minton. While both men ordinarily advocated judicial restraint, they had supported the attack on racial discrimination in the *Sweatt* and *McLaurin* cases. By 1952 they had no problem making up their minds that segregated schools should be declared unconstitutional.[8]

Black and Douglas joined them. As an ambitious lawyer in Alabama during the mid-1920s, Black had briefly joined the Ku Klux Klan. Long before 1952, however, he had disavowed this ugly aspect of his past and shown his sympathy with the plight of black people. As a Southerner he worried deeply about fierce white backlash if the Court overturned school segregation. (A better way to start challenging Jim Crow, he thought, was to protect black voting rights.) A Justice Department official recalled that Black alarmed his fellow justices by predicting that many whites in the South would fight school desegregation tooth and nail. "The guys who talked nigger would be in charge," he remembered Black saying. "There would be riots, the Army might have to be called out—he was scaring the shit out of the Justices, especially Frankfurter and Jackson, who didn't know how the Court could enforce a ruling against *Plessy*." Nonetheless, Black believed that the Court must rule against segregated schools. Segregation, he had said in a conference over *Sweatt* in 1950, was a "hangover from [the] days when [the] Negro was a slave." It was "Hitler's creed—he preached what the South believed." Like Douglas, he based his position on his loathing of racism and his liberal reading of the equal protection language of the Fourteenth Amendment.[9]

Supreme Court watchers in 1952 recognized, however, that the Vinson Court, divided on so much else, was ill-prepared to rule against segregation.[10] One justice, it seemed certain, would oppose the scrapping of *Plessy*. That was Stanley Reed. A Kentuckian, Reed had served Roosevelt as solicitor general before being elevated to the Court in 1938. He was an even-tempered, gentlemanly person, well-liked for his courtesy and simple tastes. He recognized that segregated schools in the South had led to glaring inequalities. He hoped, however, that southern states, then engaged in upgrading black schools as a defense against desegregation, could establish equality in a short time. The Court could act by enforcing, as in *Sweatt*, the equal part of separate-but-equal.

Like many white Americans, Reed also shrank from the idea of racial mixing. In 1952–53 the Court considered a case concerning racially segregated restaurants in Washington. Reed went along with the Court's decision, which was unanimous, to outlaw the practice. But he did so reluctantly. Reed lived with his wife at the city's Mayflower Hotel. Leaving the conference at which the decision was reached, he was reported to have exclaimed, "Why—why, this means that a nigra can walk into the restaurant at the Mayflower and sit down to eat at the table right next to Mrs. Reed."[11]

It also seemed likely in 1952 that others on the Court would join Reed—or at least seek some sort of delay before committing themselves on such a passionately debated issue as school segregation. Among these justices were Fred Vinson and Tom Clark. They had similar views at the time. Vinson, who had written the *Sweatt* and *McLaurin* decisions in 1950, worried greatly about leading the Court into the much bigger business of desegregating public schools. Like Black, he thought the consequences would be drastic. Unlike him, he was not prepared to decide against *Plessy*. Perhaps, he hoped, the southern states would equalize their schools. Meanwhile, delay was prudent.

Clark, it appears, largely shared Vinson's concerns, as well as his instinct to delay. He struck those who knew him, including his law clerks, as being free of racial prejudice. As a Texan, however, Clark was reluctant in 1952 to command the South to desegregate its schools. His concerns about rebellion in the South—and about the damage that such rebellion might do to the standing of the Court—in fact alarmed all the justices. They had far more than strictly legal matters to consider. Like justices throughout American history, they were well aware of social and political consequences.

Jackson and Frankfurter were also uncertain quantities in December 1952. Jackson, who hailed from New York State, had no use for segregation, and he did not feel bound by precedents such as *Plessy*. At the same time, he doubted that "putting children together" in schools would cure the disease of racism in the United States, and he did not believe that the framers of the Fourteenth Amendment had intended to outlaw segregated schools. If the Court chose to rule against *Plessy*, he thought, it should do so on frankly political grounds. It should admit that it was making new law. But if the Court tried to use other grounds to oppose segregation, he would have trouble going along. Those who watched Jackson in 1952, including Frankfurter, knew that he had not made up his mind.

Frankfurter, too, had conflicted feelings about the school cases in 1952. As a former assistant counsel for the NAACP, and as a Jewish American who had tasted prejudice himself, he detested discrimination. On the other hand, as an advocate of judicial restraint, he could not vote comfortably to overturn school segregation, a practice approved by the legislatures of twenty-one states. Moreover, like Jackson, he doubted that the men who had framed the Fourteenth Amendment had been thinking about schools. Afraid that Jackson might join Reed, Vinson, and Clark to affirm segregation in 1952, he hoped to put off the decision until the Court could speak with one voice.

Where did all these attitudes leave the Court in 1952? Opinions on this much-debated question vary. At the time, Frankfurter thought that a vote would come out five to four (with him among the five) to reverse *Plessy*. Burton guessed that the vote would be six to three to reverse. Douglas, in notes at the time of the *Brown* decision in May 1954, wrote that if the case had been decided in 1952, "there probably would have been many opinions and a wide divergence of views and a result that would have sustained, so far as the States were concerned, segregation of students."[12]

Douglas's retrospective assessment was probably inaccurate. Had the justices chosen to act in 1952, a draft opinion or opinions for a reversal of *Plessy* would have been circulated, as was common Court practice, among the justices. Doubters among them could have tailored such drafts to satisfy their reservations. Consensus might have emerged behind a final draft against *Plessy* that two-thirds or more of the justices would have signed. None of the justices, after all, was anxious by 1952 to be recorded as a defender of racial segregation. This is another way of reiterating an essential truth about *Brown*: so many larger postwar forces—rising expectations and restlessness among blacks; slowly changing white attitudes about racial segregation; the Cold War, which left Jim Crow America vulnerable to the charge of hypocrisy when it claimed to lead the Free World—were impelling the nation toward liberalization of its racial practices.

The Court, however, did not decide in 1952. Nervous about ruling on such an inflammatory issue, it stalled for time. Six months thereafter, in June 1953, it ordered a rehearing of the cases in October (later extended to December). It instructed the attorneys to come to these rehearings with answers to a number of questions. One reflected a concern of some of the justices, notably Frankfurter: what had been the intent of the framers of the Fourteenth Amendment concerning schools? Other questions suggested strongly that the Court wanted to overturn *Plessy* but was searching for a politically safe way of doing so. If the Court ruled against school segregation, should it permit the offending states to respond by means of "gradual adjustment?" Should the Court "formulate detailed decrees in these cases," and if so, "what specific issues should the decrees reach?"[13]

When the Court assembled for the rehearing on December 7, 1953— the twelfth anniversary of Pearl Harbor Day—some things had changed. Dwight D. Eisenhower, having been elected the year before, was now in the White House. Over the summer an armistice had stopped the fighting in Korea. But the Cold War and McCarthyism remained explosive national issues. The Court, meeting in special session, had refused in June to stay the executions of Julius and Ethel Rosenberg, who had been convicted of atomic espionage. In July they had died in the electric chair at Sing Sing.

For the lawyers and judges engaged in the struggle over school segregation, the most momentous change had occurred on September 8. At 3:15 in the morning, Chief Justice Vinson, sixty-three, died of a heart attack at his hotel apartment in Washington. All the justices traveled to Kentucky for the funeral. But not all greatly mourned his passing. Frankfurter, who thought the Chief had mishandled the school cases, said to a former clerk, "This is the first indication I have ever had that there is a God."[14]

A few weeks later, Eisenhower decided on Vinson's successor. The new chief was to be Governor Earl Warren of California. The president was in attendance at the Supreme Court on October 5 when Warren was sworn in on an interim basis. Although not confirmed by the Senate until March 1, 1954, Warren immediately assumed command.

Frankfurter was rumored to be disturbed by the nomination of Warren—to him a mere politician. A columnist here and there echoed this

Earl Warren dons his robe for his first day as Chief Justice, October 1953. *(Library of Congress, Prints and Photographs Division, New York World-Telegram & Sun Collection)*

view, lamenting that the president had not named a distinguished jurist to the post. The new chief justice had had no experience on the bench. Most contemporary observers, however, hailed the choice, for Warren, a white-haired, solidly built, and extraordinarily popular three-term governor, had a generally creditable record of public service. Black people, too, had reasons to be pleased. As governor, Warren had called for anti lynching and anti poll tax legislation. He supported a Fair Employment Practices Commission for California.

Earl Warren was indeed a decent, fair-minded man. Sixty-two years old at the time of his nomination, he was the son of a Norwegian immigrant who worked as a railroad repairman. He grew up in Bakersfield, California, where he had an all-American boyhood as if out of a Horatio Alger novel. He delivered papers, drove an ice wagon, and sold books door-to-door. He attended the University of California, where he received good, inexpensive public education. He then went to law school at the university and stayed to get a doctor of jurisprudence degree. Following a brief period of noncombat service in the Army during World War I he went to work as an assistant counsel for the city of Oakland. A year later he became an assistant district attorney, eventually moving up to the post of district attorney. In 1938, running as a Republican, he was elected attorney general of California.[15]

While serving as attorney general, Warren took actions that he later regretted, so much so that he did not talk about them publicly during his lifetime. In early 1942 he urged the evacuation and detention of some 110,000 Japanese Americans. Defended by Warren and many others (including President Roosevelt) as necessary to avert sabotage, the action reflected wartime hysteria and rested on racist presumptions. Outside of racial segregation, it represented the most wholesale deprivation of American liberties in the twentieth century.

White Californians, however, generally supported Warren's handling of the Japanese Americans in 1942 and considered him to be a fair, firm, and incorruptible attorney general. Pleased, they elected him governor in 1942 and again in 1946. Warren possessed great political skills and managed to amass extraordinary strength among voters. Moderately liberal and nonpartisan, he championed the building of highways, hospitals, and schools. He lowered the state sales tax and three times fought—unsuccessfully—for a state health insurance program. In 1948, failing in a bid for the Republican presidential nomination, he ran as the vice-presidential candidate on a ticket with Governor Thomas Dewey of New York, the party's presidential nominee. When Truman beat Dewey, Warren stayed on as governor and was rewarded by voters in 1950 with a third term. He tried again for the presidency in 1952 but lost the Republican nomination to the super-popular Ike. During the tense GOP convention Warren instructed California delegates to vote for the seating of contested pro-Eisenhower delegates, a decision that did much to ensure Ike's triumph over Ohio Senator Robert Taft. Eisenhower, however, claimed that he owed Warren nothing and that his selection in 1953 of the well-regarded governor as Chief Justice was based on considerations of merit.

Later, when Warren led the Court in an activist, liberal direction, Eisenhower regretted his choice. Ike, who was conservative on most issues, including race relations, then told friends that the nomination was the "biggest damn fool mistake" he had ever made.[16] There were others during Warren's highly controversial sixteen-year tenure who also denigrated the Chief. They said that he was a pedestrian stylist, a so-so administrator, and of no consequence as a legal philosopher or theorist. Critics stressed above all that Warren decided cases on his gut sense of fairness and worried only later (if at all) about judicial precedents. Even liberal admirers of the Chief thought that Warren did not provide especially strong intellectual leadership. They believed, accurately for the most part, that Hugo Black—and later, Justice William Brennan, who joined the Court in 1956—were responsible for most of the liberal vision that characterized the activist "Warren Court" of the 1960s.

There was little doubt, however, that Warren mended a badly fractured Court in 1953–54. Naturally open and gregarious, he made a special point of seeking out his new colleagues, often dropping by their offices (instead of summoning them to his) to talk. He was deferential and made no effort to pretend that he possessed the high-powered legal expertise of self-assured men like Frankfurter, Jackson, Douglas, or Black. He was courteous, graceful, a patient, retentive listener, and dignified without being in any way pompous. Within weeks he had managed to establish cordial relations with all his colleagues. No man could extinguish all the flames of discord that had flared under Vinson. But Warren worked carefully to do so. By December 1953, when the rehearings in the segregation cases began, the Court was already becoming a more harmonious and purposeful body than it had been for some time. This was one of the many important legacies of Warren's judicial career.

The rehearings lasted three days. Marshall and his fellow attorneys, having engaged in exhaustive historical research over the summer and

People lining up at the Supreme Court, hoping to get one of the fifty available seats to hear arguments in the *Brown* case, December, 1953. *(Library of Congress, Prints and Photographs Division, New York World-Telegram & Sun Collection)*

fall, came prepared to answer the first of the Court's questions, by arguing that the framers of the Fourteenth Amendment had indeed intended to prevent racial segregation in the schools. They were countered by John Davis, characteristically wearing a cutaway coat and making the last of his many appearances before the Court (he died early in 1955). Davis had lost some energy. But he was as incisive and eloquent as ever, holding the justices in rapt attention for almost an hour. He did much to demolish the hopes of those who had looked to historical researches as solid support for a case against segregation in the schools. Davis was emotionally drained when he finished. Marshall recalled seeing tears on the eighty-year-old man's face.[17]

Davis had always been contemptuous of the psychological theories of the Clarks and others. "If that sort of 'fluff' can move any Court," he had snorted privately in 1952, "God save the State." Social scientists, he added, "can find usually . . . what they go out to find." During his argument, he turned to the realities of Clarendon County in order to ridicule the psychological research and to remind the justices of the formidable practical problems involved in desegregation. Clarendon had

Editorial page cartoon, *Baltimore Afro-American*, November 28, 1953. *(Archives,* Baltimore Afro-American*)*

2,800 black pupils and 300 white ones. How should these children be mixed in a plan for desegregation? "If it is done on a mathematical basis, with thirty children as the maximum . . . you would have twenty-seven Negro children and three whites in one schoolroom. Would that make the children any happier? Would they learn any more quickly? Would their lives be more serene?" He added:

> Children of that age are not the most considerate animals in the world, as we all know. Would the terrible psychological disaster being wrought, according to some of these witnesses, to the colored child be removed if he had three white children sitting somewhere in the same schoolroom?
>
> Would white children be prevented from getting a distorted idea of racial relations if they sat with twenty-seven Negro children? I have posed that question because it is the very one that cannot be denied.

As Davis well knew, these questions anticipated serious problems of implementation. They were to perplex countless school administrators, judges, educational theorists, and experts on race relations for the rest of the century.[18]

The rehearing also featured an appearance by Lee Rankin, assistant attorney general in the Eisenhower administration, who submitted an *amicus curiae* brief in support of the Fund lawyers' case against segregation. Justice Jackson then asked Rankin the question that had consistently bothered him: if the Court demanded desegregation, how should this be carried out? In answering the question, Rankin said that local cases should be turned over to the district courts, which should apply criteria determined by the Supreme Court. Within a year, Rankin said, school districts should present plans to the lower courts, which would see to it that the plans were carried out "with deliberate speed." This was nearly the same phrase that the Court itself was to use in its implementary decision a year and a half later.

Justice Jackson, however, was not convinced. Like Frankfurter, he had worried constantly about how the Court might direct the process of desegregation. Could it dare to condemn racial segregation in the schools and then pass on the formidable practical difficulties of implementation to the district courts and communities? Rankin was saying so, recommending that the lower courts work these matters out on a case-by-case basis. Jackson observed skeptically, "I foresee a generation of litigation if we send it back with no standards, and each case has to come here to determine it standard by standard."[19]

Jackson's remarks, like Davis's, foresaw many of the complex political and administrative problems of the future. It would be one thing to declare *de jure* segregation unconstitutional, and quite another to replace it in the affected school districts, which numbered nearly 3,000 in the eleven southern states alone. When the hearings ended in mid-afternoon on December 9, neither Jackson nor the Court had satisfactory answers to these very troubling concerns.

Three days later the justices gathered expectantly for a conference on the case. Warren was quick to offer his opinion. The issue, he thought, was fairly simple: *de jure* school segregation was unconstitutional. "The more I've read and heard and thought," he explained, "the more I've come to conclude that the basis of segregation and 'separate-but-equal' rests upon a concept of the inherent inferiority of the colored race." In stating his views in this way, Warren avoided saying anything about the intent of the framers of the Fourteenth Amendment, a question that he did not think could be answered. He also avoided blaming the South, adding that the Court must not take "precipitous action" that would inflame the region. For Warren in 1953, as in later years, the issues in *Brown* were moral above all.[20]

When the other justices had finished talking that day, however, it was clear to Warren that he could not count upon unanimity, or even be certain of a substantial majority. His arrival on the Court had provided a five-man bloc for the reversal of *Plessy*—himself, Douglas, Black, Burton, and Minton. Clark seemed prepared to join them. But Reed appeared likely to dissent. Frankfurter, having lost hope that historical research might clinch the case against school segregation, was struggling to find a constitutionally satisfactory means of joining Warren and the others. And Jackson was still convinced that there was no judicial (as opposed to political) basis for reversing *Plessy*. He seemed likely to file a separate concurring opinion that would establish that point. In the end, the still-torn justices took no action on December 12. They agreed to keep talking about the issues among themselves.

That they did over the next three months, with Warren working hard to bring his colleagues together. Like Frankfurter, he much wanted the Court to reach a unanimous opinion or, if Reed held out, to announce a decision with only one dissent. He labored especially assiduously to woo the argumentative Frankfurter, and he regularly sought out Reed for lunch. He assured Reed that he (Reed) would in the end "really do the best thing for the country."

By late March, Warren was sure that he would have his way—all but Reed seemed prepared to support a decision against segregation. Warren thereupon assigned himself the task of writing an opinion. It also seems clear that the justices decided at the time on an all-important compromise: they would declare *de jure* school segregation unconstitutional but would also ask for another hearing in the fall term so as to discover the best way of implementing the decision. The South would have at least a year to cope.

Warren then set to work drafting opinions—one for the four state cases and one for the *Bolling* case concerning the District of Columbia. Within a few weeks he had done so, and he hand-delivered drafts to his colleagues early in May. He went to the hospital to leave his draft for Jackson, who had suffered a serious heart attack in late March. In a memo accompanying the drafts Warren stated that his opinion was "prepared on the theory that [it] should be short, readable by the lay public, non-rhetorical, unemotional, and, above all, non-accusatory."

Some of the justices had quibbles here and there with Warren's efforts. But these were minor and were easily patched into what he had written. Even Frankfurter, who had considered writing a concurrent version, was satisfied. So was Jackson. At some point the Chief even won over Reed, reminding him that he stood alone and that a dissent would encourage resistance in the South. Did Reed really wish to do that? Reed, assured that Warren's opinion would give the South time to dismantle segregation, gave in. Later he commented, "There was an air of inevitability about it all."[21] On May 15, a conference of the justices finally approved Warren's opinion. The long-awaited ruling on racial segregation in the schools was ready at last.

Two days later at 12:52 P.M. Warren, flanked by his black-robed colleagues, began to read his decision concerning *Oliver Brown et al. v. Board of Education of Topeka*. It was his first major opinion as Chief Justice, and he read it firmly and clearly. It did not take much time—only a half hour—for as Warren had promised, he kept the opinion short and unemotional. It was only eleven pages long. Other major decisions of his tenure, such as *Reynolds v. Sims* (concerning reapportionment of legislatures, fifty-one pages), and *Miranda v. Arizona* (concerning the rights of criminals, sixty pages), were much longer.

Warren started by explaining briefly that the "reach and intention" of the framers of the Fourteenth Amendment were unclear and that historical research to clarify the matter had been "inconclusive." Public education of blacks in the South at that time, he added, had been virtually nonexistent. It was hardly surprising, therefore, that "there should be so little in the history of the Fourteenth Amendment relating to its intended effect on public education."[22]

The Chief Justice proceeded next to allude briefly to earlier court decisions, including *Plessy* in 1896, *Cumming* in 1899, and *Gong Lum* in 1927, and moved on to the more recent cases of *Gaines* in 1938 and *Sweatt* and *McLaurin* in 1950. What really mattered, he said, was that public education had become ever more important over time in the United States. "In approaching this problem, we cannot turn the clock back to 1868 when the Amendment was adopted, or even to 1896 when *Plessy v. Ferguson* was written. We must consider public education in the light of its full development and its present place in American life throughout the Nation." Warren continued by stating a widely held American creed. Education, he said, "is perhaps the most important function of state and local governments. . . . It is the very foundation of good citizenship."

To this point, two-thirds of the way through his opinion, Warren had built up suspense among his listeners. He had not indicated what the Court had decided. Finally, he did. He asked, "Does segregation of children in public schools solely on the basis of race . . . deprive the children of the minority group of equal educational opportunities?" He answered, "We believe that it does." A few passages later he added perhaps the most widely quoted lines of his opinion:

> To separate them [black children in grade and high schools] from others of similar age and qualifications solely because of their race generates a feeling of inferiority as to their status in the community that may affect their hearts and minds in a way unlikely ever to be undone.

This line of argument, of course, relied on the psychological theories advanced by the Clarks and many other witnesses, notably at the trial at Topeka in 1951. Warren observed accurately that *Plessy*, too, had relied on psychological theories. The justice who wrote the opinion in that case, Henry Billings Brown, had sustained laws for segregated railroad cars by stressing the "underlying fallacy" of Homer Plessy's position. This was the "assumption that the enforced separation of the two races stamps the colored race with a badge of inferiority. If this be so, it is not by reason of anything found in the act [passed by the Louisiana legislature], but solely because the colored race chooses to put that construction upon it." Any stigma attached to blacks because they were relegated to nonwhite railroad cars, in short, came entirely from the eye of the beholder, not from the racist policies of whites. Warren responded:

> Whatever may have been the extent of psychological knowledge at the time of *Plessy v. Ferguson*, this finding [by the Kansas court in 1951 that racial segregation leads to feelings of inferiority and damages the motivation to learn] is amply supported by modern authority. Any language in *Plessy v. Ferguson* contrary to this finding is rejected.

Warren supported this assertion in the eleventh footnote to his opinion, or Footnote Eleven, as it was always called in later years. This listed seven works of social scientists, all of them cited earlier in briefs by lawyers for the Fund. The list began with an article by Kenneth Clark and closed with Gunnar Myrdal's *An American Dilemma*.

Only two paragraphs remained to be read. The first was clear and made the most fundamental point, the linchpin of the argument against *Plessy*. "We conclude"—here Warren departed from his printed text to add the word "unanimously"—"that in the field of public education the doctrine of 'separate-but-equal' has no place. Separate educational facilities are inherently unequal." Black children in the segregated districts involved in these cases, he said, had been deprived of the equal protection of the laws guaranteed by the Fourteenth Amendment.

The closing paragraph, also brief, dealt with implementation—a question that had stymied the justices and delayed the decision for more than a year. Warren explained that the Court would set aside time in its fall term to hear the advice of attorneys general throughout the South and the United States concerning means of compliance. In so doing, Warren made it clear that his decision would apply to all states, not just the districts involved in the five cases. He also indicated that the Court was giving the South time to participate in the complex and controversial business of implementation.

Having disposed of *Brown* and the other three state cases, Warren then moved on to the District of Columbia case, *Bolling v. Sharpe*, which he took only six paragraphs to decide. He emphasized, as Nabrit had done throughout the previous three years, that segregation in the nation's capital violated the provisions of the Fifth Amendment, which was supposed to shield people from deprivation of life, liberty, or property without due process of law. "In view of our decision that the Constitution [via the Fourteenth Amendment] prohibits the states from maintaining racially segregated public schools, it would be unthinkable that the same Constitution would impose a lesser duty on the Federal Government."

As Warren spoke these final words, tears appeared on the face of Justice Reed, whose late-stage turnabout had brought unanimity to the Court.

———

A number of legal analysts have criticized Warren's decision. Some of these critics have given Warren low grades as a craftsman and stylist. "The opinion failed to inspire," one authority later wrote. "It simply existed."[23]

More telling criticisms—Supreme Court decisions do not naturally make for great reading—focused on two other aspects of the Court's argument. The first was Warren's failure, as some liberal critics perceived it, to draw specifically upon the famous dissent of John Marshall Harlan in *Plessy*: "Our Constitution is color-blind, and neither knows nor tolerates classes among its citizens." Warren, focusing on schools, the issue at hand, did not mention Harlan or make the claim that all statutory considerations of color (such as state laws prohibiting interracial marriage) were impermissible. Many of these considerations survived with vigor into the mid-1960s.[24]

The second criticism, mainly from conservatives, zeroed in on the sociological and psychological references in Footnote Eleven. Warren scoffed at such criticisms, saying that Number Eleven was "just a note, after all," but the reference nonetheless served to antagonize many defenders of segregation. J. Harvie Wilkinson later noted that it might have been "the most inflammatory English ever in fine print." Many who attacked Warren's sources were white opponents who seized upon the note as a convenient target. Other, fairer critics have complained that social "science" changes over time: better not to rely on ephemera as the basis for a decision so important as *Brown*. These critics have also demanded to know why psychologizing was necessary. Using it to denounce racial segregation, a law professor noted at the time, was like saying that "fire burns," or that "a cold causes snuffles."[25]

Some of these criticisms gained force in hindsight. But in fact Warren and his colleagues acted thoughtfully, indeed inspiringly, in 1954. The

Chief Justice came to the bench convinced that racial segregation was evil. Determined to break with existing jurisprudence, he was ready to strike down *de jure* racial segregation in the public schools. Anticipating strong opposition from southern whites, he was eager to arrive at a unanimous or near-unanimous decision and to write an opinion that would not greatly rile the South. He was unwise to employ social science: both Hugo Black and Tom Clark, Southerners, told him in advance that citing Myrdal, a "leftist" in the minds of many people in the South, would feed resistance.[26] But Warren in fact approached his formidable task carefully, showing considerable awareness of its social and political ramifications. That is why he made his decision short, unemotional, and nonconfrontational. In so doing he achieved unanimity, which many foes of segregation considered vital in 1954.

Warren's decision also led the Court to a new constitutional position that promised, at least over time, to revitalize the meaning of "equal protection" under the Fourteenth Amendment and to change race relations in the South. There was no doubting the powerful symbolic thrust of what he wrote. The decision cut through a tissue of lies that white Southerners and others had woven to maintain the subservient status of black people. It offered the possibility of long-awaited change that other political institutions—the Congress, state legislatures— seemed wholly incapable of producing. And it suggested that the Court under Warren would henceforth interpret the Constitution in light of changing circumstances, not as a fixed document whose meaning had always to be found in the intent of the Founding Fathers or of politicians in the 1860s. These were no small innovations.[27]

4

CROSSROADS, 1954–55

The long-awaited *Brown* ruling aroused great excitement among blacks during the next few days, many of whom shared Ralph Ellison's belief that it could open up a "wonderful world of possibilities" for black children. News of the case, indeed, carried to the byways of the South. Julius Chambers, a black teenager in rural North Carolina who was later to become director-counsel for the Fund, remembered hearing about the decision and gathering his schoolmates and teachers to celebrate. "We assumed that *Brown* was self-executing. The law had been announced, and people would have to obey it. Wasn't that how things worked in America, even in white America?"

Other black people wept with joy. Sara Lightfoot, a ten-year-old black girl, vividly recalled the moment that news of *Brown* reached her house. "Jubilation, optimism, and hope filled my home," she wrote later. "Through a child's eye, I could see the veil of oppression lift from my parents' shoulders. It seemed they were standing taller. And for the first time in my life I saw tears in my father's eyes. 'This is a great and important day,' he said reverently to his children." Robert Jackson, a black history professor at Virginia Union University, added,

This is a most exciting moment. I haven't seen such collective emotion since the day Roosevelt died. A lot of us haven't been breathing for the past nine months. But today the students reacted as if a heavy burden had been lifted from their shoulders. They see a new world opening up for them and those that follow them.

NAACP staff in New York City were so happy, one employee recalled, that they "just sat there looking at one another. The only emotion we felt at that moment was awe—everyone of us felt it." Marshall was more cautious, warning celebrators at a party that night, "you fools go ahead and have your fun . . . we ain't begun to work yet." But he, too, expected the decision to promote rapid and widespread change. The Court, he said publicly, had been "very clear." If the decision were violated anywhere "on one morning," he and his colleagues would "have the responsible authorities in court by the next morning, if not the same afternoon." Marshall estimated that school segregation in the entire country could be eliminated in "up to five years."

Sharing this optimism, some blacks predicted that *Brown* would have consequences extending far beyond schools. For one thing, it would bolster the American cause in the Cold War. A. Philip Randolph, head of the Brotherhood of Sleeping Car Porters, exclaimed that "the decision has given integrity, reality, and strength to the foreign policy of the United States." The *Pittsburgh Courier*, a leading black newspaper, added, "This clarion announcement will also stun and silence America's traducers behind the Iron Curtain. It will effectively impress upon millions of colored people in Asia and Africa the fact that idealism and social morality can and do prevail in the United States, regardless of race, creed, or color."

Other black leaders were hopeful that the decision would affect race relations in all dimensions of American life. Charles Johnson, the president of Fisk University, explained in the summer of 1954, "the principal enumeration was not merely that of the constitutionality of racially separate schools, but of the constitutionality of racial segregation. . . . If segregation is unconstitutional in educational institutions, it is no less so unconstitutional in other aspects of our national life."[1]

Optimists such as Johnson further believed that *Brown* reflected the swelling of larger progressive forces, notably economic growth, technological change, and rising levels of educational attainment, that since 1940 had already stimulated rising optimism in the culture and had led scholars like Gunnar Myrdal to anticipate the weakening of racist beliefs in the United States. Holding large expectations, these optimists thought that almost nothing could stop these trends in the future. They had a point about the future, for these forces grew ever more powerful during the 1960s and helped to stimulate an irresistible civil rights movement. Philip Elman, a top Justice Department official, made a similar point by observing that the ideas sustaining *Plessy* were already dying. "In *Brown*," he joked, nothing that the lawyers said made a difference. Thurgood Marshall could have stood up there and recited 'Mary had a little lamb,' and the result would have been exactly the same." Jack Greenberg put the matter a little more gracefully. "There was 'a current of history,'" he noted later, "and the Court became part of it."[2]

Not all black people, of course, shared the confidence of these optimists. Many were highly skeptical, knowing from experience how obdurate whites could be. But there were promising signs of compliance with *Brown* at the time. One night after the decision, the school board of Greensboro, North Carolina, sent a most encouraging signal by agreeing six to one to obey the ruling—or so it seemed at the time. Five of the six who voted in the majority were whites. The sixth was a black man—blacks could vote in Greensboro. North Carolina, indeed, seemed ready to accept the Court's decision. Its governor, William Umstead, was unhappy but deferential. "The Supreme Court," he said, ". . . has spoken."[3]

Some other southern governors, while careful not to endorse desegregation, also appeared resigned to changes ahead. Francis Cherry of Arkansas announced, "Arkansas will obey the law. It always has." James "Big Jim" Folsom of Alabama added, "When the Supreme Court speaks, that's the law." Leaders like Cherry and Folsom were hailed by liberal Southerners, including editorialists for major newspapers in the region: Ralph McGill of the *Atlanta Constitution*; Hodding Carter II of the *Delta Democrat Times* of Greenville, Mississippi; Jonathan Daniels of the *Raleigh News and Observer*; and Harry Ashmore of the *Arkansas Gazette* in Little Rock. Reactions such as these indicated an important fact about the South: even on the sensitive subject of race relations, it was not a monolith.

Compliance in the border states especially pleased liberals in 1954 and 1955. The governors of Delaware, West Virginia, and Kentucky said that they would stand behind the decision. Officials in Oklahoma, Missouri, and the District of Columbia generally backed the ruling. Federal district and circuit court judges concerned with these states also moved to enforce desegregation of the schools. By 1955 it seemed likely that predominantly white cities and towns adjacent to these states, such as in northwest Arkansas, would also comply.

There was, liberals lamented, one especially frightening exception to this pattern of early compliance in the border states. That was in the southern Delaware town of Milford, where blacks were roughly 17 percent of the local population. Town officials, having dawdled, belatedly decided late in the summer of 1954 to desegregate in a token fashion by admitting eleven blacks in September to the tenth grade of the previously all-white high school. (A total of 687 whites also attended the tenth grade.)[4]

When Milford High opened in September 1954, there seemed no cause for alarm. "I didn't think much about the Negro kids one way or another," one white boy recalled. The school board, however, had done little since *Brown* to promote discussion about the issue, and its late-summer edict caught many townspeople by surprise. Ten days after the beginning of school, rumors circulated that a black student had asked a white girl to the forthcoming school dance. Other rumors followed: the black boy had made a "lewd proposal"; a black student had flashed a knife in the boys' washroom during a quarrel; a black girl had used obscene language in sassing a teacher. At this point alarmed local whites, along with many from surrounding areas, flocked to a meeting of some 1,500 people. Many were poor white farmers, but whites of all backgrounds also appear to have turned out. More than 800 people signed a petition against desegregation. Amid threats of violence the school board soon shut the school down indefinitely.

After the school had been closed for four days, the state board of education ordered it reopened. The governor, however, then waffled; neither he nor other top state officials exercised strong leadership concerning the controversy in Milford. At this point, moreover, a demagogue, Bryant Bowles, appeared on the scene. Bowles was a thirty-four-year-old native of Florida, a Marine veteran of World War II and Korea, and in September 1954 a resident of Washington, D.C. Following news of *Brown*, he founded the National Association for the Advancement of White People. With the high school due to reopen the next day, a Monday, he and others hired four small planes with loudspeakers and flew back and forth over the towns of southern Delaware. The loudspeakers called for people to show up that evening at a nearby small airport. There, Bowles promised, they could take a stand: "keeping segregation as it has always been in Delaware."

At the meeting, attended by 2,000 or more people (some estimates were as high as 5,000) Bowles held up his three-year-old daughter and cried, "Do you think I'll ever let my little girl go to school with Negroes? I certainly will not!" Later that evening, Bowles addressed a second rally

Bryant Bowles, head of the National Association for the Advancement of White People, who incited protests against desegregation in Delaware, September 1954. *(Library of Congress, Prints and Photographs Division, New York World-Telegram & Sun Collection)*

a few miles away, this one attended by 1,000 people. "The Negro," he proclaimed, "will never be satisfied until he moves into the front bedroom of the white man's home, and when he tries that a lot of gunpowder will burn." Bowles then called upon whites to boycott the school.

Many white parents in the next few days responded as Bowles had asked: on Monday, it was estimated that only one-third of the white students appeared at the school. (Ten of the eleven blacks did, too.) Some of the parents supported the boycott enthusiastically; others feared violence if they sent their children to school. Bowles and his allies telephoned hesitant parents and threatened their children if they challenged the boycott. He warned that local businessmen who supported desegregation could expect to be boycotted themselves. His supporters burned crosses. Within a few days the boycott had spread to many nearby towns, even though most of them (having done nothing to comply with *Brown*) still had no black students in their all-white schools.

Amid this turbulence the Milford school board dissolved, replaced by new members who gave in to the threats of violence of Bowles and others. At the end of September the new board decided to end desegregation in the school. Louis Redding, still leading the cause for desegregation in Delaware, filed an injunction against the board. Five months later, in February 1955, the Delaware Supreme Court agreed with Redding's claim that *Brown* had nullified school segregation laws in the state. It added, however, that the Court had not yet stated when or how segregating districts had to change their ways. Redding kept litigating, but he continued to face legal obstacles. It was not until 1962 that blacks were admitted to Milford's white schools. The first black student graduated from the high school in 1965. Many elementary schools in southern Delaware continued to be segregated in the 1960s. The last all-black high school in the state (in Georgetown) finally shut down in 1970.[5]

The struggle in southern Delaware was an alarm bell that sounded two warnings to advocates of *Brown*: first, that ardent segregationists, especially if aided by demagogic outsiders, could negate the decision; and second, that integrationists in contests ahead would need forceful white community leaders to guide the masses of white people who uneasily sat on the fence. Kenneth Clark, dispatched by the NAACP to investigate the situation in Milford, emphasized this need at the time. He observed sadly but correctly that many white Delaware leaders did not stand up to be counted in 1954.

Discouraging as this battle was, many advocates of *Brown* in 1954 and early 1955 remained guardedly optimistic about developments in the border states. The open defiance that stymied efforts for change in southern Delaware, they observed accurately, was an exception to the general pattern of compliance in such areas. Wilmington, Delaware, site of one of the five suits making up *Brown*, took steps to desegregate its public schools. So did other large border state cities: Kansas City; St. Louis; Oklahoma City; Louisville; Charleston, West Virginia; and Baltimore. By the 1955–56 school year, 70 percent of school districts in the border states had biracial classrooms.[6]

The response in Baltimore, where Marshall had attended Jim Crow schools in his youth, was especially heartening. In 1954, roughly half the city's blacks lived in substandard housing. The median income of African Americans over fourteen years of age was roughly 60 percent of white median income. Most of the city's public parks remained segregated. Spending per pupil for Baltimore's black elementary school students (36 percent of total enrollment in 1953–54) was 94 percent of the level for white students, while the black high schools received 77 percent as much per pupil as the white high schools.

Some of Maryland's political leaders, including Governor Theodore McKeldin, called for caution on hearing the news of *Brown*. They said that schools should await further guidance from the Court before moving to desegregate. But Baltimore's civic leaders, politicians, and school officials had anticipated a ruling such as *Brown*. Before 1954 they had sponsored interracial workshops and staff meetings for teachers and administrators. Moreover, the city already had a free choice plan, which enabled students (with exceptions in some crowded areas) to choose their schools. When *Brown* was announced, the city's school superintendent, John Fischer, acted immediately to implement this plan for all students, regardless of race. Hard upon this announcement, the Catholic Archdiocese, which schooled 56,000 children, said that it would also abide by *Brown*. The city's housing authority then declared that it would discontinue segregation policies in its allocation of public housing units. By July 1954, six weeks after *Brown*, *de jure* segregation in the Jim Crow city of Baltimore persisted only in public parks and beaches.

When Baltimore's schools opened in September 1954, islands of resistance surfaced. Demonstrators picketed outside twelve of the city's 189 schools. On two days during the first week of October, street fighting between blacks and whites led to six arrests and caused some 2,000 students to stay away from school. Bryant Bowles, fresh from his activities in nearby southern Delaware, then showed up to rally picketers. Both Fischer and city officials, however, quickly reaffirmed their support of desegregation. Thurgood Marshall, meeting with NAACP leaders in Baltimore, praised this show of firmness. By October 8, the demonstrations had ceased.

Preexistence of the free choice plan eased peaceful acceptance of these changes. Had the city operated a pupil placement system based on neighborhoods—as most cities did—it would not have been possible to act so quickly and decisively. Moreover, the changes in 1954–55 were far

Whites demonstrate against school desegregation in Baltimore, October 1954. *(Library of Congress, Prints and Photographs Division, New York World-Telegram & Sun Collection)*

from revolutionary. Of the 57,064 black pupils in the public system that year, only 3 percent attended schools with whites. Of the city's 189 schools, only forty-seven had one or more black students. Few black teachers were assigned to white schools; no whites went to teach in the formerly all-black schools. Profound class differences continued to separate blacks and whites in Baltimore, as everywhere in the United States.

But most Baltimorians concluded that the changes in the city's schools, though modest numerically, reflected the free choice of black parents and teachers. Many black parents said they did not want to "go too fast." Observers, Marshall included, were especially happy that violence had been minor and that the business of education went on undisturbed after October. Like Clark, he was sure of the lesson to be remembered: just as Milford had shown that indecisive local leadership could sink desegregation, Baltimore proved that strong local leadership might save it.[7]

Marshall remained sanguine in 1954–55; as late as 1956 he said, "We've got the other side licked. It's just a matter of time." But he was well aware that even the border states moved slowly in places. In Maryland, for instance, only three of the state's twenty-three counties had totally desegregated their schools by 1955. Not until after 1964 did another county follow suit. Challenged by restive black leaders, the school board of Anne Arundel County, which included the state capital of Annapolis, then replied that many whites feared "the tremendous effect on children and young people of both races if they had been suddenly thrown together on a large scale."[8] Although most border state school districts eventually complied with *Brown*—90 percent by 1964—those that did not often had high percentages and numbers of blacks. Thus 45 percent of black students in border states still attended all-black schools in 1964.[9]

Marshall also recognized that states in the South, especially the Deep South states of South Carolina, Georgia, Alabama, Mississippi, and Louisiana, would come around at an even slower pace, if at all. Getting word of *Brown*, Governor Herman Talmadge of Georgia exclaimed, "I do not believe in Negroes and whites associating with each other either socially or in school systems, and as long as I am governor, it won't happen." Governor James Byrnes of South Carolina said, "South Carolina will not now nor for some years to come mix white and colored children in our schools." Fielding Wright of Mississippi, Dixiecrat vice-presidential candidate in 1948, added, "We shall insist upon segregation regardless of consequences."[10] Understanding the fierceness of such reactions, which often terrorized would-be plaintiffs, Marshall took on only a few school desegregation cases in these states during the 1950s. Instead, the Fund concentrated on converting states like Virginia and North Carolina, where "soft" segregationists like North Carolina's Sam Ervin seemed perhaps a little more amenable to legal arguments.

Virginia, however, presented severe difficulties of its own. Many white people in northeastern areas, near Washington, were amenable to change. Not so the more heavily-black "Southside," where Barbara Johns and others had struggled against segregation in 1951. There, and in many other parts of the state, officials loyal to Senator Harry Byrd, the powerful boss of state Democratic politics, dominated affairs. And Byrd reacted immediately and furiously against *Brown*. He called the decision "the most serious blow that has been struck against the rights of the States in a matter vitally affecting their authority and welfare. . . . In Virginia we are facing a crisis of the first magnitude." Governor Thomas Stanley, who owed his election to Byrd, needed no prodding. In late June 1954 he proclaimed, "I shall use every legal means at my command to continue segregated schools in Virginia."[11]

North Carolina, too, offered Marshall bleak prospects by early 1955. By then, early indications of compliance, such as Greensboro's, had largely disappeared. Governor Umstead died in late 1954, replaced by an outwardly moderate man, Luther Hodges. But Hodges had no stomach for desegregation, which he calculated was politically unpopular among whites in the state. Fearing (or pretending to fear) a "redneck revolt" if he promoted desegregation, Hodges and other leaders opposed changes in the schools. In April 1955 the General Assembly proclaimed, "The mixing of the races in the public schools . . . cannot be accomplished, and should not be attempted." It then passed a Pupil Assignment Act that turned over decision making concerning school segregation to local officials. The act clearly aimed to flout the *Brown* decision.

Greensboro's white leaders gladly supported such actions. Indeed, as early as June 1954 it became apparent that only two of the six school board members (including the sole black member) who had appeared to back *Brown* at their meeting on May 18, 1954, really intended compliance to happen soon or in anything other than a token fashion. The others blocked school desegregation, not only in 1954–55 but also for the next two years. Stonewalling angry black protests, Greensboro did not really comply with *Brown* until forced to do so in 1971, one of the last cities in the state to do so.[12]

To advocates like Marshall, one of the most worrisome aspects of resistance in North Carolina, as in many other places of stern opposition to *Brown*, was the breadth of it among white leaders. Although Hodges and others claimed to move slowly in order to forestall something worse—a nasty "redneck" revolt—in fact they raised such a specter as a ruse. The majority of the state's white elites—politicians, churchmen, businessmen, and civic leaders—were as much opposed to desegregation of schools as were the "rednecks" they professed to fear. And they rarely if ever spoke out against white violence or incendiary segregationist rhetoric. As events in Milford had suggested, Marshall and others who yearned to end segregation could do little without bold leadership in the white community.[13]

Marshall and his allies also recognized in 1954–55 that most whites in the North displayed little zeal for *Brown*. Although polls suggested that whites were becoming steadily more liberal in their attitudes about race, Northerners did not push for change in the 1950s.[14] When the decision was announced, many politically engaged people in the North (as well as in the South) were preoccupied with the dramatic Army-McCarthy hearings in the Senate, which were shown on television from April 22 to June 17. Neither the *Brown* hearings in December 1953 nor Warren's reading in May 1954 received television coverage. Northern newspapers, after giving *Brown* front-page treatment for a few days after May 17, paid relatively little attention to race relations thereafter. Not until 1955 did the *New York Times* have a regular correspondent (Anthony Lewis) covering the Court.

Supporters of *Brown* in 1954–55 especially yearned for backing from the most commanding white leader of all: President Eisenhower. Ike enjoyed enormous public standing and popularity at the time. Many white business leaders in the South, who were keys to community responses to *Brown*, especially admired him. So did many influential southern whites who had served in the armed forces. If Eisenhower were to speak out strongly for the decision, other whites would presumably have to listen. If he chastised obstructionists, they, too, might back down a bit.

Eisenhower, like millions of white Americans at the time, considered himself a racially tolerant man. As president he issued executive orders desegregating federal facilities such as shipyards and veterans' hospitals. He encouraged the desegregation of public schools in the District of Columbia. His liberal attorney general, Herbert Brownell, supported the Fund's efforts. In his second term, Eisenhower signed two civil rights bills. Both the bills were weak and had little effect; still, they were the first to get through Congress since the days of Reconstruction following the Civil War.

But—again like most white Americans—Eisenhower had grown

up in a virtually all-white world. There had been no blacks in his home-town in Kansas or in his class at West Point. He had spent much of his adult life in a Jim Crow army and had opposed as disruptive Truman's order to desegregate the armed services in 1948. He had many friends in the South who were outspoken about the incompetence, as they saw it, of their "darkies," and who adamantly supported racial segregation.

Eisenhower approached the issue of school desegregation very cautiously. Some of his top advisers, noting the gains the Republican party had made among white voters in the South during the 1952 election, urged him to move carefully lest the party forfeit possible political advantage. More important, the president was philosophically conservative about the capacity of government to change the hearts and minds of people. "The improvement of race relations," he wrote in his diary in 1953, "is one of those things that will be healthy and sound only if it starts locally. I do not believe that prejudices . . . will succumb to compulsion. Consequently, I believe that Federal law imposed upon our States . . . would set back the cause of race relations a long, long time." He wrote the daughter of Booker T. Washington, "We cannot do it [improve race relations] by cold lawmaking, but must make these changes by appealing to reason, by prayer, and by constantly working at it through our own efforts."[15]

If Earl Warren had any uncertainties about the president's attitude on such matters, they were probably resolved while the Court was considering *Brown* in early 1954. At that time Eisenhower invited him to a dinner at the White House and sat him next to John W. Davis, who was leading the defense team against Marshall. After telling Warren that Davis was a great American, Eisenhower took the Chief Justice by the arm and explained to him the southern point of view. Southern whites, he said, "are not bad people. All they are concerned about is to see that their sweet little girls are not required to sit in school alongside some big overgrown Negro."

When the Court announced *Brown* shortly thereafter, Eisenhower was unhappy. When reporters demanded to know his opinion of the decision, he responded that he was duty-bound as president to accept it. But he refused to endorse it. "The Supreme Court has spoken," he said awkwardly, "and I am sworn to uphold their—the constitutional processes in this country, and I am trying. I will obey." There was no doubting, however, his private feelings. He told a speechwriter,

I am convinced that the Supreme Court decision set back progress in the South at least fifteen years. . . . It's all very well to talk about school integration—if you remember that you may also be talking about social disintegration. Feelings are deep on this, especially where children are involved. . . . We can't demand perfection in these moral things. All we can do is keep working toward a goal and keep it high. And the fellow who tries to tell me that you can do these things by FORCE is just plain NUTS.[16]

When Eisenhower said that "feelings run deep" on the issue, he surely meant his own feelings in particular. Neither then nor at any time during the remaining years of his presidency did he endorse the *Brown* decision. In the 1956 campaign, he (like his Democratic opponent, Adlai Stevenson) stated that he could "not imagine any set of circumstances" that would lead him to send in federal troops to enforce court orders for desegregation. When a crisis over desegregating schools in Little Rock erupted a year later, he had to eat his words, but defended his action as needed to preserve order, not to liberalize race relations. As Commander in Chief he had a duty to prevent violence.

Eisenhower's decidedly cool approach to desegregation of the races was hardly unusual in 1954. After all, most white Northerners at the time were equally cool. And white Southerners did have "feelings" that "ran deep." But the president, an extraordinarily popular figure, could have used the White House as a "bully pulpit." His refusal to do so was morally obtuse, and it allowed southern intransigence—except in the case of Little Rock in 1957—to go unchallenged. With reason, it deeply angered advocates of civil rights. Roy Wilkins, executive secretary of the NAACP, exclaimed, "If he had fought World War II the way he fought for civil rights, we would all be speaking German today."[17]

The president's reluctance to climb out on a limb for civil rights made a difference to Warren, who well knew that the Court needed political support if it was to have any hope whatever for enforcement of its rulings. Such was the discouraging political context that faced the Court as it weighed what to do next about segregation in the schools. This context is well worth remembering when one engages in retrospective criticisms of judicial caution.

Many foes of segregation hoped that Warren and his colleagues, who had promised to address in 1955 the question of implementing *Brown*, would issue clear and forceful guidelines. In support of such a goal, Attorney General Brownell's brief called on district courts to require southern school administrators to come up with desegregation plans within ninety days. Thurgood Marshall also demanded that the Court fix a date for the end of segregation in the schools.

The Court, however, moved slowly, in part because Justice Jackson died of his heart troubles in October 1954. Eisenhower's nominee to replace him, John Marshall Harlan, struck most people as a first-rate choice. Harlan, a graduate of Princeton University, had been a Rhodes Scholar and then compiled a distinguished record as an attorney in New York. Impeccably tailored, he had a ramrod, patrician exterior. In early 1954 Eisenhower had named him to the federal court of appeals for the second circuit, which included New York, Connecticut, and Vermont. Harlan revered his grandfather and namesake, John Marshall Harlan, who had issued the famous dissent from *Plessy*. Southerners in Congress therefore stalled before finally acquiescing to his appointment in March 1955. Only thereafter, in mid-April, did the Court undertake the final round of rehearings. It was not until May 31, 1955, a little more than a year after *Brown*, that a unanimous Court announced what everyone soon called *Brown II*.

In the discussions leading to this decision, divisions again appeared within the Court. Black, supported by Douglas, continued to worry that the Deep South would resort to demagoguery and violence in opposing desegregation. Recalling the sad experience of Prohibition, he warned his colleagues that the Court "should not issue what it cannot enforce."[18] It should confine itself, therefore, to offering relief only to the plaintiffs in the five cases that the Court had decided in 1954. That would at least give a start to the process of desegregation. Plaintiffs in other school districts could litigate in the years ahead. Disrespect for the law, and violence, which Black much feared, might be averted.

The other justices hoped for a little better reaction from the South and determined to fashion an order that would apply to all segregated school districts. They, too, however, were afraid of antagonizing the South by setting time limits for action. Warren was especially aware that the Court by itself could not do much to enforce a firm order. Congress, he knew, was in no mood to back such a move, let alone enact strong civil rights legislation. Eisenhower was obviously reluctant to support bold action. Finally, Warren and his colleagues again wanted to speak with unanimity. For all these reasons they agreed to compromise, seizing on a phrase that Frankfurter suggested as a way of dealing with the troublesome question of time limits: the South should be directed to proceed with "all deliberate speed."[19]

Warren's brief ruling did not call upon the lower federal courts to require that school districts submit desegregation plans within any particular period of time, and it did not set any fixed date for the end of segregated schools. Instead, the Court said it would remand desegregation cases to the federal judges in the district and appeals courts of the South and border states. These courts, in turn, were instructed to "require that the defendants make a prompt and reasonable start toward full compliance" with *Brown*. The Court added that the district courts were to

> enter such orders and decrees consistent with this opinion as are necessary and proper to admit to public schools on a racially nondiscriminatory basis with all deliberate speed the parties to these cases.[20]

There is probably no Supreme Court language so hotly disputed as "all deliberate speed." Those who defended the Court's decision in 1955—and later—maintained that Warren and his colleagues had little choice but to move cautiously, given the predictably angry reaction from the Deep South and the lack of support in the North for bold enforcement of change in race relations. They further pointed out that *Brown II* did not give carte blanche to resisters. School administrators would be allowed to move with "all deliberate speed" so as to have time to work out practical problems, such as redistricting, drawing new routes for school buses, and reassigning teachers and pupils. But they were not to dawdle in order to satisfy racist opinion in local communities. The Court stated that defendants must show that extensions of time were "in the public interest and . . . consistent with good faith compliance at the earliest possible date."

Defenders of *Brown II*, then and later, stressed two other points. The first is that great social changes in history take place gradually: nothing that the Court could have said or done would quickly have reformed deeply established racial patterns in the South. In settling for "all deliberate speed," therefore, the Court acted realistically. The second is that the Court did reaffirm *Brown*. Segregated districts that resisted would be breaking the law. Americans who trusted in the power of the law believed that justice would win out in the end.

Understanding the Court's delicate position, Marshall, too, looked hopefully to the long run. Two days after *Brown II*, he told a friend, "You know, some people want most of the hog, other people insist on having the whole hog, and then there are some people who want the hog, the hair, and the rice on the hair. What the hell! The more I think about it, I think it's a damned good decision!" The South, he added, has "got to yield to the Constitution. And yield means yield! Yield means give up!" He then outlined a strategy that would entail litigating cases in state after state. Marshall concluded, "You can say all you want but those white crackers are going to get tired of having Negro lawyers beating 'em every day in court. They're going to get tired of it."[21]

Marshall, however, quickly took a jolt from the lower courts. In July 1955, Judge John Parker, ruling for a three-man federal district court in the remanded South Carolina case of *Briggs v. Elliott*, issued an important, widely noted ruling that threatened to dilute the strength of *Brown*. The Supreme Court, Parker said, did not mean that "states must mix persons of different races in the public schools. . . . What it has decided . . . is that a state may not deny any person on account of race the right to attend any school that it maintains. . . . *The Constitution, in other words, does not require integration. . . . It merely forbids the use of governmental power to enforce segregation.*" Parker's decision, which became known as the "Briggs Dictum," greatly appealed to southern officials, who began to adopt a range of ruses aimed at avoiding the appearance of using racial considerations as the basis for their assignment of pupils to schools.[22]

In mid-summer 1955, with schools set to open soon, the future of segregated schools in the South was at a crossroads. Would Marshall and his allies manage to drive straight ahead, or would white resisters in the South use Parker's opinion, and other means, to blockade moves toward change in race relations?

5

SOUTHERN WHITES FIGHT BACK

Not long after the Court issued _Brown II_, a fourteen-year-old black youth, Emmett Till, left his home in Chicago for a vacation with relatives in Tallahatchie County, Mississippi. Till did not understand the racial mores of the South. He bragged to acquaintances in Mississippi that he had had sex with white women in Chicago. He also entered a store and, it was alleged, whistled at the cashier, a young white woman. The woman's husband and his brother-in-law went to the cabin where Till was staying with his great-uncle, Moses Wright, and dragged him away. Three days later Till's mangled body was discovered in the Tallahatchie River. He had been shot in the head and tied to a heavy fan that had dragged him into the depths. His mother had his body returned to Chicago and displayed it in an open casket for four days. Thousands of people paid their respects. The media gave the story wide coverage and graphic photography.

At first it seemed as if Mississippi authorities would punish the abductors, who were soon arrested and placed on trial for murder in September 1955. And the case against them seemed solid. Wright, braving violent retaliation, testified for the prosecution and identified the defendants as the men who had snatched Till away. But the defendants, while admitting that they had taken Till from the cabin, maintained that they had let him go. A defense attorney asserted that the corpse was not Till's, although a ring on the body's finger bore the initials of Till's father.

The defense attorney closed his case by saying he was sure that the jurors (all male and all white, though the county was 63 percent black) would vote to acquit. "Every last Anglo-Saxon one of you," he said, "has the courage to free [the defendants]." After an hour and seven minutes the jurors acquitted them. One juror remarked, "If we hadn't stopped to drink pop, it wouldn't have taken that long." Later, a special grand jury declined to indict the defendants for kidnapping, even though they had confessed on the stand to doing just that. Wright moved to Chicago and never returned home.[1]

There was no direct link between the *Brown* cases and the murder of Emmett Till. But the killing merits mention for several reasons. First, the murder and trial received international attention and aroused widespread indignation, especially among black people. Perhaps even more than the infuriating southern foot-dragging concerning *Brown*, the murder of Till—and of other blacks in the next few years—stimulated rage leading in time to more militant civil rights activity. Second, the killing exposed the ultimate weapon in an arsenal that extremist southern whites wielded in their war to preserve their supremacy. White violence against blacks in the South had declined since its peak years between 1890 and 1920. Now, after 1954, it surged again, perhaps reflecting rising white anxiety about blacks getting "uppity" in the aftermath of *Brown*. If they managed to get into white schools, there was no telling what might come next—perhaps competition for jobs. Between 1954 and 1959 there were 210 recorded acts of white violence against black people in the South, including six murders, twenty-nine assaults with firearms, forty-four beatings, and sixty bombings.[2]

The Till case also bared a range of white sexual concerns. Some of those who played on these apprehensions cited statistics revealing rising rates of out-of-wedlock pregnancy among blacks and argued that black people had a less developed moral sense than whites. More commonly, white supremacists continued to insist that black men lusted after white women and that mixing would pollute the purity of the white race.[3] State Senator Walter Givhan of Alabama argued that the true goal of the NAACP was "to open the bedroom doors of our white women to Negro men." A South Carolinian, Herbert Ravenel Sass, wrote an article for *Atlantic Monthly* in November 1956 entitled "Mixed Schools and Mixed Blood." He emphasized that most adults found "mixed mating" "disagreeable or even repugnant." If black and white pupils were to go to school together, "among those new generations mixed matings would become commonplace and a greatly enlarged mixed-blood population would result."[4]

Reactions such as these revealed the uniquely sensitive place that schools were to maintain in forthcoming battles over race relations. In the 1950s, as earlier, working-class southern whites commonly "mixed" with blacks in places of employment, especially on farms and plantations. Later, when civil rights laws forced them to do so, most southern whites also learned to associate with blacks, though often uneasily, in public places, such as restaurants, parks, and buses, and even in a wider range of jobs. Desegregation of schools, however, always remained an extraordinarily problematic matter for many white parents, and for emotionally powerful reasons: they wanted the very best education for their children and they worried about social mixing, dating, and even marriage.

Whites who openly expressed feelings of this kind normally raised the specter of sexually aggressive black males. But at some level they also worried that their own children might come to enjoy the company, even sexual relationships, with blacks. Perhaps, just perhaps, these parents harbored deep, scarcely conscious doubts about the durability of white supremacy—and therefore about their ability in the long run to maintain their social and economic superiority over people of color. In any event, the idea of racial mixing in the schools remained especially frightening to whites in the years to come. It was therefore ironic that segregated public schools were among the first institutions to be seriously challenged by the NAACP and the Fund, and therefore to be ruled upon by the Supreme Court.

No one reiterated opposition to the desegregation of schools more purposefully than Senator James Eastland of Mississippi. A relentless, humorless man, Eastland was also a staunch Cold Warrior. Five days before the Court issued *Brown II* he gave a major speech on school segregation and ordered his office to send it to some 300,000 people. Following *Brown II* it was cited again and again by southern editorialists and other speakers and became one of the most important documents of the southern resistance. The speech concluded, "It is evident that the decision of the Supreme Court in the school segregation cases was based on the writings and teaching of pro-communist agitators and other enemies of the American form of government."[5]

Eastland surely did not speak for all whites in the South. The notion that "the white South" was uniformly racist was a flawed, often self-gratifying northern notion. To be sure, states of the Deep South, which

Senator James Eastland, the powerful segregationist leader from Mississippi, 1960. *(Library of Congress, Prints and Photographs Division, New York World-Telegram & Sun Collection, 1960 photo)*

had the highest percentages of blacks, remained as immovably defiant after *Brown II* as earlier. Other areas of the South, however, particularly local regions with small percentages of blacks, seemed more accommodating. Most of west Texas and northwestern Arkansas desegregated after 1955 without incident. Throughout the South, there were white people here and there—parents, school principals, school board members, other community leaders—who were prepared to support *Brown*. Many more whites, especially parents, were moderates. Although they did not consider segregation to be morally wrong, they were law-abiding and concerned more about the quality of their children's schools than about defending all aspects of segregation. Their reactions to *Brown* and *Brown II* often depended on the actions of local white leaders.

Even within Black Belt areas, patterns of white resistance varied: in the heavily black Delta area of Mississippi, for instance, white leaders vehemently opposed desegregation, but many of them tended to be paternalistic and to have doubts about the most extreme behavior of violently racist groups like the Ku Klux Klan. Parts of nearby southwestern

Mississippi, a very poor region that also had high percentages of blacks, witnessed a rawer, cruder style of white racism, including rising levels of violence, in the aftermath of *Brown*.[6]

Variations developed in cities, too. Many whites in urban areas such as Birmingham ("Bombingham," liberals called it) had long shown themselves willing to spill blood if necessary to stop civil rights activity. Even in Birmingham, however, folkways proved fluid over time: moderate whites in the early 1960s slowly turned against such tactics. By the mid-1960s, when the federal government finally cracked down on Jim Crow, many white businessmen and professional people in southern cities, including Birmingham, concluded that unbending insistence on white supremacy alienated Northerners, isolated their region, and impeded economic development. Further resistance, they recognized, was both futile and counterproductive. White attitudes, in short, changed over the years. The egalitarian message of *Brown*, once given teeth, ultimately helped to liberate white Southerners as well as blacks.

It is one thing, however, to identify variations in southern opinions about race and another to imagine that liberals in the South had wide influence in the 1950s. On the contrary, southern liberals almost everywhere remained weak and on the defensive. In the late 1940s conservative business leaders had spearheaded a successful coalition against Operation Dixie, an ambitious effort by the Congress of Industrial Organizations to promote labor unions in the South. In so succeeding they had weakened liberal elements in southern politics. The mass of blacks, meanwhile, still lacked the vote in the 1950s. On labor as well as racial issues, there were only a few southern politicians of stature—Governor "Big Jim" Folsom of Alabama was one—who managed in the early 1950s to forge liberal-populist coalitions. Fewer still dared to call for substantial changes in Jim Crow.

Systems of political apportionment further weakened southern liberals, whose potential strength, as in the North, lay primarily in urban and suburban regions. Rural, Black Belt areas, often the most committed to white supremacy, continued to be overrepresented in the governments of many southern states. In Georgia, the most egregious example, a county unit system made it possible for 121 of the most rural counties, with one-third of the state's population, to nominate a governor. In Alabama, sixteen Black Belt counties had 12 percent of the population but elected 25 percent of the state legislators. As one observer of southern politics put it, "The political South is far more conservative than are southerners themselves."[7]

The southern judiciary, too, was hardly a bastion of liberalism in the mid- and late 1950s. Although a few of the fifty-eight federal judges in the South—keys to interpretations of "all deliberate speed"—were to emerge as defenders of desegregation, most of them showed little stomach for change until the mid-1960s. Of the forty-eight federal district judges in 1960 (the other ten sat on the circuit courts), forty-three had been born, raised, and educated in the South. All were white males. A few openly championed Jim Crow. Judge J. Robert Elliott in Georgia denounced "pinks, radicals, and black voters" who were trying to topple racial hierarchies. Judge Harold Cox of Mississippi described blacks who tried to vote as "niggers" who were "acting like a bunch of chimpanzees." Judge Armistead Dobie, who had ruled against the Fund in the Farmville case in 1952, lamented later that a "foreign Communistic anthropologist" (Gunnar Myrdal) had stimulated civil rights activity.[8]

Those judges who challenged segregation encountered fierce reactions from whites in their communities. One of the first to face such hostility was Judge Waties Waring, a Charleston, South Carolina, native who had dared in the late 1940s to support Joseph DeLaine and his fellow black plaintiffs in *Briggs v. Elliott*. Out-voted by the other two judges, Waring had then been threatened by local rowdies who hurled a large lump of concrete through the front window of his house, barely missing him and his wife. Erstwhile friends ostracized him. In 1954 he resigned from the bench and moved to New York City. When he died in 1968, his body was returned to Charleston for burial. He was lowered into the earth in the presence of 300 black people who gratefully remembered his stand. Only three white people—his widow, the undertaker, and the minister— took part in the ceremony.[9]

Other judges who dared to defy local white opinion also suffered. Judge Richard Rives, who in 1956 upheld Montgomery blacks against the city's segregated bus system, discovered that racists had littered his son's gravesite and painted his tombstone red. When he and his wife attended services at their Presbyterian church, long-time friends made a point of sitting far from their pew. Frank Johnson, who joined Rives in the bus case decision, encountered a still nastier ostracism in Montgomery. Opponents bombed his mother's house in the city and burned crosses on his lawn. George Wallace, a former classmate at the University of Alabama Law School who was to become governor of the state in the 1960s, later denounced him as an "integratin', carpetbaggin', scalawaggin', baldfaced liar."[10]

Brown II should have mollified adamant foes of change such as those who had driven Waring out of his state. The ruling, after all, fixed no time for compliance and left important decisions in the hands of southern school officials. Even so, many southern leaders continued to preach defiance. Georgia Governor Marvin Griffin announced, "No matter how much the Supreme Court seeks to sugarcoat its bitter pill of tyranny, the people of Georgia and the South will not swallow it." The *Richmond News Leader* in Virginia editorialized:

> Yesterday's opinion of the Supreme Court ended nothing. And if it be said that the Court's opinion was conciliatory, we would reply that the South is no more of a mind to conciliate on Wednesday than it was on Tuesday. When the Court proposes that its social revolution be imposed upon the South "as soon as practicable," there are those of us who would respond that "as soon as practicable" means never at all.[11]

Statements such as these were obviously demagogic. But they were plentiful in 1955 following *Brown II*, and they apparently resonated well with many poor white people—small farmers and sharecroppers in the countryside and working-class people in the cities, especially where large numbers of blacks lived in proximity. Holding black people down offered many of these white people consolation—protection against job competition as well as some dearly sought sense of status or of superiority to compensate for the hardships of their lives. But "rednecks" such as these were hardly alone in fighting against *Brown*. Most middle-class white business and professional people, too, continued after 1955 to support white supremacy. Negrophobic attitudes, in short, still permeated all levels of southern white society, especially but not only in the Deep South. The urge to suppress black people, though varying over time, had deep roots in southern history.

Many conservative white politicians who held high office in the South during these years readily identified with these feelings, and they naturally championed white supremacy. Others opportunistically fanned the flames of racism during the late 1950s in order to advance their political fortunes. George Wallace of Alabama offered the best example of this turn to demagoguery. Intensely ambitious, Wallace had started as a supporter in the 1940s of Folsom, who avoided racist appeals. In 1948 Wal-

Governor George Wallace of Alabama. *(Library of Congress, Prints and Photographs Division, New York World-Telegram & Sun Collection, 1964 photo)*

lace had refused to join the Dixiecrats who walked out of the Democratic national convention in protest against Truman's initiatives for civil rights. But racist reactions to *Brown* pushed Alabama politics to the right and helped to end Folsom's career. In 1958 Wallace lost the Democratic gubernatorial nomination in a battle against an avid segregationist. Thereafter he pandered to racist feelings. "They outniggered me," he said of his foes in 1958, "and boys, I'm not goin' to be outniggered again." Seeking the gubernatorial nomination in 1962, Wallace waged a racist campaign and won the largest number of votes of any gubernatorial candidate in Alabama history. He proclaimed in his inaugural address in 1963, "I draw the line in the dust and toss the gauntlet before the feet of tyranny, and I say, 'Segregation now! Segregation tomorrow! Segregation forever!' "[12]

Violence. Intimidation. Anguished alarms about social and sexual mingling. Emotional appeals to the Cause of the Confederacy. Raising the specter of communism. These were among the many southern white reactions to *Brown* and *Brown II*. But opponents of change in the South believed after *Brown II* that they had to do four other things: litigate, organize at the local level, agree on a sectionwide statement of resistance, and— most important—devise strategies for assignment of students that would satisfy the federal courts without giving away anything of substance.

In litigating, white Southerners lost a few cases in the late 1950s: relying on the precedent of *Brown*, federal courts ruled against segregated public golf courses and segregated bus systems such as the one that provoked the dramatic boycott led by Martin Luther King and others in Montgomery in 1955–56. The Supreme Court allowed these rulings to stand. But in hotly contested school cases white litigants had considerable advantages over Marshall and his colleagues at the Legal Defense Fund. The first was money, which never ran low, thanks in part to generous funding from state legislatures. South Carolina, for instance, paid two attorneys working on the Clarendon County case $25,000 each. In 1957 Texas lawmakers appropriated $50,000 to help the state attorney general manage legal resistance. White litigators, moreover, had a big edge in the numbers of talented people they could draw upon, thanks to the Jim Crow system that had kept blacks out of law schools. A shortage of resources—of attorneys as well as of funds—hamstrung Marshall and prevented him from undertaking a good many suits.[13]

Disagreements among black attorneys added to Marshall's problems in these years. Infighting at the Fund, much of it centered on conflicts between Marshall and Robert Carter, grew especially sharp. Carter and many other attorneys came to believe that Marshall was spending too much time fund-raising. Eager to litigate a wave of cases in support of *Brown*, they also wondered if "Mr. Civil Rights" had become too accommodating and too ready to rest on his laurels. Marshall, proud of his accomplishments, was certain that Carter and others were scheming to kick him upstairs and take over leadership of the Fund. Meanwhile, the Fund split totally from the NAACP, which engaged in desperate legal battles to keep its state membership lists out of the hands of Alabama officials. When the NAACP refused to turn over the lists in 1956, it was slapped with a $100,000 fine for contempt of court. It had to close its offices in Alabama and appeal. In 1958 the Supreme Court ruled in its favor, but the NAACP's effort was costly and exhausting.[14]

The fight over membership lists revealed the largest problem that Marshall and other black attorneys faced: trying to cope with endlessly imaginative legal offensives waged by their white opponents. Often, the first weapon of the whites was intimidation of blacks who seemed ready to stand up as plaintiffs. As earlier, many blacks had to back away when threatened with loss of employment—or worse. When intimidation failed, whites resorted to a strategy of "all deliberate delay."

Litigation concerning schools in Dallas well exemplified this strategy of delay. Beginning in 1955 after *Brown II*, Marshall and local allies fought white resisters for two years in three separate district court cases, but seemed to get nowhere in their efforts to force Dallas to come up with a desegregation plan. At yet another hearing, this time in November 1957, the attorney for Dallas, Andrew Thuss, was mildly upbraided by federal circuit court judge W. L. Jones, as follows:

> *Jones:* You've taken two years and you're not a step further.... When do you expect to present a [desegregation] plan?
> *Thuss:* I think this summer.
> *Jones:* What do you think deliberate speed means in this situation?

Jones smiled.

He had reason to, for the judge—like many of his colleagues on the bench—was in no hurry to contemplate the mixing of black and white children in the schools. He vacated a district court order that had called for desegregation and set no date for action by the city. Attorneys for the local NAACP finally forced another district court hearing in mid-1959. Marshall turned up at the hearing to assist the local lawyers handling the case. The school board, Marshall complained, was just going through "tongue-in-cheek steps." He was correct, for the judge in this case, T. Whitfield Davidson, had no sympathy for his efforts. Davidson, eighty-two years old, was a former lieutenant governor of the state and had been on the bench since 1932.

Integrationists persevered and secured yet another circuit court hearing in early 1960. At this one, judges Rives and John Minor Wisdom ordered Dallas to present a plan quickly. Three months later, it did so, recommending a "stair-step" procedure under which first grades in the public schools would be desegregated in September 1961. Subsequent first grades were also to be desegregated, so that all twelve grades would be mixed by 1973. Davidson, however, rejected the plan. It moved too fast, he declared. Besides, it would lead to "an amalgamation of the races." He called instead for the "voluntary" desegregation of a few schools. Marshall, who had travelled to Texas again, was bewildered. "I don't know what the ruling is . . . let me out of here."[15]

The litigation in Dallas was far from atypical. J. W. Peltason, a careful observer of these legal contests, estimated that federal judges held more than 200 hearings concerning school desegregation between 1955 and 1960. By the end of that year court orders had achieved token desegregation in Miami, Little Rock, Nashville, and Houston. A few cities in Virginia and North Carolina had also introduced token plans in order to forestall court orders. Atlanta, Chattanooga, Knoxville, and Galveston, having just come under court orders, were slated to start desegregating by 1961. This was indeed "all deliberate delay."[16]

The second effort of southern segregationists—organizing—developed rapidly after 1954. The KKK gathered strength in these years, mainly in rural, Black Belt areas of the Deep South. Mississippi sanctioned creation of a State Sovereignty Commission in 1956. Funded with taxpayer dollars, it employed spy tactics, jury tampering, and false imprisonment to intimidate blacks over the next decade. Most important, however, were White Citizens' Councils. The first of these had formed in Indianola, Mississippi, in July 1954. Many others sprang up after *Brown II*, especially in Mississippi and Alabama. The Citizens' Councils recruited mainly among the middle classes, pursuing—as one historian has put it—"the agenda of the Klan with the demeanor of the Rotary."

Exposed!

A Bob Howie cartoon for *The Citizens' Council, October 1956*. Segregationist groups such as the Citizens' Councils also hinted that Communist agitators were behind NAACP integration efforts.

They too, enjoyed their greatest successes in Black Belt regions of the Deep South.[17]

In mid-1956 the Citizens' Councils claimed 60,000 adherents in Alabama. By the end of the year they had attracted 85,000 members in Mississippi. Overall membership peaked in 1957, probably at around 250,000. Many thousands more sympathized with and applauded their efforts, which included virtually all forms of resistance. Publicly, however, the councils focused on economic intimidation. Blacks who tried to vote or considered sending their children to white schools discovered that they could not get mortgages or other forms of credit. Loans were called in. Medical care and insurance were refused. What the South was doing, council members proclaimed, was resisting a northern-imposed "Reconstruction II."[18]

The quest for a sectionwide statement bore fruit in March 1956, when Senator Strom Thurmond of South Carolina, abetted by such influential southern colleagues as Sam Ervin of North Carolina, Harry Byrd of Virginia, and Richard Russell of Georgia, championed a so-called Southern Manifesto. This widely circulated document accused the Supreme Court of "clear abuse of judicial power." It promised to use "all lawful means to bring about a reversal of this decision which is contrary to the Constitution and to prevent the use of force in its implementation."

Nineteen of the twenty-two southern senators, including moderates such as J. William Fulbright of Arkansas and Lister Hill and John Sparkman of Alabama (who had been the Democratic vice-presidential candidate in 1952), signed the Manifesto. So did seventy-seven of the 105 southern representatives. Moderates who supported it feared political retribution from white constituents. Many, including Fulbright, also held out hopes that better education and economic development would ultimately liberalize white attitudes as well as improve the lives of blacks. But neither in 1956 nor later did these men do anything substantial to better the racial climate in their states. Their silence in the face of white resistance and violence during the 1950s gave great encouragement to racist demagogues and others who resisted *Brown*. Within a few years, it helped to fire very great rage among militant black people, who led the civil rights movement into a thunderously effective direct action phase.[19]

The only southern senators who did not sign were Democratic leader Lyndon Johnson of Texas and the two senators from Tennessee, Albert Gore and Estes Kefauver. All three had presidential or vice-presidential

ambitions that they knew would suffer if they became too closely identified with southern racist opinion. Seventeen of the twenty-eight House
members who refused to sign were from Texas, which with a black
population of 13 percent had the smallest proportion of blacks of any
southern state.[20] Other southern congressmen who resisted pressure to
sign represented major urban centers (such as Miami and Nashville) in
non-Deep South areas—from Florida, North Carolina, and Tennessee.[21]

Easily the most effective resistance of southern whites came at the
state level, in laws and constitutional amendments aimed at evading
compliance with *Brown*. Many of these whites liked to say, "As long as
we can legislate, we can segregate." Georgia made it a felony for any
state or local official to spend public funds on desegregated schools, and
thus there were no such schools in Georgia. Mississippi and Louisiana
declared it illegal for children to attend racially mixed schools. South
Carolina repealed its laws requiring compulsory school attendance and
eliminated tenure clauses in teachers' contracts. It also said that teachers
could not belong to the NAACP. Other states tried to emulate Alabama
and bar the NAACP from operating within their borders. Intimidation
and restrictive laws were instrumental in cutting southern membership
in the organization from 130,000 in 1955 to 80,000 in 1957.[22]

Virginia's white population included many moderates who were un-
easy with tough responses. But the powerful political machine of Senator
Byrd overrode the moderates, and the state pioneered the strategy of
Massive Resistance in 1956. This authorized the closing of any public
schools ordered to desegregate and approved state-supported tuition
grants for white students attending "private" schools. In late 1958 and
early 1959 officials closed public schools in Norfolk, Charlottesville, and
Warren County (in the northern part of the state) rather than subject
white students—some 13,000 in all—to biracial classrooms. Students in
Norfolk received no education for several months. When a federal court
ruled against this plan in 1959, token desegregation began in Arlington,
Alexandria, and Norfolk. But Prince Edward County, where Barbara
Johns and other students had carried out their electrifying strike against
segregation at Robert R. Moton High School in Farmville in 1951, responded by shutting down its schools and setting up "private" schools
for whites. These schools, which accommodated 1,400 white students,
received support from white organizations such as Parent Teacher As-
sociations, the Jaycees, and churches, and from state and county funds.

The Reverend L. Francis Griffin, who had forcefully backed Johns in

1951, again moved into action, launching efforts to help the county's 1,700 black children find schooling of one kind or another. Approximately 300 were placed in "free schools" in other communities or states—some of them in 1963–64 at Moton High in Farmville. Many of the black students, however, did without formal education for four years until the Supreme Court (in *Griffin v. County School Board*) ruled against the county in 1964.[23]

The most widely adopted white strategies were "pupil placement" laws, approved during the mid- and late 1950s in ten states. These were shrewdly designed statutes that avoided mention of "Negro" or "race." They stipulated that local districts should assign students to schools according to very complicated psychological and "academic" criteria, such as student preparation and aptitude, and the "morals, conduct, health, and personal standards of the pupil." The goal, of course, was to perpetuate segregated schools. Under Virginia's law, school authorities considered hundreds of thousands of placements without discovering one black student qualified to be placed in a white school.

Aided by Marshall and others in the Fund, blacks challenged statutes such as these in the district courts. But their efforts were frustrating, in part because the pupil placement laws had the effect of requiring black students individually to establish qualifications for admittance to a white school. If one student somehow managed to do so, she or he did not open the way for others. And the courts, dealing with evasion on a case by case basis, were slow to put a stop to such tactics. In November 1958, the Supreme Court allowed Alabama's law to stand, affirming without hearing oral argument the judgment of a court of appeals that had said race had played no role in the case.[24]

Southern whites also relied heavily on "freedom of choice" statutes. On paper these seemed fair, for they permitted parents to send their children to schools of their choice. In practice, however, virtually no white children applied to black schools. And black parents who considered sending their children to white schools had to initiate the transfer process individually, and then to combat a range of bureaucratic obstacles such as those in pupil placement laws. Black parents had other matters to worry about. Would mixed-race schools take their children seriously? Protect them against white hostility? Give them a better education? How would their angry white neighbors react to such a revolutionary change in local custom?[25]

A young black student in rural Virginia, Stanley Trent, recalled the way in which he, his younger brother, and parents reacted when told that a "freedom of choice" plan was to be implemented in their district. His parents asked him, "Which school do you want to attend?" Trent quickly replied, "I don't want to go to no white school." His brother concurred. Trent added, "My father signed the form indicating that we wished to remain in our same school, and that was the end of our family conference. We returned outside and continued to shoot some hoops." Reflecting later, Trent concluded that his parents worried that enrollment in one of the white schools "would place us in physical, psychological, and emotional danger. They feared that our mere presence in one of the newly integrated schools would aggravate and intensify the hatred that had maintained our segregated communities, our segregated existence, for centuries."[26]

A number of struggles—some of them resulting in heralded controversies—illustrate the ways that whites and blacks contested for the future of their schools in the late 1950s.

Blacks managed to eke out minor victories in a few of these struggles. The first was in Hoxie, Arkansas, a small, predominantly white town in the northeastern part of the state. There, the school board decided in mid-1955 to admit twenty-five black students to the public schools (which had 1,000 whites) because, it said, "integration is right in the sight of God, obedience to the Supreme Court . . . and it's cheaper." Some local whites, however, protested. Galvanized by the Citizens' Council, they forced the closing of an early summer session of the schools. But Eisenhower's Justice Department filed a brief in support of the board, and a federal court of appeals upheld it. This was a small, isolated instance, but it illustrated the point that had been made in Baltimore a year earlier: if local officials acted quickly, they could seize the initiative. If they received help from federal officials and the courts, they might prevail.[27]

In 1956 blacks seeking desegregation also managed a victory—of sorts—in Clinton, Tennessee. There, a federal court had ordered desegregation at the opening of school in August. In a token gesture, the local board admitted twelve black students, who were to join 750 whites at Clinton High School. At this point, however, John Kasper entered the scene. Kasper was executive secretary of Seaboard Citizens' Council of Washington, D.C., and an irrepressible activist. Within two days he had

Negro students arrive in September 1956 at Clinton High School in Tennessee. *(Library of Congress, Prints and Photographs Division, New York World-Telegram & Sun Collection)*

rallied local whites to picket the school. Black parents were threatened over the telephone. A crowd of whites attacked one black pupil outside the school. A federal judge served Kasper with a restraining order, and when he violated it, sentenced him to a year in jail. Kasper went free on bail and resumed his demonstrations. When disorder mounted, local police despaired of controlling it, whereupon the governor called in the National Guard. By Labor Day the black students were back in class, and order was restored.

Kasper, however, did not quit. In November a local jury acquitted him and several of his followers of charges that they had incited riots. Kasper and fellow picketers again surrounded the school, and white violence erupted. Frightened local leaders asked for federal assistance, but it was slow in coming. Whites again resorted to violence, including an attack on a popular local minister, and officials decided to close the school. At this point the department of justice took action, charging Kasper and sixteen others with contempt. The school reopened. In July

1957 he and six others were convicted and jailed. The turbulence at Clinton, which was in predominantly white northeastern Tennessee, demonstrated the ease with which a skilled agitator could disrupt even a token effort at change. Still, law and order, belatedly assisted by the federal government, had ultimately been restored.[28]

Blacks also derived a bit of satisfaction from tense struggles in Nashville, where nineteen black first-graders were tapped to inaugurate desegregation in August 1957. This was assuredly a token move, for there were 1,400 black children waiting to enter the first grade in Nashville at the time. Once again, however, Kasper arrived in order to lead picketers against the plan. On the first day, whites shouted catcalls at the black children, and scuffling broke out. That night a school was bombed. Local officials then acted firmly. The next day they set up barricades to block the picketers, and they arrested Kasper and others on a variety of

Mary Brent, principal of Glenn School in Nashville, which introduced token desegregation in 1957. Glenn had previously been an all-white school. *(Library of Congress, Prints and Photographs Division, New York World-Telegram & Sun Collection)*

charges, including resisting arrest. Local prosecutors later succeeded in convicting him of stirring up a riot.

Spared more disturbances, Nashville proceeded in the next few years to desegregate each subsequent first grade in the stepwise fashion that was to become a common means of token compliance in other southern cities. This outcome was hardly a resounding triumph for *Brown* or *Brown II*. Indeed, only nine of the original nineteen harassed black children remained in the white school at mid-year of 1957–58. The struggle in 1957, however, at least indicated that law and order could prevail, even without federal intervention, if local police and politicos were willing to stand behind their plans. Although few white people in Nashville, an Upper South city, spoke out against the immorality of segregation, they showed that they would accept token change in preference to lawlessness.[29]

These were some of the "happy" results for blacks among the great many struggles that recurred every year in southern towns and cities during the 1950s and 1960s. But Marshall and others, looking at this larger number, had every reason to feel despondent. In Mansfield, Texas, for instance, black litigants secured a federal court order that called for desegregation of the white high school in August 1956. (There was no local high school for blacks, who were expected to find their own transportation to a school seventeen miles away in Fort Worth.) A mob, however, turned out at the school in Mansfield and threatened violence. Some people carried signs saying, "A Dead Nigger is a Good Nigger." Defying the court order, Governor Alan Shivers called in the Texas Rangers to bar the blacks from the school. Blacks appealed to the Eisenhower administration, which replied that the trouble was a local matter. In Mansfield, segregation lived.[30]

It also managed to live almost everywhere else in large southern cities during the 1950s. A case in point was Atlanta, where white officials began spending more money for black schools, in the hope that blacks would become content with separate-but-more-equal. The officials deliberately situated new schools in the middle of the most heavily black neighborhoods, not in areas where blacks and whites lived closer together. This strategy, which many cities (in the North as well as South) employed, attempted to ensure that schools would be highly if not totally segregated in the future.

In 1959 litigation from blacks finally induced Atlanta to agree to a plan whereby a few black twelfth-graders would be accepted in white schools in 1960. More legal fighting held up the plan for a year, and in September 1961 Atlanta at last admitted some Black eleventh- and twelfth-graders to white schools. As white officials had anticipated, however, few black students wished to leave their long-time classmates for the last year or two of their schooling, especially if they were to be in a tiny minority. And the city's plan used very stringent pupil placement procedures to winnow out black applicants. In 1961 only 133 black students applied. Ten were accepted, and nine actually went to the white schools. In 1962, forty-four of the 266 applicants were admitted to the top three grades. More than 4,000 blacks remained in overcrowded black high schools. And whites, alarmed by small changes such as these, moved even more rapidly than earlier to white suburbs. In Atlanta, as in many other places, gloom enshrouded the possibilities for desegregated education.[31]

Dramatic as some of these controversies were, they paled in visibility compared to four others between 1956 and 1960.

The first involved a young woman named Autherine Lucy, a black college graduate who had sought admission in 1952 as a graduate student to the University of Alabama. After more than three years of litigation she was admitted and showed up for classes in February 1956. She was then twenty-six years old. On her second day, a crowd of some 1,000 students, mostly male, demonstrated against her presence on campus. Some burned a cross at the scene. Others, perhaps 500-strong, marched to downtown Tuscaloosa. Singing "Dixie," they chanted "Keep Bama White," and "To Hell with Autherine." On the next day Lucy was pelted with rotten eggs. Students, along with members of the Klan, shouted, "Lynch the Nigger," "Hit the Nigger Whore," and "Kill Her! Kill Her!" Governor Jim Folsom, a liberal who might have backed Lucy, was away on a three-day fishing and drinking trip and could not be located during the crisis. That night the university's board of trustees voted unanimously to exclude her from the campus. A little later they expelled her. "Bama" remained an all-white university into the early 1960s.[32]

The second example, widely noted, involved fifteen-year-old Dorothy Counts, who tried in September 1957 to enter an all-white high school in Charlotte, North Carolina, that offered token desegregation so as to avoid a court order. She survived the first day, but on the way home

Fifteen-year-old Dorothy Counts enrolls at the previously all-white Harding High School in Charlotte, Sept. 1957. Leaving school later that day, she was pelted with sticks and pebbles. A white girl spat in her face. *(Library of Congress, Prints and Photographs Division, New York World-Telegram & Sun Collection)*

from school an abusive crowd of young white people threw sticks and pebbles at her. A white girl spat in her face. Counts kept her poise and walked on with dignity. A white girl who had tried to befriend her in school was shoved into a bathroom and locked inside by other girls. When the white girl got home, she found a note attached to her door: "We know where she lives." Later the girl told Dorothy that they could not be friends. Counts stayed away from school for the next two days, but then returned to face shoving in the hallways and the ransacking of her locker. She was hit in the head with an eraser. Whites smashed a window in her father's car, in which she was being transported from school. Counts's family could endure no more. She was sent to Philadelphia, where she attended a nonsegregated school.[33]

Three years after Counts was driven from home, District Court Judge J. Skelly Wright ordered his native city of New Orleans to put in place a long-postponed plan to desegregate its public schools. The plan required the schools to be desegregated in token fashion, one year at a time, beginning with the first grade. Liberal optimists hoped for compliance: New Orleans, after all, was a cosmopolitan city. It had desegregated its parks and buses in 1958. Schools, however, were as everywhere a much touchier matter, and New Orleans was in the Deep South, where no desegregation of public education at the elementary or secondary level had yet occurred. Many whites in the city, incited by Negrophobic state legislators, were clearly seething about what Wright—"Judas Wright," "a traitor to his class"—had ordered.

Ruby Bridges, six years old, was nonetheless taken by her mother to an all-white school in November. Pigtailed, dressed in starchy white, she was shielded by armed United States marshals from 150 white people, mostly housewives and teenagers. Some of these people threw tomatoes and rotten eggs and spat at her. Others sang, "Glory, Glory, Segregation," to the tune of the "Battle Hymn of the Republic." Still others chanted, "Two, four, six, eight. We don't want to integrate. Eight, six, four, two. We don't want a chiggeroo." Ruby endured the abuse and entered the school, whereupon she burst into tears. Lead stories in many northern papers that day gave the story relatively little play. They featured instead a meeting between President-elect John Kennedy and his vanquished foe in the 1960 election, Richard Nixon.

Two days later whites rioted and beat black people on the streets. Four were hospitalized. Leander Perez, a powerful political boss, told a huge rally of the Citizens' Council, "Don't wait for your daughters to be raped by these Congolese. Don't wait until the burr-heads are forced into your schools. Do something about it now!" By the fifth day, white parents had withdrawn all their children from Ruby's classroom and placed them instead in "private" schools financed by public funds. Ruby, while apparently calm amid the turmoil, was deeply frightened by the insistent, shrill threat of one white woman outside the school, "We're going to poison you until you choke to death." When school staff

Six-year-old Ruby Bridges in the doorway of her home in New Orleans, November 1960. *(Library of Congress, Prints and Photographs Division, New York World-Telegram & Sun Collection)*

cleaned out her locker at the end of term, they discovered that it was jammed with sandwiches that her mother had given her for lunch. Ruby had been afraid to eat.[34]

Repercussions quickly followed. Ruby's father, a Korean War veteran who had earned a Purple Heart, was fired from his job at a local service station. Her grandparents, who lived in Mississippi, had their credit cut off at local stores. White segregationists called the Bridges home at all hours and threatened violence if she kept going to the school. Fighting broke out here and there across the city. Judge Wright took a large share of abuse. At the steps of the Louisiana Capitol in Baton Rouge, he was hanged in effigy, with a swastika painted on his back and a sickle on his front. A placard read, "J. Wrong." Police camped in his basement to guard him day and night. His friends ostracized him. Among the few consoling gestures were letters from Judge Waties Waring, the South Carolinian who had moved to New York six years earlier, and from Mrs. Elizabeth Black, wife of the Justice.

The tension in New Orleans eased a little after the Christmas break. With Mardi Gras approaching, some white leaders worried that the controversy was bad for tourism. Ruby, however, studied alone, instructed by a white teacher who had been brought in from Massachusetts because no one in New Orleans would do the job. Four years later Norman Rockwell captured part of her ordeal with a much-admired painting, "The Problem We Live With." It showed Ruby walking stoically to school through a crowd of hard-faced white people.

Advocates of desegregation found little to cheer about in New Orleans during the next few years. In the 1961–62 school year, stern placement guidelines resulted in acceptance to white schools of only twelve black students, who attended six schools with 951 whites. One of the blacks was Ruby Bridges, who returned to the same school. More than 5,000 other black students stayed in increasingly crowded all-black schools. Many of the white parents who continued to boycott the public school system in protest received state grants-in-aid so that their children might attend "cooperatives" or private schools. Other whites, as in Atlanta, moved in droves to all-white suburbs.[35]

Easily the most heated confrontation of these heralded struggles over school desegregation erupted at Little Rock, Arkansas, in September 1957. In some ways that arena was unexpected, for Arkansas until then had been more moderate concerning racial issues than Deep South states. In 1948 it had desegregated its state university. Ten of its school districts announced in 1955 that they would gradually comply with *Brown*. One of these was Little Rock, which had desegregated its parks, buses, and hospitals and had approved a token plan that was to admit six black girls and three black boys to Central High School in 1957. The governor of Arkansas, Orval Faubus, was a product of the largely white Ozark hill country. He had been elected in 1954 as a progressive advocate of economic development. In 1955 Citizens' Council leaders dubbed him "Awful" Faubus. Challenged by a staunch advocate of segregation in 1956, he had taken a relatively moderate course on racial issues and had been reelected to office.[36]

Even in 1956, however, Faubus had operated behind the scenes so as to rally Arkansas senators and representatives in support of the Southern Manifesto, and by 1957 he was looking for an issue to help him win a third term. He thereby announced that desegregation of Central High School in Little Rock could not be managed without violence. To avert trouble (which Faubus alone foresaw) he called out the National Guard, which surrounded the school on opening day, September 3. No mob materialized, and the soldiers had nothing to do. But Faubus had whipped up racist feelings.[37] And white community leaders, having devised a plan that would have isolated desegregation within the largely working-class neighborhoods in the Central High school district, did virtually nothing in the struggles that followed to counteract Faubus's demagogic stance. The next day, when the nine black students sought to enter the school, they faced crowds of irate whites and were barred from the building by the troops. Elizabeth Eckford, a slim, short girl who tried to enter alone, had a terrifying experience. Furious whites snarled, "Nigger go home," and "Hang her black ass." She escaped only when two whites helped her board a bus to go home.[38]

For more than two weeks the Little Rock nine were unable to enter the school. Then, on September 20, a federal district judge finally enjoined Faubus from preventing the attendance of the students. The governor thereupon ordered the troops away, leaving the nine black students at the mercy of a howling, spitting mob on September 23. When the students managed to slip into the building, white people shouted, "The niggers are in our school." Violent whites attacked black people as well as "Yankee" reporters and news photographers. Local police were clearly sympathetic to the mob and did little to stop the violence. One policeman took off his badge and walked away. The students were spirited out of the school at midday and sent home.

The standoffs during these three weeks captured national and international attention. Integrationists demanded that President Eisenhower intervene on behalf of the embattled black students. Television, by now a fixture in millions of American homes, showed many of the ugly scenes. Eisenhower hesitated, however, hoping that local authorities could resolve the crisis. At one point he conferred with Faubus, who flew to the president's summer retreat in Newport, Rhode Island. But the confrontations of September 23 left Ike with little choice, and he sent regular army troops as well as federalized Arkansas national guardsmen to the city. Some 1,100 troops protected the children as they entered for a full day of school at last. Eisenhower's reaction earned him low marks abroad as well as from liberals at home, who damned him for his dawdling. Southern firebrands, however, condemned his intervention. Senator Richard Russell of Georgia, who was normally moderate in speech, compared the federal troops to "Hitler's storm troopers."

Some of the white students at Central High cursed, pushed, kicked, and spat on their black classmates. Segregationists in 1957–58 set thirty

The army escorts black students at Central High School in Little Rock, October 1957. *(Library of Congress, Prints and Photographs Division, New York World-Telegram & Sun Collection)*

fires, provoked forty-three bomb scares, and threatened to kill the school superintendent (one such effort was later made but failed). Other extremists fired bullets into the Little Rock home of Daisy Bates, president of the Arkansas branch of the NAACP. Authorities bathed her house in floodlights at night to lessen the chance of further attacks. Eisenhower refused to consider federal prosecution of alleged instigators of violence, but he did keep the guardsmen at Central High for the remainder of the academic year. Eight of the students stuck it out. The only senior among them, Ernest Green, graduated and went on to Michigan State.

The Little Rock school board, meanwhile, claimed that disorder in the city necessitated a further delay, until September 1960, of previous court orders to desegregate. Thurgood Marshall led the opposition to this claim. When the case, *Cooper v. Aaron*, reached the Supreme Court in August 1958, Warren called his colleagues to a special term. In September the justices, angry that Arkansas was openly flouting *Brown*, unanimously rejected the claim. They insisted that threats of violence could not be used by public officials as justification for obstructing school desegregation. The Court's decision in *Brown*, they emphasized, was paramount. In an unusual move the nine justices individually signed the decision. "It is emphatically the province and duty of the judicial department," the justices declared, "to say what the law is." *Cooper v. Aaron* was the first occasion since *Brown II* that the Court issued its own opinion concerning racial segregation in the schools.[39]

Segregationists in Arkansas still resisted. Faubus ordered all four high schools in Little Rock to be closed for the 1958–59 school year. He became a hero in these years to many in the white South and was reelected four more times before retiring as governor in 1966. When the schools reopened, following a federal court order in 1959, Little Rock police dispersed protesters with fire hoses and arrested twenty-one. This response was effective and contrasted sharply with police behavior in 1957. But black students had only a token presence in 1959. Three blacks attended each of two high schools. No black pupils went to the city's white junior high or elementary schools. Four years later, in 1963, sixty-nine of the 7,700 students in Little Rock's once all-white junior and senior high schools were black.

The Court, meanwhile, returned to the position of judicial restraint that it had adopted since *Brown II*. Not until the mid- and late 1960s

did it press forcefully for the great change in southern educational practices that it had tried to begin in *Brown*.

———

Critics of the Court's continuing reliance on "all deliberate speed" in
the late 1950s and early 1960s emphasize three points. The first is that
the Court did not give clear guidance to the lower federal courts covering
the South. Lacking unambiguous instructions, the fifty-eight judges on
these courts faced extraordinarily difficult decisions. If they took a strong
stand for desegregation, as Rives, Wright, and others sometimes did,
they could not cite clear language from Warren and his colleagues. They
risked exposure to the most extreme southern hostility, including
violence.

The second main criticism of *Brown II* overlaps with the first. A
phrase such as "all deliberate speed," detractors say, may indeed have
been an understandable compromise in 1955. Marshall, after all, had
thought so at the time. But when southern white officials resorted to all
manner of ruses to evade the ruling, the Court should have stepped in
to give backbone to the district and circuit courts. The fault was not so
much the phrase as the failure, as these critics see it, of the Court to
insist after 1956 that the South not abuse the language of its decision.
Southern resisters were thereby able to claim that there was a legal alternative to speedy compliance, and to overrun the lonely desegregationists who argued otherwise.

The third criticism, following from the other two, enjoys the benefit
of hindsight: racial patterns in southern schools changed very little between 1955 and the late 1960s. Compliance in much of Dixie, one scholar
has noted, moved "with the pace of an extraordinarily arthritic snail."
By early 1964, only 1.2 percent of black children in the eleven southern
states attended schools with whites. Virtually all southern black children
who had entered the first grade in 1954 and who remained in southern
schools graduated from all-black schools twelve years later.[40]

Given this outcome of *Brown II,* it is hardly surprising that many
people have wondered if Warren and his colleagues were right about the
virtues of gradualism. It would have been better, they have argued, to
administer some sort of "shock therapy." At the very least this would
have required school districts quickly to draw up plans promoting significant desegregation and to meet deadlines for action. Such a therapy

might also have warned procrastinating federal judges that the High Court would summarily reverse them. There was no way, these critics pointed out, that shock therapy could have provoked more disrespect for the law than in fact occurred. How could things have moved more slowly than they did?[41]

Kenneth Clark, drawing on his expertise as a psychologist, emerged as an especially vehement articulator of these criticisms. *Brown II,* he complained, "led to more rather than to less disruption." He argued that the Court should have demanded full and rapid compliance, thereby giving opponents no time to organize opposition: "Prompt, decisive action on the part of recognized authorities usually results in less anxiety and less resistance [than] a more hesitant and gradual procedure. It is similar to the effect of quickly pulling off adhesive tape—the pain is sharper but briefer and more tolerable."[42]

Another criticism of *Brown* and *Brown II,* known later among scholars as the "backlash thesis," stresses an additional point: after 1955 the decisions did little to inspire blacks or liberal whites. True, *Brown* had large symbolic value—the law, at last, was on the side of racial justice. But how practically powerful was symbolism? Not very, perhaps. The "backlash thesis" maintains, moreover, that the two decisions—especially *Brown*—may in fact have made matters worse for advocates of desegregation, at least in the short run, by arousing demagogues who incited massive resistance. This extreme response—"backlash"—isolated white moderates, further racialized southern politics, and halted incipient amelioration of Jim Crow practices (mainly in the less sensitive areas of public transportation and voting rights, not schools). In so doing, massive southern resistance retarded the possibility of gradual, more peaceful progress and exposed the impotence of the Court as an agent of social change.[43]

In the 1960s, the backlash interpretation continues, massive resistance finally backfired, because it unleashed ever angrier reactions among black people, who then mobilized a much more effective civil rights movement. By the time of the widely televised demonstrations that Martin Luther King and others staged in Birmingham in 1963, the movement became strong enough to force federal officials to introduce and, in 1964, to enact civil rights legislation. Considerable desegregation of southern schools then followed—in the late 1960s. Only by this circuitous, unintended, highly divisive, and very slow process, this backlash argument holds, may *Brown* and *Brown II* be said to have accomplished much racial mixing in southern schools. Overheated southern resistance, followed by outraged black reactions and civil rights legislation with teeth—not unenforceable Court decisions of the 1950s—finally advanced significant change.

The historian following the trail of might-have-beens such as these is well advised to tread carefully. From the vantage point of hindsight, integrationist critics of *Brown II,* like Kenneth Clark, seem to have a good case. Clearly, they are correct that *Brown II* failed to promote change in the South. Most southern whites, perceiving the caution of the Court, may have been bolder (though we cannot know for certain) than they would have been had the justices left them less room to maneuver. Stonewalling successfully in 1955, they proceeded thereafter to defy the Court, evoking no effective countermoves until the late 1960s. Lawyers for these stonewallers relied repeatedly on Judge Parker's ruling in the *Briggs* case in 1955: *Brown* did not require *integration,* only the ending of state-sponsored segregation. By 1957, Marshall himself conceded that the case by case legal process was painfully slow and that the Deep South would never tire of fighting in the courts. Recalcitrant whites would not surrender unless forced by other political institutions to comply.

The backlash thesis is in part plausible, for *Brown*—and even *Brown II*—surely infuriated southern white segregationists: Yankees, they complained, were once again meddling in their affairs. Their effective resistance indeed outraged blacks and laid bare the limitations of courts as advocates of reform. It is also arguable that the Court's targeting of *schools,* which were so sensitive as institutions, did more to arouse white obstructionists than decisions attacking other aspects of segregation (for instance, voting rights or seating on buses) might have done. Had the Court initially steered clear of schools, this argument goes, the South might have gradually and more peacefully bent to the winds of change that were inexorably pushing the nation toward the liberalization of race relations.

Might-have-been arguments such as these, however, are highly debatable. The backlash thesis, for instance, tends to assume that whites in the South were already showing signs of agreeing, though slowly, to changes in race relations (notably concerning transportation and voting) prior to *Brown.* Except for the school decisions of the Court, this assumption continues, much white backlash—and ensuing black rage—might have been avoided. In fact, however, one looks in vain for evidence of significant change in southern racial practices prior to the early 1960s. As earlier, the majority of white community leaders were not ready to support civil rights for blacks. All but a few politicians incited or deferred to racists. Even in the 1960s, when the government began to crack down on segregation, white extremists in the Deep South resorted to violence to prevent blacks from gaining voting rights. Then, too, moderate white leaders were slow to step in against the agitators and the demagogues. It is doubtful, therefore, that *Brown* or *Brown II* set back the advance of more progressive southern race relations in the 1950s.

What would have happened if the Court had postponed a decision on the highly delicate question of segregation in the schools? This might-have-been is highly provocative, for school desegregation indeed proved especially hard to accomplish in later years. Given the resistance of southern whites to reform in the early 1950s, however, it is difficult to imagine that the larger white backlash that followed *Brown* considerably retarded change in the late 1950s. Again, one is struck by a central point: southern white intransigents, scarcely challenged by southern moderates, would not be mollified or moved. Their obduracy so greatly antagonized blacks that militant civil rights activity soon spilled beyond the courts. The force of this activity, indeed, shocked veteran advocates like Thurgood Marshall.

By 1954, moreover, it would have been difficult indeed for the Court to skirt questions about the constitutional status of school segregation. With understandable feeling, blacks (like whites) in America had long believed that schools offered the best hopes for a decent start in life. Well before 1954—indeed, as far back as the 1930s—leaders of the NAACP and the Fund had calculated that segregation in higher education was the weakest link in the steel chain of Jim Crow. By the late 1940s Marshall and others at the Fund were confronting separate-but-equal in the public schools, and by 1950 they had cast the die that led to the challenge against segregation. By 1954, Warren and his colleagues no longer had the option—stalling—that the Vinson Court had employed. By postponing guidelines for implementation in 1954 and by steering a calm course for "all deliberate speed" in 1955 they did their best to calm the waters. But it is scarcely imaginable, given the evolution of opinion by 1954, that they could have dared to uphold *Plessy*.

But why did the Court not step back into the arena in the late 1950s, by which time it was abundantly clear that most southern whites were thumbing their noses at its handiwork? The answer to this question, in part, is that it had decided in 1955 to turn controversies involving school segregation over to the lower courts, and it continued to do so thereafter. Indeed, the last thing the justices were prepared to do was to act as a gigantic school board, engaging endlessly in the details of student assignments and redistricting. Moreover, the High Court justices did take some actions in the late 1950s, endorsing lower court decisions that struck down racial segregation in municipal golf courses, bus systems, and parks. In the Little Rock case of *Cooper v. Aaron*, it made it clear that threats of violence were no excuse to ignore *Brown*. Finally, the Court could point to progress that *Brown* was slowly forwarding in the border states.

The wider political context following *Brown II*, moreover, discouraged further judicial activism in the late 1950s. Eisenhower still refused to endorse *Brown*. And Cold War fears issues continued to be the most absorbing national concerns. In one sense, of course, the Cold War bolstered the stance of integrationists, who argued tirelessly that Jim Crow advertised American hypocrisy to the rest of the world. But liberals and integrationists were on the defensive during the late 1950s. Southern Democrats and conservative Republicans enjoyed considerable power in Congress until 1959 and became increasingly critical of civil libertarian decisions that Warren and his colleagues delivered between 1954 and 1957. Joining forces with southern segregationists, these politicos championed legislation to curb the jurisdiction of the Court. In 1958 they almost pushed such a bill through the Senate. Alarmed by threats like these, apostles of judicial restraint, notably Felix Frankfurter and John Marshall Harlan, urged their fellow justices to move cautiously during the late 1950s.

Warren and his colleagues in the mid- and late 1950s were inescapably conscious of a final fact: courts by themselves could not greatly change American society. Well into the 1960s litigation for more humane race relations continued to encounter very strong resistance from most southern whites. Until 1963 it received little encouragement from Congress. Needing powerful allies, liberally inclined judges often stood alone. Only a potent civil rights movement that forced other political actors onto the stage could bring about the reforms that the Court had hoped to dramatize in 1954.

6

STRIVING FOR RACIAL BALANCE
IN THE 1960s

Three days into the new decade of the 1960s a somewhat chastened Thurgood Marshall confessed to reporters that litigation alone was not likely to destroy racial segregation. "I consider the lawsuits to be a holding action," he said, "a way of getting things open so that they can operate. But the final solution will only be when the Negro takes his part in the community, voting and otherwise."[1]

Marshall had ample reason to be cautious. As he spoke, the Legal Defense Fund could claim victories in a handful of recently decided cases involving racial discrimination in the hiring, assignment, and salaries of black teachers. But it had forty-six suits still pending, most of them against segregated schools in the Upper South. The case by case judicial process moved, as before, at a glacial pace. Even in Topeka, the courts were still dealing with litigation surrounding the city's efforts to comply with *Brown II*. Outside of encouraging changes in parts of the border states, it was hard to predict whether *Brown* or *Brown II* would ever promote significant desegregation of schools in the United States.[2]

Although Marshall did not say so, he would also have been correct in January 1960 to wonder whether *Brown* had greatly helped to promote broader demands for civil rights in the United States. To be sure, many northern whites believed that the decision gave them a responsibility to make the white South behave. When blacks became more militant in the 1960s, this sense of responsibility (along with guilt) grew appreciably, at least as measured in polls on the subject. Moreover, *Brown* stimulated some veteran activists—A. Philip Randolph, Ella Baker, Medgar Evers—

to continue their agitation. On occasion they invoked the decision in order to arouse protests. When Martin Luther King decided on a prayer pilgrimage to Washington in 1957, he set it for May 17, the anniversary of *Brown*. Randolph sponsored a number of events he called Youth Marches for Integrated Schools in 1957 and 1958. Members of the NAACP's Youth Council, who led sit-ins against segregation in Wichita drug stores in 1958, cited the decision (among other events) as an inspiration for their efforts. And Marshall still found black people in the South willing to stand up as plaintiffs. "The federal government," they said, "is on our side."³ As later events were to suggest, the symbolic value of *Brown*, though impossible to measure exactly, helped at least to to reassure a number of people who participated in the rising protests of the 1960s.⁴

Still, *Brown* had not obviously stimulated an effective civil rights movement as of January 1960. Most northern whites at the time still seemed relatively uninterested in improving the lot of blacks. One poll in February 1958 had indicated that only 4 percent of Americans identified "integration" to be the most important problem facing the nation. During the 1960 presidential campaign, civil rights did not become a major issue. As late as 1964, by which time white attitudes had become considerably more liberal, a poll of whites indicated that 64 percent favored school desegregation but that only 38 percent believed that Washington should have a role in bringing this about.⁵

Most blacks in the South, too, were not openly militant as of January 1960. As before, many were ambivalent about sending their children into predominantly white schools. Understandably, they dared not engage too aggressively in protests. There was no increase in the number of demonstrations for civil rights following the *Brown* decisions in 1954 and 1955. By 1959 there were fewer demonstrations than there had been during the late 1940s.⁶

Even the much-publicized, dramatic bus boycotts that convulsed Montgomery in late 1955 and 1956 seemed to owe relatively little to the example of *Brown*. Blacks in the city surely welcomed the decision, but they did not focus on desegregation of the schools, and their boycott did not at first go so far as to demand the end of segregation on the city's buses. Rather, boycotters began by calling for fairer, gentler regulations—passengers should be seated on a first-come, first-served basis, with blacks filling up the back of buses and whites the front. Martin Luther King, who earned fame as a leader of the boycott, was moved primarily by Christian and nonviolent ideals, not by *Brown*. Although he urged the Supreme Court to defend the Montgomery movement—which the Court did in 1956, citing *Brown* in the process of effectively striking down segregation on the buses—he generally placed little reliance on litigation. Like many militant civil rights leaders after 1955, King favored direct action.[7]

Many of the young southern blacks who emerged as militant civil rights activists in the 1960s had been children in 1954. *Brown* had not greatly affected their lives in the late 1950s; in 1960 they still attended segregated schools and lived in an apparently unchanging Jim Crow world. More inspiring than *Brown*, they often said, was the Montgomery boycott, an example of direct action that had had some measurable success. More enraging were acts of violence such as the murder of Emmett Till. Litigation continued to engage leaders like Thurgood Marshall, but the courts still moved slowly and seemed to make little difference to the folkways that put blacks down.

A month after Marshall's statement, four freshmen from all-black North Carolina A&T College in Greensboro entered the local Woolworth department store to protest against being barred from the lunch counter. They then conducted a sit-in at the counter to force management to change its ways. Their courageous effort attracted widespread attention and sparked enormous growth in direct action by blacks, mostly in the South, against racial discrimination. Within two weeks, fifty-four sit-ins were underway in fifteen cities in nine states in the South. Although whites resisted strongly—some 3,000 protestors were sent to jail in 1960—demonstrators normally held firm. Often, they succeeded: Greensboro's Woolworth finally backed down in July, after suffering an estimated loss of $200,000, or 20 percent of anticipated sales, during a black boycott that accompanied the sit-ins.[8]

The sit-ins touched off an acceleration of civil rights activity in the next few years: the creation of the Student Nonviolent Coordinating Committee (SNCC) in April 1960, "freedom rides" to desegregate southern bus terminals in 1961, James Meredith's effort to desegregate the University of Mississippi in 1962, Martin Luther King's struggles to desegregate public accommodations in Albany, Georgia, in 1961–62 and in Birmingham in 1963, the March on Washington in August 1963 at which King preached to multitudes about his "dream" for racial integration. Whites continued to resist, sometimes violently: between 1961 and 1965, twenty-six civil rights workers lost their lives in the South.

Why the civil rights movement quickened so much after February 1960 is the subject of a host of books and essays.[9] Many ongoing postwar forces, notably rising prosperity, higher levels of education, and demographic movements (especially of blacks to urban centers in the South as well as the North) were keys to this process. These forces promoted rising expectations from blacks as well as whites concerning the potential for progress in all ways of life, including more equitable race relations in the future. Also vital to the successes of the movement in the 1960s was the leadership of people like King and Marshall and the bravery of thousands of grassroots activists, who were enraged by the violence that southern whites were inciting in resistance to change.

One source of the accelerating movement is particularly clear: the increasing impatience of black people, especially the young, with the pace of change since World War II and *Brown*. In this way the decision played a role of its own in arousing black expectations—a role that was symbolic to most, but direct to some. For instance, three of the four black students who started the Greensboro sit-in had grown up in the city and had reacted with escalating fury as the school board's promise to desegregate their schools, made on the night after *Brown*, was betrayed. For another example, the freedom riders planned their itinerary through the South in 1961 with the idea of arriving at their destination, New Orleans, on May 17, the anniversary of *Brown*. (Violence by whites bloodied the riders and disrupted their schedule.)

The rapid spread of militant civil rights activity in 1960, however, surprised many Americans, including leaders of the Legal Defense Fund, who were besieged by jailed activists seeking bail and other forms of legal assistance. Marshall, Robert Carter, and others had surely not anticipated activism such as this, and at first they did not altogether welcome it. Carter, then working for the NAACP, sensed that a new group of black leaders was about to displace the lawyers. To divert scarce resources to the protestors, he said, "would tie us to something that some other organization has taken and run with." Marshall appears to have reacted uneasily at first to the trouble caused by the activists. He was later described by a young aide as having "stormed around the room proclaiming . . . [that] he was not going to represent a bunch of crazy colored students who violate the sacred property rights of white folks by going in their stores or lunch counters and refusing to leave when ordered to do so." Marshall faced strong pressure, however, from younger aides to help, and he soon calmed down. Both the NAACP and the Fund gave valuable and costly legal assistance to civil rights activists in the next few years.

Still, Marshall's initial response indicated that the path toward the much expanded civil rights movement of the 1960s was crooked and uncertain, and that *Brown*'s precise part in paving that path is difficult to chart. His attitude also exposed divisions in a movement that featured a determined new generation of blacks who were angrily pushing from the bottom up for change and who were committed to direct action. These and other divisions later helped to rend the movement asunder.[10]

As his response to the sit-ins suggested, Marshall was also wearying of having to lead the drawn-out legal struggles that had absorbed him for nearly twenty-five years. Tired also of infighting within the Fund—and especially between the Fund and NAACP attorneys loyal to Robert Carter—he was receptive to new challenges. When President John Kennedy offered in October 1961 to nominate him to a federal judgeship on the court of appeals in New York, he accepted. Southerners in the Senate opposed the nomination and forced six separate hearings before finally giving in. The Senate confirmed him, fifty-four to sixteen, in September 1962. Marshall pressed his colleagues on the Fund to name Jack Greenberg, the only top attorney at the office who was white, to succeed him.[11]

Marshall then raised the eyebrows of some of his long-time friends and allies. As a judge for the next four years he hired only white clerks, mostly from Yale and Harvard. He sent his two young children to a predominantly white private school, not to public schools in Harlem. "I think they should have the best education I can afford," he told critics. He remained cool to tactics of direct action and refused to endorse the march on Washington in 1963. Asked his opinion of the march, he replied judiciously, "No comment."[12]

The Kennedy administration's response to mounting civil rights activism was also ambivalent. Raising liberal expectations by calling for a new frontier, Kennedy excited many young Americans who flocked to Washington. Many were to staff the federal bureaucracies that rapidly expanded, demanding enforcement of liberal goals, as a result of congressional legislation in the 1960s. But the president's main interests lay in foreign affairs. In 1961 and 1962 he was absorbed by several Cold War crises, including the invasion of the Bay of Pigs in Cuba, a standoff over the status of Berlin (which led the Soviets to erect the Berlin Wall), and the near-cataclysmic missile crisis of 1962. During these years he only sporadically turned his full attention to domestic matters.

Although JFK held moderately liberal views on most domestic issues, including civil rights, he also worried about losing valuable backing from politically influential southern Democrats if he seemed to sympathize too much with embattled civil rights workers. Some of his judicial nominations aimed to please southern extremists such as Senator Eastland of Mississippi, chairman of the judiciary committee. Both John Kennedy and Robert Kennedy, his brother and attorney general, were cautious about assisting freedom riders and other foes of Jim Crow in 1961 and 1962. Knowing that a civil rights bill would encounter ferocious opposition in the Senate, JFK declined to introduce one. By 1962 many blacks, having hoped for help from a supposedly more liberal administration than Eisenhower's, had become bitter at the Kennedys.

Still, blacks and liberal whites refused to give up hope for governmental assistance, and they pressed onward with increasingly effective protests and demonstrations. By mid-1963, the movement had become a near-irresistible moral force that politicians could not ignore. When Martin Luther King and others staged demonstrations in Birmingham, public safety commissioner T. Eugene "Bull" Connor and his all-white police responded by blasting protestors with streams of water from fire hoses. Police dogs lunged at the demonstrators, among them women and children. Television relayed many of these ugly scenes to viewers throughout the world. When Alabama governor George Wallace then attempted to prevent the token integration of the University of Alabama, Kennedy decided that he had to act. In June 1963 he introduced a civil rights bill aimed at abolishing Jim Crow in public accommodations.

From the start it was clear that Kennedy's action did nothing to tame the behavior of southern white extremists. Indeed, on the night that he introduced his bill, a sniper shot and killed Medgar Evers as he arrived home to join his wife and three children in Jackson, Mississippi. Further bloodshed caused by whites, notably the bombing of a black church in Birmingham in September, stained the long road to passage of the bill. The blast killed four black children. Kennedy himself was assassinated two months later, whereupon Vice President Lyndon Johnson took control.

Johnson, a Texan, evoked suspicion among many advocates of civil rights. But once he came to the presidency he demonstrated a stronger commitment to racial justice than any of his predecessors in the White House. Like many of the younger liberals who were beginning to swell the government bureaucracy at the time, he also believed that the national government could—indeed must—develop what he later called a Great Society. Government leaders for civil rights, he also believed, must no longer tolerate the kind of evasions that had been permitted under the guise of "all deliberate speed."

For all these reasons, Johnson proved a stalwart advocate of Kennedy's civil rights bill, which liberals in Congress helped him strengthen in late 1963 and early 1964. Guided in the Senate by Hubert Humphrey of Minnesota, the measure in 1964 endured the longest filibuster in American history. The president well understood why Southerners fought so hard, for the new bill was aimed directly at them, not at all at *de facto* segregation in the North. As strengthened, it promised to attack racial discrimination in employment as well as to banish Jim Crow in public accommodations. It also authorized the attorney general to bring suits against officials, including school administrators, who tried to advance *de jure* programs of racial discrimination—thereby lifting the burden of litigation from black people. The bill further threatened southern white schools with cutoffs of federal aid if they continued to segregate. In May 1964, Johnson told Humphrey that the bill, if approved, would provoke "mutiny in this goddamn country."[13] A month later, the filibuster was broken, and the measure finally passed.

For most blacks who lived in the South, news of the Civil Rights Act of 1964 did not prompt immediate demands for changes in the schools. It was wonderful enough, they thought, to anticipate an assault on Jim Crow in public accommodations and employment. Revamping school procedures, they recognized, would be especially difficult to accomplish. For Matthew and Mae Bertha Carter, however, passage of the law was inspiring. The Carters, who were sharecroppers, and their thirteen children lived in Drew, Mississippi, not far from where Emmett Till was thought to have been killed almost ten years earlier. They inhabited a small house that had no indoor plumbing. Mae Bertha, Matthew, and their children worked long hours in the cotton fields. The children went to ill-equipped, badly staffed black schools.

Mae Bertha, an indomitable woman, had left school after the fifth grade and yearned to help her children escape a lifetime of chopping cotton. In 1955 she had joined the NAACP, an unusual and daring move for a woman in the countryside of the Delta. Hearing of the Civil Rights

President Johnson signs the Civil Rights bill of 1964 into law on July 2. *(Library of Congress, Prints and Photographs Division, New York World-Telegram & Sun Collection)*

Act, she and Matthew decided to take advantage of the local "freedom of choice" plan and to demand that the white schools in Drew admit seven of her children. (Five had already graduated from black schools, and one was not yet in school.) No other black family in the region dared to do so.

White authorities in Drew were afraid of challenging the Civil Rights

Three plaintiffs in school desegregation cases attend a press conference in 1964, ten years after the Brown decision. They are (*l. to r.*), Harry Briggs Jr. (South Carolina), Linda Brown Smith (Kansas), and Spottswood Bolling (District of Columbia). *(Library of Congress, Prints and Photographs Division, New York World-Telegram & Sun Collection)*

Act, which authorized Washington authorities to cut off federal aid, and they grudgingly complied in 1965. The seven Carter children went to the white schools, where they faced abuse. White students called them "nigger" and jostled them in the halls. Mostly, though, the Carter children were ignored; no one would play with the younger ones at recess or befriend the older ones at the high school. Much of the time they dreaded going to school. And one night someone riddled their house with bullets. But the Carters, with federal law firmly on their side at last, did not break. Mae Bertha concluded that the teachers were generally fair. She also believed that her children were getting a better education than they could have received in the local black schools. So the children persevered, alone for three years among the whites. In 1968 the first of the seven enrolled at Ole Miss, which by then had been desegregated. Six more followed; all seven graduated between 1972 and 1982.

Nothing remotely like this outcome could have been imagined prior to 1964.[14]

Southern whites, having lost the struggle over the Civil Rights Act, gradually learned to live with most requirements of the law. While old folkways died slowly in rural Black Belt regions, blacks and whites managed to mix peaceably, if often awkwardly, in theaters, restaurants, parks, and other public places in most areas of the South by the 1970s. Thanks to dramatic demonstrations in Selma, Alabama, Congress also approved a Voting Rights Act in 1965 that guaranteed southern black people the franchise. These tough-minded, firmly enforced laws, among the most far-reaching in American history, did more to change the legal status of blacks than had the decades of litigation that Thurgood Marshall and his fellow-attorneys had pursued.

The transcendent moral strength of the civil rights movement, moreover, did more than promote federal civil rights legislation, important though that was. It also stimulated broader popular expectations that in turn sparked an ever more wide-ranging, group-oriented rights-consciousness in American society. Within a few years, many other groups—Native Americans, Hispanics, women, the elderly, the welfare poor, gay people, the handicapped—emulated blacks by demanding their rights, too. From the mid-1960s to the early 1970s Congress approved a remarkable body of liberal legislation that sought to respond to such demands, notably Medicaid and Medicare, signed into law by Johnson in 1965, and substantial liberalization of Social Security in 1972. Liberal laws mandated environmental protection, expanded bilingual and special education, provided for consumer protections, and attacked gender inequities in universities. In the late 1960s federal officials adopted affirmative action guidelines that called on employers and unions to take race and gender into consideration in all their operations. Many of these guidelines went far beyond anything that Congress had anticipated in the Civil Rights Act of 1964, which was presumed to promote a color-blind society.[15]

Minority groups benefited during the 1960s in other ways, too. The decade featured extraordinary, uninterrupted economic growth, which facilitated increased public spending aimed at alleviating domestic problems. In the South as well as in the North, to which millions of black people were still migrating, real spending per pupil in public schools increased considerably. Young people, including blacks, were encouraged to stay in school longer and began attending colleges and universities in much higher numbers. Unemployment dropped, and prices remained stable. Government, perceived by politically ascendant liberals as a fount of support for the downtrodden, expanded at all levels and created hundreds of thousands of white-collar jobs for black as well as white people. Economic progress not only promoted the rise of an ever-larger black middle class; it also stimulated a further surge of grand expectations and of rights-consciousness, which climbed to unprecedented heights by the end of the 1960s. As life became better, everyone, including advocates of racial justice, demanded even more from it.

———

Amid these encouraging developments, the tenth anniversary of *Brown* arrived in May 1964. Although contemporary editorialists reminded their readers that southern schools were still segregated, they were also optimistic about the future. *Brown*, the *New York Times* maintained, "stands as the great turning point in the battle for civil rights." Much remained to be accomplished, but "the commitment to equal opportunity is irrevocable, the outcome certain." The *Times* added that there was "no end in sight to the sweeping revolution in racial codes and customs generated by nine justices' unanimous ruling. . . . Further, the psychological effects of the ruling have been immense. Negroes frequently observe that, while the Emancipation Proclamation freed them physically, the Supreme Court decision freed them mentally."[16]

The Supreme Court seemed eager at the time to advance this freedom. By the mid-1960s Hugo Black was becoming increasingly irascible, as well as cool to the rising militancy of the civil rights movement. But he still sided on most occasions with the other two senior liberals on the Court, Earl Warren and William Douglas. Moreover, these three usually had the support as well of Justice William Brennan, Jr., of New Jersey. Brennan, one of eight children of a Catholic labor leader and municipal official, had gone to Harvard Law School and become a judge on New Jersey's Supreme Court. He had joined the High Court in 1956, when Eisenhower—seeking Catholic support in his reelection campaign—had named him to replace Sherman Minton.

At Harvard, Brennan had studied under Felix Frankfurter, but he did not echo Frankfurter's great faith in judicial restraint. Once on the Court, Brennan quickly became a close friend and confidant of Warren, thereby nettling Frankfurter, who was reputed to have said, "I always encouraged my students to think for themselves, but Brennan goes too far." By the early 1960s, Brennan, a gregarious, intellectually confident man who worked hard to bring fellow liberals together, had become a major force on the Court—maybe more influential than Warren himself.[17]

When Frankfurter retired in 1962, President Kennedy replaced him with Arthur Goldberg, his secretary of labor. Goldberg embraced the judicial activism of the other four liberals. When he left the Court three years later to become America's ambassador to the United Nations, Johnson named as his replacement the equally liberal Abe Fortas, a well-connected Washington attorney who specialized in corporate law. Fortas had many talents, including skill as a violinist. As a student at Yale Law School in the early 1930s he had become a protégé of Douglas, who taught there at the time. Fortas was a confidant of and adviser to President Johnson, whom he had met in Washington during the 1930s. Like Goldberg before him, he regularly sided with Warren, Black, Douglas, and Brennan.[18]

In 1967 Tom Clark retired, and President Johnson had a chance to enlarge this liberal bloc on the Court to six. As early as 1965, when LBJ had sounded Marshall out as a possible nominee for the post of solicitor general, he had been anxious to elevate blacks to visible federal positions. At that time Marshall had demurred, whereupon Johnson exclaimed to him, "I want folks to walk down the hall of the Justice Department and look in the door and see a nigger there." Marshall accepted the offer and was easily confirmed. In 1967 Johnson wanted very much to appoint a black man to the Court—and it had to be Marshall, "Mr. Civil Rights." When an aide to LBJ suggested that he name instead Leon Higginbotham, an African American whom Johnson had placed on the federal bench, Johnson leaned forward and said, "The only two people who ever heard of Judge Higginbotham are you and his momma. When I appoint a nigger to the bench, I want everyone to know he's a nigger." Johnson went ahead with the nomination, and after a two-month struggle to overcome southern opposition in the Senate, Marshall was confirmed by a vote of sixty-nine to eleven. The first black Supreme Court justice joined the Court on September 1, 1967.[19]

There remained, of course, apostles of judicial restraint on the Court in the 1960s, notably John Marshall Harlan; Potter Stewart of Ohio, a well-regarded, moderate federal judge whom Eisenhower had appointed in 1958 when Harold Burton retired; and Byron "Whizzer" White, an all-American football player, Rhodes Scholar, classmate of Stewart at Yale Law School, and one-time law clerk to Chief Justice Vinson. White was a friend and political supporter of Kennedy, who elevated him to the Court in 1962.[20] Harlan was a powerful intellectual presence and clashed often with Black until both retired in September 1971. But between 1962 and June 1969, when Warren stepped down, the Chief could normally count on at least a narrow majority. This second "Warren Court," carrying forward the activism that it had begun with *Brown*, delivered during these years a series of path-breaking, controversial decisions: banning required prayer in the public schools, demanding an end to malapportionment of state legislatures (and of the House of Representatives), striking down a state law outlawing the sale of contraceptives, broadening the rights of welfare recipients, and widening the legal standing of defendants in criminal cases. The Court promptly affirmed the constitutionality of the historic civil rights acts of 1964 and 1965. In June 1967 it even overturned Virginia's law barring interracial marriage. Such a decision, which was unanimous, had been unthinkable in the 1950s.[21]

Still, Lyndon Johnson had been prescient in May 1964 to worry that something like a "mutiny in this goddamn country," at least in the South, would eventually occur. Running in the fall against conservative Senator Barry Goldwater of Arizona, who had defiantly voted against the Civil Rights Act, Johnson failed to carry the five Deep South states of South Carolina, Georgia, Alabama, Mississippi, and Louisiana. He lost no other states, save Goldwater's Arizona. A majority of white voters in Arkansas, North Carolina, Tennessee, and Virginia also rejected the president. From 1964 forward, the Democratic party, identified since the LBJ years as the party of civil rights, had to struggle against a rising tide of white conservative Republicanism in the South.

Even more than in the 1950s, southern extremists resorted to violence in 1964. Civil rights workers who engaged in Mississippi Summer, an effort to support "freedom schools" and voting rights, confronted especially vicious responses. In June three young activists (two white, one black) were murdered. A bloody summer followed. By the end of August, foes of the movement had burned or bombed thirty-five homes, churches, and other buildings in Mississippi. Thirty-five volunteers were shot at, eighty were beaten, and three more were killed.[22]

Violent acts such as these understandably enraged civil rights workers in the South. Many directed their wrath at the FBI—and the federal government in general—for failing to protect them. One activist wrote on the wall of a building, "There is a town in Mississippi named Liberty, there is a department in Washington called Justice."[23] When Johnson refused to recognize the legitimacy of the Mississippi Freedom Democratic Party, a biracial group of delegates favoring civil rights, at the Democratic National Convention in September 1964, most of the black activists in the party lost faith in white liberals. Some soured on Martin Luther King, who supported LBJ's position at the convention and who persisted in calling for Christian nonviolence.

By 1965 many black militants were ready to take matters into their own hands. In 1966 they forced whites out of SNCC and the Congress of Racial Equality (CORE) and embraced the cause of Black Power. Their boldness revealed the extent to which their gains since 1960 had whetted their expectations for more. It also suggested that scholar-activists like Kenneth Clark may have been wrong to maintain that school segregation deeply damaged the self-esteem of young black people. The militants—many of them educated in segregated schools—surely did not *seem* passive or unsure of themselves. Black Power, however, had a cost. By 1967, the once nonviolent, biracial, and morally inspiring civil rights movement had splintered, never again to recover its strength. Meanwhile, blacks from 1965 through 1968 rioted in scores of cities, causing rising backlash among whites.[24]

In the North, polls suggested after 1965 that most whites continued to support peaceful moves toward racial justice, including the civil rights acts and the desegregation of southern schools. These attitudes, having changed rapidly in the early 1960s, persisted. Truly, much had changed. But most northern whites in the late 1960s also believed that the civil rights acts had effectively turned the tide. They thought that blacks, having achieved legal equality, had won most of what they needed in order to advance in American life. Further gains, they said, were up to the blacks, not the government, to achieve. As in the past, moreover, northern whites did not always practice at home what they preached for others. Backing the civil rights acts because they hoped to remedy a "southern" problem, they continued to do little to combat racial inequality in the North. This remained striking. As in the past, *de facto* segregation in housing confirmed black isolation, often in poverty-ridden ghettos. The median family income among blacks, though rising in real terms, remained relatively low, about half that of whites.[25]

White Northerners, meanwhile, continued to discriminate in jobs and to resist, sometimes violently, the efforts of black people to move into their neighborhoods. George Wallace of Alabama, seeking the presidency in 1964 and 1968, ran thinly disguised racist campaigns to capitalize on such feelings. In 1964 he received 34 percent of votes in a Democratic primary in Wisconsin, 30 percent in Indiana, and 45 percent in Maryland. Much of his support came from white working-class people who felt threatened by in-migrations of blacks. In 1968, Wallace ran as a third-party candidate and was the choice of some 10 million voters, 13 percent of the total. Johnson, meanwhile, failed to get strong open housing legislation through Congress. Most northern school districts remained as segregated *de facto* as ever.[26]

During the mid-1960s, a few white liberals, including Johnson, turned their attention to these social problems. One of these liberals was Daniel Patrick Moynihan, a social scientist who had become assistant secretary of labor under LBJ. Early in 1965 Moynihan fashioned a graph-laden report entitled "The Negro Family: The Case for National Action." It emphasized that rates of unemployment, family breakup and welfare dependency among black families, always very high compared to those among whites, were rapidly increasing. He urged vigorous federal policies, "National Action," to fight such problems. In June, Johnson adopted Moynihan's position, proposing in a widely reported speech at Howard University to support legislation for blacks that would promote not only equality of opportunity but also "equality as a fact and equality as a result."[27]

Given the deep structural roots of racial problems, this was a very bold promise, and it further excited expectations for social change. Unfortunately for Johnson's hopes, however, the Moynihan Report linked its discouraging statistics about black families to the legacy of slavery, thereby suggesting that black men had become emasculated as a result of bondage and could not take charge of their own fate. Moynihan also wrote about a "tangle of pathology" that devastated black families and inner-city neighborhoods. Kenneth Clark and others had reached similar conclusions, arguing that living in the "dark ghetto" (as Clark entitled a book he published in 1965) damaged the psyches of black people. But the Moynihan report seemed to go beyond Clark, to imply that flaws in black institutions themselves helped to create "pathology."

A few years earlier, before the civil rights movement greatly enhanced black pride and activism, Moynihan's argument might not have aroused excited controversy among black leaders. After all, the report called for vigorous national action to alleviate social problems. By 1965, however, the racial climate had changed. Militant black leaders then rejected any notion that historically based racial oppression, awful though it had been, had destroyed their culture or damaged their personalities. Black institutions, they retorted, remained rich and dynamic, not "pathological." Some blacks—Muslims as well as other black nationalists—not only sang the praises of African-American culture; they also went so far as to disdain desegregation. For these reasons many black leaders responded with fury to the Moynihan report, broke with white liberals, and consigned Johnson's hopes for new social legislation to oblivion. CORE leader James Farmer called the report a "massive cop out for the white conscience. We are sick to death of being analyzed, mesmerized, bought, sold, and slobbered over, while the same evils that are the ingredients of our oppression go unattended."[28]

Moynihan was not the only white social scientist at the time who advanced controversial ideas to account for the socioeconomic plight of blacks. Other liberals, worried that black children—even in nonsegregated schools—scored poorly on standardized academic tests, began devising remedies for "cultural deprivation." Blacks, they said, were surely not inferior by nature, but all too often they grew up in racially isolated, poverty-stricken, and "culturally deprived" surroundings, thereby testing more poorly than whites when they started school—and falling ever farther behind as they reached high school. One answer to this situation was to enrich the educational opportunities of black children (and other "culturally deprived" minorities). This argument could be advanced to bolster efforts for desegregation—placing minority students with achievement-oriented white children, reformers assumed, would help blacks advance. It also informed passage in early 1965 of a centerpiece of Johnson's Great Society program, the Elementary and Secondary Education Act. A core of this much-celebrated law, which at last provided significant general federal aid to public schools, was money for "compensatory education" to aid culturally disadvantaged children.[29]

As early as 1966, however, leading social scientists began to question such assumptions. A major report submitted at that time to the Office of Education by the sociologist James Coleman and others, *Equality of Educational Opportunity*, confirmed the well-known fact that the academic achievement of black schoolchildren lagged badly behind that of whites. When blacks started school, they were on the average one to two grade levels behind whites; when they reached the twelfth grade, they were three to five years behind. But the Coleman report, as it was called, was unenthusiastic about compensatory education. Surveying schools throughout the nation, it pointed out the obvious: most American children still went to virtually all-white or all-black schools. Because local property taxes were the primary source of support for schools, large differences in financing and physical facilities continued to characterize American education across districts. Within districts, however, these differences had narrowed appreciably by 1966. In this respect, Coleman said, blacks and whites normally went to schools that were separate-but-almost-equal in resources.

Some black children who were enabled to attend mostly white schools, the report continued, seemed to become more motivated to learn than those who remained in heavily black schools. Desegregation of this sort, therefore, could lead to better academic results. But black children in these nonsegregated schools, the report added, did only slightly better on most standardized achievement tests than did blacks in highly segregated schools. Northern black children scored only a little better than blacks in the South. Most important, the report argued, the class and family situations of children were primarily responsible for levels of academic achievement. School facilities alone, Coleman said, accounted for "only a small fraction of differences in pupil achievement." Coleman and his colleagues offered a sober conclusion that challenged high expectations from schools alone:

> Taking all these results together, one implication stands out above all: That schools bring little influence to bear on a child's achievement that is independent of his background and general social context; and that this very lack of an independent effect means that the inequalities imposed on children by their home, neighborhood, and peer environment are carried along to become the inequalities with which they confront adult life at the end of school.[30]

The widely publicized Coleman report did not much appeal to the most avid integrationists, liberal school teachers and administrators, or federal education officials, many of whom had strong reasons to emphasize the transcendent virtues of desegregation as well as high levels of government spending for compensatory education. Like millions of Americans, they also persisted in thinking that good schools, per se, were the keys to the promotion of greater academic achievement and therefore of greater equality in life. Spending money on schools, moreover, seemed to many liberal reformers to be a simpler, more straightforward means of promoting racial equality than trying to undertake the task of dealing seriously with the numerous other structural problems afflicting the black poor. Indeed, they argued—then and later—that compensatory education programs deserved far higher levels of support than they received. Federal assistance to education, including compensatory aid, therefore received fairly steady congressional funding over the years ahead, while other large sources of racial inequality, given less political attention, persisted.[31]

The Coleman report has sometimes been misunderstood. It did not argue that school resources, let alone quality, did not matter. After all, how many children learn algebra at home? How many poorly educated teachers have the capacity to challenge ambitious students? Doesn't learning suffer when it is conveyed through dated textbooks or offered in ill-heated, badly equipped libraries, classrooms, and laboratories? Parents, of course, were very much aware of these matters, which was one reason so many of them moved to districts that had well-financed schools. Nor did the report dismiss the academic advantages, in some circumstances, for desegregation. In fact, by noting the potential value of bringing black children into classrooms with academically oriented whites, it encouraged many liberals after 1966 in their belief that better racial balance in schools (of teachers as well as of students)—to be achieved if necessary by court-ordered busing of children—might help to soften the power of social class differences and thereby lessen, a little, black-white gaps in academic achievement.

But the implications of the Coleman report were nonetheless unsettling to people who held great faith in the potential of schools to reform society at large. Did racial mixing in schools advance the self-esteem or academic motivation of black children? Sometimes, perhaps. Did it promote tolerance among white children? Maybe, but it was hard to tell. Would spending for "compensatory education" narrow large racial gaps in academic achievement? By itself, probably not. What really determined such achievement, the report emphasized, were the educational and social situations of families, the ethos of neighborhoods, and the academic ambitions of peers in school. Substantial progress in the academic achievement of black children might therefore require large social programs—public as well as private—that would strengthen the economic status of black parents as well as enhance the home environments of their children. Programs like these would presumably have to go well beyond spending more money on schools or promoting greater desegregation in education.[32]

Some blacks, meanwhile, began expressing rising doubts concerning the emphasis of liberal reformers on the virtues of desegregated schools. In 1954, Warren and his colleagues had declared that "the doctrine of 'separate-but-equal' has no place. Separate educational facilities are inherently unequal." For many black leaders—Thurgood Marshall, Kenneth Clark, and others—these remained inspiring phrases. By the mid-1960s, however, increasing numbers of black leaders found the phrases patronizing. Why, they asked, did liberals keep measuring the quality of schools by the percentages of white children in attendance? What was wrong with "community" schools run by blacks in their own neighborhoods? Many of these schools, they asserted, had in the past demanded high standards of their students and had instilled pride in black institutions.[33]

Blacks who doubted the great advangages of desegregated schools remained, as before, a minority in the late 1960s. The star of desegregation still shone brightly, for blacks as well as liberal whites, amid the darker racial atmosphere of the times. Still, eminent social scientists such as Coleman had questioned expansive assumptions about the educational and social virtues of school desegregation alone. Rising calls for black-run "community schools," echoing the concerns of W. E. B. Du Bois in the 1930s and Zora Neale Hurston in the 1950s, exposed the continuing ambivalence of some black people about racial mixing. And louder demands for affirmative action, which desegregationists like Marshall had not imagined in 1954, further challenged the idea that America should expect to be a wholly color-blind country—at least not in the short run. Some of the liberal beliefs that had seemed self-evident in 1954 were coming under siege amid the turbulent and divisive racial politics of the late 1960s.[34]

Most top federal officials, however, remained committed in the late 1960s to desegregation of the schools. This was a high tide of expectations, especially among the rapidly expanding officialdom of Washington, about the capacity of liberal public policy to create a more egalitarian society. Between the mid-1960s, when Johnson and his advisers drove the civil rights acts and the Elementary and Secondary Education

Act through Congress, and 1973, when the Supreme Court delivered the last of several strongly voiced opinions that strengthened *Brown*, all three branches of government broke with the gradualist guidelines of *Brown II* and moved with unparalleled and sometimes passionately cooperative determination to promote desegregation in schools. The cooperation of the three branches accomplished far more than the Court, since *Brown*, had been able to accomplish alone.

The first of these actions, the Civil Rights Act of 1964, mainly sought to attack racial segregation in public accommodations and employment. But it also featured a Title VI empowering federal officials to cut off aid from school districts that practiced *de jure* segregation. The bill passed only after apprehensive congressmen—from the North as well as the South—managed to insert what they thought was a clause that would protect their constituencies against the imposition of racial quotas. " '*Desegregation*,' " the clause read, "*shall not mean the assignment of students to public schools in order to overcome racial imbalance.*"[35] To this extent the Civil Rights Act advanced a color-blind vision of the good society. It sought to promote equal opportunity by ending Jim Crow in the South, not to promote affirmative action or guarantee equal results for blacks either in the North or the South.[36]

Within the next five years, however, eager liberal officials in the swelling federal bureaucracies established under the auspices of the Great Society were interpreting the law so as to strive for "racial balance"—one of the most controversial phrases concerning school desegregation to emerge from the late 1960s. What the phrase meant was often maddeningly unclear in the details—hence some of the controversy—but its confident supporters relied on three assumptions: heavily black or all-black schools were generally inferior, thus (as the Clarks had argued in 1954) sabotaging the desire for achievement among students who were forced to attend them; low-income black pupils who were enabled to mix with motivated middle-class white students would achieve more; and mixing would promote racial tolerance over time. The goals of enhancing academic achievement and interracial understanding lay at the core of the rising quest for racial balance.

To achieve this balance, school officials practicing *de jure* segregation were expected to mix the races in rough accordance with the percentages of blacks and whites of school age in their districts. They were also supposed to attain greater balance in the hiring and assignment of teachers, and within classrooms as well as within schools. Moving toward such a standard, ardent liberals in the Department of Health, Education, and Welfare (HEW), which oversaw federal spending for public schools, began pressuring southern school districts as early as December 1964. In March 1966 they called for a doubling or tripling of the percentage of black students in "formerly white schools" for the 1966–67 school year. Johnson eagerly supported these moves, on one occasion wandering in and out of HEW offices, where he urged officials to come down hard on southern resisters. "Get 'em!" he called. "Get 'em! Get the last ones!" In March 1968, HEW told segregating school districts to submit plans for complete racial balance by the fall of 1969 (in majority black districts by the fall of 1970). The firmness with which HEW insisted on these percentage-specific, result-oriented standards had been largely unanticipated by Congress after passage of the Civil Rights Act in 1964. Demanded by nonelected liberals in the executive branch of government, they outraged southern school officials. Districts that resisted risked losing federal funding for education.[37]

Enforcement of the Elementary and Secondary Education Act, which increased federal aid to public schools, raised the stakes of this controversial business in 1965. Federal funding for schools jumped from $2.7 billion in 1964–65 to $14.7 billion in 1971–72. More than earlier, when federal aid had been small, HEW officials who allotted the money had power to help or to hurt. Moreover, most of the federal school aid was earmarked for compensatory education—it was a key part of the larger, highly touted antipoverty program of Johnson's Great Society. In urging such aid, the president reflected the very high expectations that Americans were expressing in the buoyant 1960s concerning the role of schools in American life. "I know that education is the only valid passport from poverty," he said. No law of the 1960s better reflected the central assumption of the Great Society's "can-do" liberalism: government could equalize opportunity, and equal results would follow, at least for those who worked hard, over the course of time.[38]

Scholars and others have labored hard to assess the impact after 1965 of federal aid to schools and of compensatory education. Understandably so, for these policies affected many of the 80 million "baby boomers" who were born between 1945 and the early 1960s. Expectations about such policies, the Coleman report notwithstanding, remained high among liberals. Francis Keppel, commissioner of education between 1962 and 1965, led ardent liberal officials who believed that nonsegregated schools not only must expand to provide equal access to all young people; schools must also improve so as greatly to advance the achievement of students. Like many goals of American liberals in the mid-1960s, these educational aspirations were highly ambitious, especially compared to the more modest expectations that had dominated during the 1950s.[39]

Did federal aid to schools manage to achieve these goals? Some liberals have perceived progress. Between the 1964–65 and 1965–66 school years, pressure from HEW helped to increase the percentage of black students who attended majority-white schools—a definition of "desegregated" schools that HEW soon adopted—from 10.9 percent to 15.9 percent. Most of this change occurred in the Deep South, where the percentage rose from 2.23 to 6.01 percent, and to 13.9 percent by 1967–68. Then and later, liberals have also argued that compensatory education programs have been beneficial. The proportion of seventeen-year-olds with very low scores on standardized science and mathematics achievement tests, for example, fell between the early 1970s and the mid-1990s.[40]

Most scholars, however, offer mixed assessments. Federal aid, to begin with, affected school districts in varying ways. In some southern districts it was significant, amounting to as much as 20 or 30 percent of school budgets. In areas like these, segregationist school officials protested angrily against the ever tougher desegregation guidelines, but liberals in key federal bureaucracies created during the Johnson era—notably the Office for Civil Rights within HEW—stood their ground, and resistance often crumbled. In other districts, federal aid was relatively small: nationally, it hovered after 1965 between 6 and 9 percent of spending on public schools. Some segregating districts where the aid was modest dared to ignore the guidelines, lost federal funding, and carried on as before. Cutting off aid, moreover, struck many officials, including advocates of desegregation, as a draconian option—an all-or-nothing response that would penalize pupils who needed help. From the beginning, federal bureaucrats employed the option, but they were sometimes hesitant to go that far.

Other southern officials resorted to evasion, or sought to stall for time, thereby turning the avidly desegregationist Office for Civil Rights into a den of controversy. Almost everywhere, southern white officials who made a pretense of complying reassigned black students to formerly white schools, not whites to formerly black schools. And they instituted tracking procedures whereby blacks and whites were separated in different classes. Tracking of this sort had determined defenders who pointed out—then as well as later—that white students on the average scored much better on standardized tests than blacks (and many poor whites), and therefore should be taught on a faster track of their own. More often than not, however, this sort of tracking left the majority of blacks unprepared to do well on college admissions tests or to cope with demanding university standards. [41]

Northern areas, meanwhile, did not expect to worry about cutoffs—after all, they did not practice *de jure* segregation. When Keppel nonetheless threatened Chicago Mayor Richard Daley with a deferral of aid in 1965, in order to promote greater mixing in the city's highly segregated system (90 percent of black public school students in the city attended all-black schools, many of them crowding into mobile classrooms imported to already teeming ghetto schools), Daley erupted in fury. Johnson normally backed Keppel, but on this occasion Keppel and his aides overstepped their authority and failed to keep the White House well informed. LBJ, moreover, needed Daley's powerful political support. So he called Keppel into the Oval Office and blistered him for his temerity. HEW backed off, whereupon federal funding to Chicago's school system continued, as it did to other heavily segregated systems in the North. The United States Civil Rights Commission reported in 1979 that two-thirds or more of students in the North and West were in "moderately segregated school districts."[42]

Other limitations of the federal aid program developed in its operation: a good deal of compensatory education money aimed in the 1960s at the poor missed its targets. Employees of HEW's Office of Education, a small agency, lacked the resources to monitor carefully how the money was spent. Nor did they consider monitoring to be their job: they were to allot the money, not to micromanage the way recipients spent it. For these reasons, local school officials continued as in the past to make many important decisions, and they often diverted the money to cover administrative and transportation costs. Other local officials used the funds to enhance the social skills of students, to promote nutrition, or to develop medical services. In many districts, little of the money earmarked for compensatory education went directly into classroom instruction for "culturally deprived" children—or other children, for that matter. Carl Kaestle and Marshall Smith, leading scholars of education, later concluded, "After almost two decades of intervention, the Title I program [for compensatory education] stands primarily as a symbol of national concern for the poor rather than as a viable response to their needs."[43]

For other reasons it is hard to evaluate federal intervention. In preparing their report in 1966, Coleman and his colleagues tried to identify the factors that affected educational achievement. But neither they nor anyone else knew a great deal in the 1960s about how teachers might significantly advance the achievement of the masses of pupils, including minorities and poor children with complex and varying needs who were by then moving in ever larger numbers into the elementary schools and for the first time in American history staying to finish high school and to seek entrance to college. In this rapidly changing new world of high educational expectations, how was one to do a good job of educating all students, especially if the goal was to help them achieve at notably higher levels? What educational strategies might greatly narrow the gaps that separated low-achieving pupils from others? (Later studies that addressed this question estimated that compensatory education programs may have accounted for at most 10 percent of a modest narrowing of the gap that took place by 1990.) Managing formidable tasks such as these required, in the words of education expert Diane Ravitch, "intensive, individualized instruction in an encouraging, supportive environment."[44]

The fact was that by the 1960s Americans were asking much, much more of schools than they had ever done before. In the past, they had mostly embraced lesser goals, such as the development of literacy and good citizenship. Prior to the 1950s the majority of students had not even finished high school. To imagine that schools could quickly achieve the more ambitious educational goals of Americans in the 1960s—without having clear ideas about how to attain them—was utopian. When federal reforms of the 1960s were later judged—by overexpectant parents and critics in the 1970s and 1980s—to have "failed" to do so, a huge hue and cry arose inaccurately lamenting the apparent deterioration of American education. That is another story.[45]

Still, what the Congress did in 1964–65—passing the civil rights and education laws—gave the government powerful new weapons to fight the long-running battle for desegregation of the schools. Equally important was the manner in which the new breed of morally motivated, idealistic federal officials brandished these weapons in the late 1960s. The move toward affirmative action and racial balancing led to the growing use of enforcement strategies that Congress had scarcely imagined in 1964, let alone at the time of *Brown* ten years earlier.

The effectiveness of these new strategies, however, still depended on the reactions of the courts, which could conceivably have ruled that policies such as affirmative action and racial balancing, unauthorized by legislation, were unconstitutional. Many congressmen surely thought that this was the case: beginning in 1966 the House voted for bills that forbade the reassignment of children away from their neighborhood schools in order to achieve racial balance. It also sought to whittle away the discretionary scope of the Office for Civil Rights within HEW. As always, the vision of the "neighborhood school" continued to evoke warm feelings.

In 1964, however, the Supreme Court began to act more decisively on behalf of school desegregation. In May of that year, ten years after *Brown*, it decided unanimously in *Griffin v. County School Board of Prince Edward County* (Virginia) that the county, which had closed its public schools in 1959 rather than desegregate, must reopen them and obey the Court. Justice Black wrote, "There has been entirely too much deliberation and not enough speed in enforcing the constitutional rights which we held in *Brown*." The *Griffin* decision did not work wonders, at least in the short run, because white parents made it known that they would keep their children in the "private" schools that had sprung up in the 1950s. Prince Edward County's public schools, therefore, would be nearly 100 percent black. Still, advocates of forceful judicial action were encouraged. Robert Carter, general counsel for the NAACP, hailed the ruling as the beginning of a new era. The decision, he said, "has broken the back of the South's unlamented 'massive resistance' and marked the end of open defiance of the Supreme Court's decree."[46]

Federal district and circuit court judges further challenged the South after 1964. They drew their new forcefulness, in part, from observing the inspiring valor of civil rights activists and from the Civil Rights Act of 1964. Chief among them was Judge John Minor Wisdom of the Fifth Circuit Court of Appeals, which handled cases in Deep South areas such as Alabama and Mississippi. Appointed to his post by Eisenhower in 1957, Wisdom had grown impatient with dodges such as pupil placement and freedom of choice laws and resolved to end them. In 1965–66 he seized his chance, when a series of Mississippi school cases reached his

Handwriting On The Wall

From *Straight Herblock (Simon and Shuster, 1964).*

court. In the most widely cited of these cases, *United States v. Jefferson County Board of Education*, decided in December 1966, Wisdom directly challenged the still influential ruling that Judge John Parker had made in *Briggs* in 1955. This was the "Briggs Dictum." At that time, Parker had written, "The Constitution . . . does not require integration. . . . It merely forbids the use of governmental power to enforce segregation." Wisdom emphatically disagreed, stating that "the only school desegre-

Judge John Minor Wisdom, the federal circuit court judge in the Deep South whose decisions in the late 1960s greatly accelerated the pace of school desegregation. *(The United States Court of Appeals Fifth Circuit)*

gation plan that meets constitutional standards is one that works." He added, "The only adequate redress for a previously overt system-wide policy of segregation against Negroes as a collective entity is a system-wide policy of integration."[47]

Jefferson reflected the rapidly changing times. Wisdom, indeed, had dared not act so boldly in the late 1950s, when popular support for equal rights had been much weaker. In 1966, however, he said that school districts practicing *de jure* segregation must take affirmative steps toward racial balance—and do so quickly. Such a process required carefully color-conscious assignment of children. Endorsing the ever-tougher guidelines of HEW, Wisdom then gave detailed instructions to school boards. In so doing he engaged the courts in the nuts and bolts of school operations—districting, pupil placement, transportation, teacher assignment, and a range of smaller details. As critics noted, *Jefferson* marked a long stride in the direction of judicial supervision of public education in the United States. This was soon to become an extraordinarily complex and controversial effort.

Wisdom's challenge, while important, would make little difference if the Supreme Court shied away from endorsing it. Would the Court, having tolerated southern obstructionism for many years, follow Wisdom's lead?

Racial turbulence in 1967 and 1968 created a climate that may have encouraged the High Court to do so. Urban race riots peaked in 1967, devastated cities such as Newark and Detroit, and further exposed the depth of America's racial divisions. An assassin gunned down Martin Luther King on April 4, 1968. The day before this assassination, the Court heard oral arguments in *Green v. County School Board of New Kent County, Va.* The case involved a freedom of choice plan established in 1965 in predominantly rural New Kent County just east of Richmond. Like most such plans, it resulted in little desegregation: 115 black high school students, of 736 in the district, went to the "white" high school; no white pupils, of 519 in all, chose to attend the "black" high school. The federal circuit court had approved the plan, but Greenberg and others at the Legal Defense and Educational Fund carried an appeal to Washington.[48]

The Court debated the issues in *Green* amid racial rioting in Washington following King's death. Reflecting the impatience that it had shown four years earlier in *Griffin*, it sided unanimously with the black plaintiffs. Warren was relieved and happy. As his friend Justice Brennan prepared to read the decision on May 27—fourteen years after *Brown*—Warren passed him a note: "When this opinion is handed down, the traffic light will have changed from *Brown* to *Green*. Amen!"

School officials, Brennan's opinion declared, had an "affirmative duty" to desegregate so that the county would run a "unitary system in which racial discrimination would be eliminated root and branch." The school board "must be required to formulate a new plan ... which promises realistically to convert promptly to a system without a 'white' school and a 'Negro' school, but just schools." The opinion did not go so far as to declare that all freedom of choice plans were unconstitutional, but Brennan's language indicated that such plans must be judged severely and approved only if effective in achieving desegregation. *Green* was broad, affecting the hiring and assignment of faculty, quality of facilities, and transportation. Reacting angrily, Governor Lester Maddox of Georgia ordered all state flags to be flown at half-mast.[49]

The Court's ruling focused on ending *de jure* racial segregation, and therefore it mattered only in the South and many border regions. It made no claims for what desegregation might mean for academic achievement or for racial attitudes among children. Still, the decision marked a major milestone in the history of judicial steps toward desegregation of public schools. It gave specificity to the vague and ineffective phrase, "all deliberate speed." Together with rulings soon to follow, it was to transform racial patterns in southern public schools in an amazingly short period of time.[50]

Green delighted Justice Thurgood Marshall, the Court's junior member. It was also the last major school segregation case in which Chief Justice Warren, then seventy-seven years old, participated. Worried that his old political enemy from California, Richard Nixon, would win the presidency in November, he resolved to quit so that President Johnson would have time to replace him. A little later he told Johnson that he wished to retire as soon as a successor could be confirmed.

7

THE BURGER COURT SURPRISES

Rarely in American history has the membership of the Supreme Court changed as rapidly as it did in the next three years to the end of 1971. President Johnson, a lame duck in the summer of 1968, resolved to replace Earl Warren by elevating his friend and close adviser, Justice Abe Fortas, to the position of Chief. Republicans, however, anticipated victory in the angrily contested presidential election of 1968. Nixon, their candidate, had angrily denounced the Court for "coddling criminals" and was eager if elected to name a conservative Chief. His yearning to do so exposed a lasting legacy of the Warren years: appointments to the Court, which had come to play a key role in American life during Warren's tenure, were becoming ever more contested. A host of controversial constitutional issues—involving the Vietnam War, the death penalty, affirmative action, busing, abortion, and welfare rights, among others— might reach the Court in the near future. If Nixon could name a conservative, he might begin to banish the curse, as he saw it, of liberal judicial activism.[1]

For these reasons, Johnson's effort encountered unyielding opposition from congressional Republicans, who argued that Fortas, by privately advising the president, was guilty of conflict of interest. They also criticized Fortas for unethical financial behavior. Filibustering, they prevailed: at Fortas's request, Johnson withdrew the nomination. Further revelations in May 1969 then provided still more alarming evidence concerning Fortas's personal finances. Although Fortas denied any wrongdoing, he was unconvincing, and he left the Court in mid-May 1969 rather than prolong the controversy. His departure meant that the newly elected Nixon had a chance to name two justices—one to replace Fortas, the other to replace Warren, who had reluctantly stayed on while these controversies lasted.[2]

Nixon's first nominee, to succeed Earl Warren as Chief, was Warren Burger, a sixty-one-year-old Republican who had been named by Eisenhower in 1956 to the Court of Appeals in the District of Columbia. Nixon had met Burger at the GOP national convention of 1948 when Burger was floor manager for the presidential candidacy of fellow Minnesotan Harold Stassen. Looking for a conservative with judicial experience, the new president was attracted to Burger, a broad-shouldered, white-maned man whom one scholar accurately described as a "casting director's ideal of a Chief Justice." Many people found Burger to be pompous and aloof, but Nixon correctly recognized him as a fellow supporter of "law and order." Burger had scant respect for Warren, whom he considered a careless and politically motivated judge. Disgusted by what he considered to be the liberalism of the *New York Times*, he pointedly subscribed to the more moderate *Christian Science Monitor*. Later, when Nixon announced in 1970 that the United States had invaded Cambodia—an action that inflamed many college and university campuses and led to the killing of four students at Kent State University—Burger went to the White House and congratulated the president for his speech.[3]

When Nixon asked him to serve, Burger was delighted. It was a mark of those highly partisan times, however, that Burger entered into the confirmation process unsure that the Democratic Senate would support his nomination. After all, Fortas had resigned under pressure only a week earlier; no doubt liberal Democrats like Senator Edward "Ted" Kennedy of Massachusetts, a member of the judiciary committee, would retaliate. The Court, too, seemed a hotbed of politics. Visiting the Court building to pay his respects to the justices, Burger entered the space where William Brennan's law clerks worked. There he saw a grotesque rubber mask of Nixon hanging on the wall. Also displayed was a Black Power poster featuring a clenched fist. No institution was immune from the passionate feelings aroused by the Vietnam War, urban race riots, and other controversies of the late 1960s.[4]

As it turned out, Burger need not have worried. The judiciary committee, headed by Eastland of Mississippi, quickly forwarded his nomination to the floor of the Senate, which confirmed him as Chief Justice by a vote of seventy-four to three. With Nixon in attendance, Burger was sworn in by Warren as Chief Justice on June 23, 1969. Warren retired the same day, having served for more than fifteen years. Nixon seemed to be on his way toward turning the Court in a more conservative direction.

The president had a much more difficult time, however, filling the vacancy left by the departure of Fortas. He tried twice in the next eleven months, first nominating a conservative South Carolinian appeals court judge, Clement Haynsworth, and then naming another appeals court judge, G. Harrold Carswell of Florida. His choices reflected a larger "southern strategy" aimed at consolidating Republican political gains in Dixie. But liberal Senate Democrats (and a few Republicans) resisted, claiming that the nominees were not only opposed to civil rights but were also mediocre in general. In bitter Senate battles, both Haynsworth and Carswell went down to defeat. Like the struggles over Johnson's effort to make Fortas Chief Justice, these controversies showed that the Supreme Court had become a battleground for partisan fighting.

Nixon finally succeeded with his third choice, Harry Blackmun of Minnesota. Sixty-one years old at the time of his nomination in April 1970, Blackmun, too, was an appeals court judge, having been named by Eisenhower to the post in 1959. Some Court watchers worried that the nominee, who seemed insecure and indecisive in 1970, would become an echo of Burger—a "Minnesota twin," or "Hip Pocket Harry." Indeed, Blackmun had gone to school with Burger and had been best man at his wedding. In naming Blackmun, however, Nixon gave his southern strategy a rest. Senate Democrats, moreover, had made their point by stopping the nominations of Haynsworth and Carswell. Blackmun, a moderate, was confirmed unanimously in May 1970, a year after Fortas had resigned.[5]

Sixteen months later, in September 1971, two more vacancies suddenly occurred. Black, long in ill health, retired at the age of eighty-five after thirty-four years on the bench. He died eight days later. Harlan, who had served more than sixteen years, had maintained an influential presence until the late 1960s, despite failing eyesight that made him nearly blind. His handwriting had become almost illegible. Diagnosed with cancer, he, too, retired in September (and died in December). With the new term set to open in October, Nixon moved quickly to name their replacements. His choices were Lewis Powell, Jr., and William Rehnquist.

Powell, sixty-four, was a rail-thin and courtly Virginian who had been shocked when he had heard the news of *Brown* in 1954. Then, and until 1961, he had been head of the school board in Richmond. Although he had opposed the strategy of massive resistance, he and fellow board members (like most southern whites at the time) had done nothing to promote desegregation. When he stepped down from the board, there were only two black children among the 23,000 students in the city's public schools. Powell, however, had a distinguished record as an attorney and had served a term as president of the American Bar Association. The Congressional Black Caucus opposed his nomination but failed to win over the Senate, which confirmed him in December 1971 by a vote of eighty-nine to one.[6]

Rehnquist, then forty-seven, was a considerably more controversial choice. In 1952, as a law clerk for Justice Robert Jackson, he had written a memorandum that favored the separate-but-equal doctrine of *Plessy*. Challenged during his confirmation hearings in 1971, he maintained (unconvincingly, most scholars think) that the memo reflected Jackson's views, not his own. In 1953 he moved to Arizona to practice law and plunged into Republican politics. He campaigned for GOP presidential nominee Barry Goldwater in 1964. As an assistant attorney general in Nixon's justice department he had frequently testified before congressional committees in support of a range of strongly held conservative positions. Liberals conceded that Rehnquist, an affable man, was articulate, intelligent, and gifted as a writer. But some senators could not abide the thought of him on the Court. When his nomination reached the Senate floor, sixty-five voted for it and twenty-six opposed. With Powell, he was sworn in on January 7, 1972.[7]

No president since Warren Harding in the early 1920s had been so fortunate as to name four Supreme Court justices during his first term. (FDR, of course, had not had the chance to name even one between 1933 and mid-1937, when he chose Black.) It was hardly surprising, therefore, that liberals expected the worst of the Burger Court, as it came to be called. The cartoonist Herblock dubbed it the Nixonburger Court.

Liberals had other reasons to worry about the Court in these years. Brennan, having emerged as an intellectual leader of the liberal bloc early in the 1960s, continued to be a strong member. In the last years of his tenure on the Court, however, Black disappointed liberals. Weakened by a stroke, he was both more testy and more conservative than he had been earlier. Douglas, who turned seventy-one in late 1969, kept the liberal faith. But he seemed more crotchety than ever. Worse, he struck many of his colleagues as indifferent to much of the Court's business. Whenever possible, he left Washington for his isolated retreat in Gopher Prairie, Washington, where he was virtually incommunicado.

Marshall, sixty-one in late 1969, also disappointed people who had hoped he would be a major intellectual force on the Court. He remained a wholly dependable liberal. But he was restless as a justice and seemed content to follow in Brennan's shadow—so much so that some people referred to him as "Mr. Justice Marshall-Brennan." He told his clerks (only half in jest), "I'll do whatever Bill [Brennan] does." Marshall also suffered a number of health problems—pneumonia that hospitalized him for thirty days in 1970, stomach ulcers, and an emergency appendectomy in 1971. Refusing to moderate his heavy smoking and drinking, he ballooned in weight to 230 pounds by the mid-1970s. He spent a good deal of time watching television in his office and regaling his clerks—all but one of whom (a god-child) between 1967 and 1977 were white—with stories about his past.

"Mr. Civil Rights," in short, had tired. Proud of his accomplishments, certain of his place in history, he displayed little patience for people— fellow justices included—who presumed to contradict him. He also grew increasingly uncomfortable amid the rising tide of conservatism that descended on the nation (and on the Court) in the 1970s and 1980s. For these reasons, and unlike Brennan, he made little effort to forge alliances or compromises with colleagues. Worse, in the eyes of most of the other justices, he did not bestir himself to master complicated issues outside of his experience. Douglas, who shared Marshall's liberal views, came to regard him as a lightweight. Marshall, he wrote later, "was named simply because he was black." A leading legal historian, Bernard Schwartz, has delivered an even harsher evaluation: "next to [Charles] Whittaker, he [Marshall] was arguably the least able Justice to sit on the Warren Court."[8]

Observers of the Court in these years, therefore, thought that the Burger Court might overturn much that Warren and his fellow liberals had done. After 1971, Nixon's nominees—Burger, Blackmun, Powell, and Rehnquist—needed the vote of only one more justice, perhaps Potter Stewart, a Republican named by Eisenhower, or Byron White, a devotee of judicial restraint who had often sided with Harlan—to gain a majority of five. Moreover, the national mood was in many ways more conservative during the Nixon years. Although public opinion polls revealed that most white people still favored desegregation—much had changed since the early 1950s—people also indicated that they no longer regarded civil rights as a high priority. More important, they said, were such emotion-laden issues as Vietnam, drugs, and crime. Led by the president, many Americans exhibited a growing backlash against the excesses, as they saw them, of the liberal 1960s. Would the Court, historically sensitive to the world about it, dare to defy such a mood by preserving the work of the Warren Court?[9]

Surprisingly, it did, at least in the early years of Burger's tenure between 1969 and 1973. While the new Chief was undeniably a conservative, he recognized that the Court should not attempt a rapid reversal of what his predecessor had done. To do that, he understood, would not be easy, given the conflicting views of his colleagues. It would also arouse con-

The Supreme Court, 1973. First row (*from left*), Potter Stewart, William Douglas, Warren Burger (chief), William Brennan, Byron White. Second row (*from left*), Lewis Powell, Thurgood Marshall, Harry Blackmun, William Rehnquist. (*Library of Congress, Prints and Photographs Division, New York World-Telegram & Sun Collection*)

troversy that could damage the image of the already embattled Court. It was better, he believed, to undertake a holding action. Burger, moreover, was sensitive to criticism and worried about how he would appear in the press if he led an overly aggressive conservative charge. He was sensitive also to predictions that he would merely do Nixon's bidding. Many critics of Burger thought that he was inconsistent and that he too often changed his mind at the last minute. Unlike Warren, who stamped his strong personality on the Court from the start, Burger was a cautious and uninspiring Chief. Neither liberals nor conservatives much admired him.

Liberals were nonetheless gratified that Burger and his fellow justices did not move quickly to the right. Between 1969 and 1974 the Court rejected the effort of the Nixon administration to halt publication of the classified "Pentagon Papers." It struck down existing death penalty laws and gave strong support to affirmative action procedures in employment. Corporate leaders were stunned and irate at the unanimously decided pro-affirmative action decision, *Griggs v. Duke Power Co.*, reached in March 1971. In January 1973, Justice Blackmun, writing for a seven to two Court, delivered the opinion in *Roe v. Wade* that legalized abortion. Rehnquist and White dissented. In July 1974 the Court again defied Nixon, ruling unanimously, Rehnquist abstaining, in *United States v. Nixon* that the president must turn over tapes relating to the Watergate crisis. Two weeks later, the president was forced to resign. Clearly, the Burger Court did not sit under the thumb of the president.[10]

Decisions extending *Green* and school desegregation offered the greatest surprises in these years. The first of these cases, considered by the Court at the start of Burger's first term in October 1969, stemmed directly from Nixon's southern strategy. Seeking to gain favor in the South, the president told the Department of Health, Education, and Welfare to approve a request for delay, until December 1, 1969, of earlier court orders that would have forced thirty school districts in Mississippi to produce effective plans for desegregation by the start of the school year. The administration's action outraged civil rights activists and attorneys for the Legal Defense Fund, who appealed to the High Court. Chief Justice Burger suddenly faced a visible, highly controversial case. Like *Brown* fifteen years earlier, it would force his Court to rule on this most inflammable of racial issues.[11]

From the start the case sparked sharp debate among the justices, with Black insisting that the Court move quickly to hear it so as to order the plans to be adopted right away. "Too many plans, not enough action," he exclaimed during hearings. A tense and expectant audience, jamming the chamber, erupted in laughter. Harlan, however, thought that the Court ought at least to take time to draft a decision giving lower courts some guidance. Irritated by Black's demand, he complained, "You don't give in to blackmail." For six days, the embattled justices exchanged drafts but got nowhere. A Burger draft, which largely supported the Nixon administration, satisfied no one. It seemed for a time that the Court would divide, four to four. In the end, however, Burger and others feared to turn against *Brown*. Accepting a draft by Brennan, the Court decided unanimously that the desegregation plans must quickly be implemented. The standard of "all deliberate speed," the Court said, was no longer constitutionally permissible. It added, "The obligation of every school district is to terminate dual school systems at once and to operate now and hereafter only unitary schools." These were schools in which "no person is to be effectively excluded from any school because of race or color."

The decision, *Alexander v. Holmes County Board of Education*, stung southern segregationists. George Wallace of Alabama observed that the Burger Court was "no better than the Warren Court." The judges were "a bunch of limousine hypocrites." Governor Lester Maddox of Georgia exclaimed that the ruling was a "criminal act by the government." Mississippi governor John Bell Williams added, "Once again the schoolchildren of our state have been offered as sacrificial lambs on the altar of social experimentation." An editorialist for *Crisis*, the journal of the NAACP, predictably disagreed. The ruling in *Alexander*, he wrote, was a "great decision and a giant step forward." Emmitt Douglas, head of the Los Angeles NAACP, commented simply, "Deliberate speed is dead, dead, dead."[12]

Douglas's comment was accurate, for the decision in *Alexander*, following on continuing pressure from HEW and on *Green* eighteen months earlier, made it clear that the Supreme Court—whether Warren-led or Burger-led—would no longer tolerate delay in the implementation of *de jure* school desegregation. But many white Southerners still resisted, so loudly that a second surge of massive resistance—to rival that of the 1950s—seemed imminent. In Lamar, South Carolina, a mob of whites turned over and smashed two school buses filled with black elementary schoolchildren, who barely escaped with their lives. Elsewhere, thousands of white parents in heavily black areas pulled their children from the public schools. It was estimated that white public school enrollment in the Mississippi districts directly affected declined by 25 percent. The drop was as high as 90 percent in some heavily black areas, and 100 percent in one.[13] In Drew High School, where Matthew and Mae Bertha Carter's children had broken the color line in 1965, white children left in droves after 1970 and went to tax-supported "private" academies. By 1973 the school had become 80 percent black.[14]

Still, the Court had spoken. Nixon, moreover, acted responsibly, urging the South to obey the ruling.[15] At the same time he let it be known to southern whites that his officials in HEW, unlike Johnson's, would lay down their axes in the allotment of federal aid to segregated schools. (Cutoffs of aid, he believed, punished children more than school districts.) He also made it clear that he would appoint conservative judges to the federal bench. In time, he reassured white Southerners, his appointees would reverse the tide of social engineering that liberals from Warren on had tried to implement. This approach promised to protect Nixon politically. Turning over the sensitive issue of school desegregation to the courts would make the judges, not the president or his Justice Department, the locus of controversy.

Needless to say, Nixon's calculated policies did not please staunch advocates of desegregation. Many branded him a racist. But his request that Southerners obey the rulings of the Court did help to prevent a resurgence of massive resistance in the 1970s. Indeed, the changes that soon occurred in the South were extraordinary and dramatic. At the time of *Alexander*, most southern school districts still maintained dual— that is, separate black and white—systems. These districts then had to move rapidly toward creating unitary systems. The percentage of black students in majority-white schools in the South jumped up again—as it already had after *Green*—from 23.4 percent in the 1968–69 school year to 33.1 percent in 1970–71.[16]

In October 1970 the Court placed at the top of the agenda for its fall term another controversial school case, *Swann v. Charlotte-Mecklenburg County Board of Education*. It dated to late 1964, when Darius Swann, a black Presbyterian missionary, and his wife Vera returned to Charlotte from service in India and were told that their eldest child, aged six, must attend an all-black school. Engaging the Legal Defense Fund, the Swanns brought suit against the local school system, which since 1960 had included not only the city of Charlotte but also the surrounding county of Mecklenburg. There was no doubting that Charlotte-Mecklenburg operated a dual school system featuring *de jure* racial segregation.[17]

In the years of controversy after 1964, the system inched toward desegregation: by 1969, two-thirds of its 21,000 black pupils, who were 29 percent of the overall enrollment in the system, attended schools with whites. But many whites resisted more than token desegregation. The stubborn federal district judge who demanded change, James McMillan, drew on precedents such as *Green* and *Alexander* and insisted that Charlotte-Mecklenburg achieve true desegregation by the start of the 1970 school year. He called for a range of methods to do so, including much greater use of school busing to promote racial balance. He received death threats and was hanged in effigy. Crosses were burned on his lawn. The law office of the Fund's chief attorney on the case, Julius Chambers, was later fire-bombed.

Unusual alliances developed among the justices when they heard the case. Black, who had been obdurate for immediate desegregation in the *Alexander* case a year earlier, now made it clear that he had little use for large-scale court-ordered busing to achieve racial balance. He was of course well aware of the obvious: black children had long been bused past nearby schools to faraway locations. But Black cherished the tradition of neighborhood schools, especially for city children in the elementary grades. He rested his position in part on his characteristically literal reading of the Constitution, a copy of which he still carried in his pocket. "Where does the word 'busing' appear in the Constitution?" he demanded. He added, "I don't like this trying to condemn a whole way of living. You want to haul people miles and miles in order to get an equal ratio in the schools. It's a pretty big job to assign to us, isn't it?" Two weeks later Black wrote a friend, "My father walked five miles to get to his nearest neighborhood school." Black especially feared that whites, if confronted with orders to bus their children long distances to black schools, would abandon the public school system.[18]

Burger joined Black in opposing substantial court-ordered busing, which a number of American school systems were then beginning to employ in order to desegregate. Busing of this sort—the only way, many people thought, to counter residential segregation—was indeed becoming one of the most incendiary issues in American politics. The Nixon administration had frequently denounced the practice. It sent its attorneys to the Court with arguments opposing Judge McMillan's order.

Between October 1970, when the Court heard the case, and April 1971, when it finally issued its opinion, the justices circulated a host of memoranda and draft opinions. From the start, however, Black and Burger were outnumbered. While their colleagues also had qualms about "forced" busing, they were reluctant, as they had been in the *Green* and *Alexander* cases, to reverse the momentum of *Brown*. It was clear to them that Charlotte was practicing *de jure* segregation. In the end, Black and Burger gave way and joined a unanimous decision. Burger, who assigned the opinion to himself, wrote that a range of tools, including busing, were appropriate to promote racially desegregated schools.

Contemporary observers noted that the Court's ruling in *Swann* left a few holes for segregationists to hide in. Burger stopped short of saying that all single-race schools were unconstitutional. He did not mandate fixed, judicially specified racial balances. He was willing to let school officials take into consideration the age of children to be bused. The decision did not require Charlotte-Mecklenburg (or other districts) or district courts to readjust school boundaries every year once the affirmative requirement to desegregate had initially been undertaken.

The decision, moreover, applied only to school systems that segregated *de jure*. *Swann*, therefore, did not affect the North, even though many public authorities there continued to pursue housing and school districting policies that separated blacks and whites. Jimmy Carter, governor of Georgia, was one of many who pointed this out. *Swann*, he said, was "clearly a one-sided decision; the Court is still talking about the South; the North is still going free." Senator Abraham Ribicoff of Connecticut, a liberal, went further, accusing some of his northern colleagues of "hypocrisy." Many northern senators, he said, did not have "guts to face their liberal white constituents, who have fled to the suburbs for the sole purpose of avoiding having their sons and daughters go to school with blacks."[19]

Ribicoff surely had a point. Southern schools in general were already more desegregated—thanks to the powerful and rapid impact of *Green* and *Alexander*—than northern or western schools. The effect of *Swann*, moreover, remained to be seen, even in the South. Nixon, a consistent critic of busing, responded to it by telling HEW officials to hold busing to the "minimum required by law." And Burger issued a statement in August 1971 that revealed his considerable ambivalence. "The constitutional command to desegregate schools," he said, "does not mean that every school in every community must always reflect the racial composition of the school system as a whole." Opponents of busing took heart from this and other signs of doubt about the guidelines of *Swann*.[20]

In the next two years, Charlotte-Mecklenburg experienced some difficulties in carrying out the decision of the Court. Brawls between white and black students forced all of its high schools to shut down for short spells at one time or another. Many white parents who could afford to do so pulled their children out of the public schools and paid for private education. Desegregation in Charlotte-Mecklenburg, as in most places, had a greater impact on poor and working-class whites than on wealthier families. Five years after *Swann*, some 10,000 white children in Charlotte-Mecklenburg attended private schools.

Still, *Swann* represented another large step forward on the path toward serious enforcement of *Brown*. Roy Wilkins, executive director of the NAACP, spoke for many when he exulted, "The neighborhood school . . . is toppled from its perch as the determinant of desegregation policy." District court judges, while not required to call for year-by-year readjustment of school boundaries, were permitted to do so, and often did in order to seek racial balance. In part for this reason, the decision had far-reaching effects, leading to mandatory busing plans to promote school desegregation in more than 100 southern school districts. Southern cities that so complied included Little Rock, Jacksonville, Tampa, Savannah, Greensboro, Memphis, Nashville, Dallas, Fort Worth, and Norfolk.[21]

The decision also changed Charlotte. Many of its top leaders, white as well as black, worked hard to see that it was enforced, and by 1974 all of the district's schools had achieved racial balance. As whites resegregated thereafter, city leaders reacted in order to maintain these balances. In the mid-1980s (by which time Charlotte had elected its first black mayor, Harvey Gantt) this process entailed reassigning some 2,000 pupils per year. Although the growth of private schools revealed that many people were opting out of the system, most parents stayed put. They had little choice: outside of paying for private education, they could escape the city-county system only by moving out of the county and sending their children to poorly equipped rural schools that were for the most part desegregating themselves.

The majority of parents in Charlotte seemed to grow proud of what they had accomplished. Standardized test scores increased after 1975 for children of both races and especially for blacks. The black-white gap in

In September 1970, a volunteer helps children at Hidden Valley Elementary School in Charlotte, N. C., site of bitter controversies over busing of students. *(The Charlotte Observer)*

scores narrowed a bit until the mid-1980s. In 1984, President Ronald Reagan came to the city and denounced busing as the "social experiment nobody wants." He expected enthusiastic applause, but received only silence. The *Charlotte Observer* ran a lead editorial the next day, "You Were Wrong, Mr. President." School desegregation, it added, was the city's "proudest achievement."[22]

In October 1972, the Court heard another controversial school case that had the potential of giving still more rigor to *Brown*, then nearly twenty years old. This one concerned Denver, the first nonsouthern city to have its school policies challenged in an important case concerning race at the High Court level. The issues were different. Denver did not practice *de jure* segregation, southern-style, of its schools. Its black population (14 percent of the city) was relatively well off. The average family income of blacks in the city was estimated to be $1,500 higher than the national average for black families. Black children had two more years of schooling than black children nationwide.

With the rise of rights consciousness in the 1960s, however, local black leaders became more insistent than ever in demanding better school facilities. Some of the largely black schools in Denver, located in heavily black neighborhoods, featured crowded, trailerlike portable classrooms. Black leaders, however, assailed segregation as well as inequality. Nearly 40 percent of black children, they said, attended identifiably black schools. They insisted that policies of the Denver school board had deliberately kept black children out of predominantly white schools in the Park Hill area of the city. This intentional segregation, they said, so affected pupil placement in the other schools that it made the entire district a dual system. *De facto* segregation, in short, rested on a bed of public policy in the city: it was a thinly disguised form of *de jure* segregation. A lower court judge agreed, ordering greater busing to eliminate such segregation, and the case went to the High Court.[23]

As in the *Alexander* and *Swann* cases, the often divided Burger Court struggled to deal with these complicated issues. Douglas argued in conference that "what had been called *de facto* is in most cases *de jure*." But others disagreed. For a while it seemed that the Court, which by then had the four Nixon appointees on it, would divide four to four, with Douglas, Brennan, Marshall, and Stewart supporting the black plaintiffs and Burger, Blackmun, Powell, and Rehnquist opposing them (White, a Coloradan, recused himself). But both Powell and Blackmun came around to Douglas's view, and Burger finally shrank from the prospect of appearing to backslide on the issue of desegregation of the schools. In June 1973, nineteen years after *Brown*, all but Rehnquist, who dissented, supported the complainants. The burden of proof, the Court said, lay with the Denver school board to show that its actions had not been intentional. If it could not do so, it was constitutionally obligated to desegregate the entire system. The Court all but ordered Denver officials to institute citywide busing. It was the first time that such an order had affected any city outside the South.[24]

This decision, *Keyes v. Denver School District No. 1*, did not attract nearly so much attention in the media as had *Green, Alexander,* and *Swann.* Newspapers gave more play to revelations about Watergate by Nixon adviser John Dean, to a visit to the United States by Soviet Premier Leonid Brezhnev, and to another Court decision on the same day that enlarged the capacity of public officials to regulate obscene materials. Moreover, Brennan, who wrote the *Keyes* decision, was careful to say that the existence of *de facto* school segregation was insufficient grounds for judicial intervention. If a school board could show that it did not *intend* to segregate—that is, if the segregation had stemmed from other sources, such as segregated housing arising from uncoordinated private decisions—the board need not take steps to establish greater racial balance. Integrationists in other cities thus faced the daunting task of exhuming old school board decisions to build cases proving that school segregation had been intentional.

Because this task was costly and time-consuming, white officials in many northern cities managed to stave off court orders. They persisted in operating schools that were heavily white or black. In the next ten years, for instance, school officials in highly segregated cities such as

The dynamiting of buses at the Denver Public Schools Service Center in 1970 signaled violent opposition to busing. *(The Denver Rocky Mountain News)*

New York, Chicago, and Philadelphia did not have to cope with court orders.[25] Small wonder that Southerners, forced as *de jure* offenders to toe the Supreme Court line, continued to seethe with indignation at the legal double standard that persisted.

Keyes, moreover, led to considerable inconsistencies in a wave of litigation that did follow. What seemed like school board intent to one district court was adjudged otherwise in another. As predicted by Justice Powell, who had joined the majority but opposed the Court's retention of a *de jure/de facto* distinction, many subsequent decisions were fortuitous and unpredictable. And in Denver, which established citywide busing, the results of judicial intervention seemed mixed at best. White parents there, unlike those in Charlotte, had an easily available option if they wished to avoid the effects of busing: move to the suburbs. It was estimated that white public school enrollment in Denver decreased by 30 percent between 1970 (when concerns over the long-running case began to intensify) and December 1974. Other suits seeking "comprehensive plans" soon made race-based busing an even more incendiary political issue than it had been in the early 1970s.

Still, many supporters of desegregation considered the *Keyes* decision to be modestly encouraging. At last, the North, too, risked serious court intervention. As Justice Powell said, "The focus of the school desegregation problem has now shifted from the South to the country as a whole. . . . We must recognize that the evil of operating separate schools is no less in Denver than in Atlanta." If the Burger Court held to the course in the school cases that it had been following since 1969, who could tell where it might take the nation?[26]

———

Americans who favored school desegregation in 1974, the twentieth anniversary of *Brown*, indeed had reasons to be pleased with much that had happened in the previous ten years. Thanks to pressure from the civil rights movement, President Kennedy and, even more so, President Johnson had placed the strong arm of government behind racial justice. And courts had finally given force to *Brown*. Indeed, the Court had gone further than anyone, Warren included, could have imagined in 1954. *Brown* had called for an end of state-sponsored segregation in public schools. The decisions of the Burger Court had insisted on greater racial balance, to be achieved if necessary by court-ordered busing and other bold strategies. Change between 1954 and 1964 had been glacial; progress in the next decade, especially between 1969 and 1973, had been stagger-ingly rapid. Jack Greenberg, celebrating in 1974 his twenty-fifth year with the Legal Defense Fund, proclaimed that further progress would bring "full citizenship for blacks and other minorities."[27]

Optimists at the time pointed to places where the mixing of blacks and whites in schools seemed promising. A white teenager in a newly desegregated school in New Albany, Mississippi, told an interviewer in November 1969, "Well, I guess one thing I learned is that they're [black classmates] not so dumb as lots of us figured." A black girl down the hall said, "They're [the whites] not as mean as I thought."[28]

Jim Hill, describing his feelings when he was bused at that time to a desegregated elementary school in Louisville, later echoed these opti-mistic reactions. Transferring to a once all-white school had filled him with terror. "I remember my scalp itching," he said. "I was so uncom-fortable and under such stress that literally my scalp began to burn." But Hill, who became a lawyer and professor of political science, insisted that the stress had been worth it. The black schools, he said, had been inferior. Moreover, mixing dispelled ugly stereotypes:

> It's much more difficult to maintain the wall of racism when you're faced with the humanity of those other people. When you sit with them and talk with them they're no longer evil demons, they're friends who end up at your birthday parties and go with you to football and baseball games.[29]

Liberals who visited the grass roots cautiously seconded hopeful views such as these. Racist pressures, they thought, came mainly from the most prejudiced of grown-ups—backed by enlightened teachers, well-meaning kids could surmount them. Liberals further argued that racial mixing worked well when school authorities acted quickly to stop fights and maintained stern and consistent discipline. Desegregation, they added, was taking place peacefully in an encouragingly large number of districts, especially in not too heavily black rural areas, in small towns and cities where there was but one high school, and in schools where blacks and whites started off together in the first grade.

Advocates of desegregation emphasized above all—as they had in crit-icizing the evasion encouraged by the "all deliberate speed" language of *Brown II*—that change happened peacefully wherever courts and com-munity leaders, as those in Charlotte, took pride in their schools and held firm for desegregation. Faced with determined leadership of this kind, liberals said, whites would soon get used to racial mixing in schools. Some day, perhaps, desegregation might even lead to greater integration of the races—a multicultural world in which black and white people began to judge one another by their character, not their color.[30]

Others who commented on the twentieth anniversary of *Brown*, however, were less hopeful. They were distressed, first of all, by developments in the North. By then, "white flight" of northern families hurrying to suburbs was becoming a widely headlined issue. This had surely preceded court-ordered busing—suburbanization for racial reasons had a considerable history—but it seemed especially frenetic during the 1970s in many large metropolitan areas. And some largely black inner-city schools left behind in these areas became awful places. At predominantly black Maggie Walker High in Richmond, from which massive white flight had occurred, blacks walked along hallways ugly with graffiti. Classrooms featured broken windows. Students milled in the hallways, periodically fighting with one another. One teacher complained, "Things are so bad that kids come to school without pencils, without paper, without books—and go home the same way. I have to keep a supply of everything and pass it out each day at the start of classes. This isn't education; this is chaos."[31]

Kenneth Clark had become an especially dour pessimist by 1974, pointing dejectedly to trends in the North. As the struggle moved north of the Mason-Dixon line, he said, America was reaching an "end of an age of innocence." Events in Topeka seemed to confirm his pessimism. There, where Oliver Brown had challenged the system in 1951, some of the schools remained segregated in 1974. HEW, losing patience with Topeka officials, insisted that the city close down seven black elementary schools and redraw boundaries so as to achieve racial balance. Topeka officials refused, setting the stage for litigation later initiated by the American Civil Liberties Union. Linda Brown-Thompson, of *Brown v. Board* fame, who was by then a mother of two school-age children, was one of the plaintiffs.[32]

Developments in the South during these years evoked more mixed reactions among advocates of desegregation of the schools. Liberals were of course delighted that many school districts there were finally obeying the law. Indeed, the rapid turnabout that occurred in the early 1970s seemed almost miraculous given the resistance that had stymied compliance with *Brown* in the past. But proponents of desegregation also deplored other trends in the South during these years. As before, many white parents, especially in heavily black areas such as Summerton, continued to pull their children out of the newly desegregated schools and to place them in private "white academies." Only the poor whites were likely to remain with the blacks. Friends of desegregation complained also that whites continued to control the school boards, that blacks almost never rose to become principals, and that race-and class-based tracking was spreading, thereby creating high levels of racial and social segregation in classrooms. Moreover, white school officials throughout the South continued to desegregate by sending black students to formerly white schools. The old black high schools frequently became junior high or elementary schools and were renamed. White leaders defended this widespread practice by arguing reasonably enough that the white schools were generally newer and better equipped. To many black people in these communities, however, it seemed that the price of "progress" was the loss of black institutions and traditions. As a later observer noted, "these changes deprived the black community of a sense of historical continuity, the continuity of memories of fellow students and favorite teachers, athletic teams, graduations and proms, and public events, all of which are part of a rich school life."[33]

For black students who were the first to desegregate, often in token numbers, the tension could be as unbearable as it had been for the Little Rock nine in 1957 or for Ruby Bridges in New Orleans in 1960. In Selma, Alabama, Jo Ann Bland was told by her father that she was to be part of the "integration team" that in 1970 would break down the racial barrier at a local high school." "It was *awful*," she remembered. "It was already traumatic enough just to be going to high school for the first time. To go to a place where you're not wanted by the students and teachers because they felt we were forced upon them made everybody unhappy. There were just eight of us, and sixteen hundred and ninety-two of them, dedicated to making our lives miserable. I cried every day."

Bland bitterly recalled a white boy who regularly spat on her. When she complained to the principal, he did nothing about it. She then told her father, who said that she should follow the boy wherever he went; if he spat on her again, she should report him. She did so, but the boy denied it. In desperation, she finally left his spit on her as proof, and appealed again to the principal. He berated her for not being in class. Bland then ran to a pay phone and called her father, a taxi driver. "When he arrived at school," she recalled, "I was hysterical. He stormed into the principal's office with me in tow and the principal said, 'Wait just a minute. You don't just walk into my office.' That made my father angry. They went 'round and 'round until the principal calmed daddy down enough for them to talk. So the principal sends for the kid and he denied it again. Then I started crying and my father got mad again. So he beat up the kid and then beat up the principal until the secretaries called the police."

The outcome of this extraordinary confrontation was mixed. As Bland recounted it, "The police came and took Daddy to jail. . . . later they got him out of jail. But I noticed from then on, I *never* had the problems I had before. Whenever I had a complaint, the principal *did* something. But it was rough."

Conflicts such as these among students were widely reported at the time. A black youth in Valdosta, Georgia, complained that whites made him feel unwanted. "Like trespassing, man," he said. "That's how it is when you step on the man's property." Along with 300 others, he had recently been suspended from high school for protesting against the Confederate embellishments of the football team. Some white students seemed equally resentful. "What's the use?" one white student asked. "They resent us for being forced to come here. Last year, when there was only a few of them, it was better. You could get them to eat lunch with you. Now they wouldn't be caught dead eating lunch with you."[34]

Interracial harmony seemed particularly hard to promote at the junior high and high school levels. "The younger kids couldn't care less," one HEW official explained. Echoing Marshall's hopeful predictions in 1954, he added, "They eat together, ride to school together, horse around together." But children tended to separate along racial lines between the fourth and sixth grades. Thereafter they rarely associated in school clubs, social events, class elections, or student government. Fights were frequent, often featuring white and black girls. A day or so later, it seemed, the boys would go at it as well.

Given the fears that accompanied the truly awesome task of school desegregation in the South, it is hardly surprising that progress toward harmony moved slowly at best or that fights sometimes broke out. We can wonder, in fact, that so much change took place in Dixie during the early 1970s: the North, after all, was doing little. Still, the interracial hostility that persisted in many school districts testified to the gap that was to remain between once high expectations of progress and the reality of day-to-day experience after 1970.

The process of change, moreover, might have taken hold a bit more firmly if local white leaders, perceiving that some form of desegregation could not be avoided, had focused more creatively on advancing quality education. But many white leaders kept resisting, complying only grudgingly and slowly to court orders. Even those who came to accept change, moreover, stepped to the tune played by civil rights attorneys and federal judges—litigators and jurists, not educators. And local black teachers and parents had even less say in the process as it slowly unfolded. Some time passed before black educators managed to secure much if any say in educational planning—or in the awarding of contracts. The freezing out of these knowledgeable black people intensified interracial hostility and left legacies of bad feeling that were to plague the operation of schools in many areas of the South for years thereafter.[35]

Were the students learning more in the desegregated schools? In the early 1970s, when the process of desegregation was just beginning to start in the South, it was hard to say. Some parents, of course, thought so. A black cab driver from Maryland was delighted that his fifteen-year-old daughter could go to school with whites. In the black schools, he said, "all they learn to do is to shoot dope—that won't get you into college." A white principal of an integrated school agreed: "Look, nobody anywhere can prove anything one way or another. All I know is that my kids, black and white, do O.K., and the blacks are no longer going to school in tarpaper shacks." His point deserves to be remembered: nostalgia notwithstanding, there was little to romanticize about black education in most communities of the Jim Crow South.[36]

On the other hand, many white parents remained certain that black children pulled down academic achievement. One father said, "I think the quality of education is going to drop in the next few years because I don't believe the colored children can learn the same as white children." Attitudes such as his, of course, had deep roots in the United States. Perceptions that blacks were intellectually inferior—whether because of their genetic makeup or because of the "cultural deprivation" of their lives—were weaker than in the past, but they remained formidable obstacles to white acceptance of desegregation of the schools.[37]

Some black people, meanwhile, openly admitted second thoughts about the much-celebrated virtues of desegregation. In cities where race-based busing became widespread, even in Charlotte, it was often the black pupils who had to endure the longest rides and were most often tracked in nonacademic courses. When white and black schools merged, black principals often lost their jobs. The number of black principals in North Carolina elementary schools, where 30 percent of public school students were black, is estimated to have dropped from 620 to 170 between 1963 and 1970. The number of black secondary school principals fell between 1963 and 1973 from 209 to three. Twenty-one percent of black teachers in the state lost their jobs between 1963 and 1972.[38]

In some places, blacks organized to resist these developments. A few of these protestors, as in Greensboro, advocated black power. Others fought to prevent the shutting down of black schools. In Hyde County, a rural area on the coast of North Carolina, blacks in 1968–69 staged five months of daily nonviolent protests against the closing of two such schools. In the process they set up their own alternative schools. When Klansmen tried to stop the protests, blacks armed themselves and drove off the Klan in a gunfight. This was perhaps the most sustained civil rights protest in the history of the state, and it resulted in a desegregation plan more satisfactory to the blacks. Smaller, similar protests followed in North Carolina between 1970 and 1972.[39]

By the early 1970s, a few black leaders were openly echoing the doubts that W. E. B. Du Bois had expressed in 1935. "It is easy to put black kids in white public schools," said Ruby Martin, a former director of HEW's Office for Civil Rights. "But just to integrate will simply compound the problems we have and polarize the community more. I would not close a black school without going into the community to find out what will be the impact." Constance Baker Motley, a leading attorney for the Fund, made a different point: "*Brown* has little practical relevance to central city blacks. Its psychological and legal relevance has already had its effect. Central city blacks seem more concerned now with the political and economic power accruing from the new black concentrations than they do with busing to effect school desegregation."[40] And Robert Carter, who had long aided Marshall at the Legal Defense Fund, added his own doubts about integration. In 1980, by which time Carter had become a federal judge, he wrote, "Integrated education must not be lost as the ultimate solution. That would be a disaster in my judgment. For the present, however, to focus on integration alone is a luxury only the black middle class can afford. They have the means to desert the public schools if dissatisfied."[41]

A Wilmington, North Carolina, black woman also wondered about desegregation. She had attended Williston High School, which had been dedicated as a new facility—for blacks alone—on the very day, May 17, 1954, that *Brown* had been decided. There she had been happy and motivated. "We were in a cocoon bathed in a warm fluid, where we were expected to excel," she recalled. In 1968, however, "something called desegregation" arrived in Wilmington and "punctured" the cocoon. Williston High ceased to exist as a black school, later becoming instead a middle school for whites as well as blacks. The woman sighed, "We went from our own land to being tourists in someone else's. It never did come together."[42]

Citing scattered opinions such as these cannot provide solid conclusions concerning black attitudes or white attitudes in the early 1970s. Nor does impressionistic evidence capture the immense variety of responses in the thousands of school districts, mainly in the South, that were coping with the often traumatic business of desegregation. Like Kenneth Clark, however, many integrationists in the 1970s were losing some of the optimism on the subject of race that they had had during the heady, expectant year of 1964. At that time courageous activists had provided the firepower driving LBJ's efforts for powerful civil rights acts that were expected to bring equality to black people. Ten years later, Jim Crow was dead in the South, as was *de jure* school segregation. These were huge changes that few people could have imagined in 1960.

But hopeful integrationists in the 1960s had come to expect more, and by 1974 they were worrying that true racial equality would remain a distant dream. So would true integration. To these once optimistic integrationists, as to many others, it was becoming clear that racial conflict would continue to be a vast and complicated national problem that blighted the North as well as the South. And it remained unclear whether schools, repositories of all sorts of utopian expectations, could greatly promote interracial understanding. Twenty years following *Brown*, much had been accomplished, and much remained to be done.

8

STALEMATES

Daniel Patrick Moynihan, while serving as a top domestic policy adviser to President Nixon, seemed to shelve the faith in government that had animated his call in 1965 for "national action" to help poor black families. In January 1970 he recommended privately that Nixon settle for "benign neglect" of the political agenda of militant blacks. When his advice to that effect leaked to the public in March, liberals reacted with predictable outrage.

Many Americans, however, were coming to share Moynihan's doubts about governmental activism. A host of discouraging events, notably defeat in Vietnam and Watergate, combined by 1974 to weaken once high expectations about government, especially as exemplified by the liberalism of Lyndon Johnson's Great Society of the 1960s. Many of these programs, Americans now complained, had fallen far short of the grandiose promises that Johnson and others had made for them. The much-touted "war on poverty," they said, had fizzled. Federal aid to public schools had been greatly oversold. Medicare and Medicaid were costing far more than liberals had predicted. And the activism of liberal judges and bureaucrats on behalf of civil rights—policies such as busing and affirmative action—had become increasingly contested and divisive.

Rising criticisms of these liberal programs, which had aroused high hopes in the 1960s, led to stalemates that discouraged advocates of reform, including racial desegregation. Nixon, who had little interest in domestic policies, was quick to heed Moynihan's advice. Although he approved politically popular new programs to protect the environment and to advance consumer protections, he showed little faith in further governmental social engineering, and he continued to criticize court-ordered busing. Black leaders shunned him. His reelection by a huge margin in 1972 seemed to signal the growth of a vociferous conservative backlash against the perceived excesses of American liberalism.[1]

Other developments in the 1970s further disposed Americans to lower their opinions of governmental action. Chief among these was the souring of the once vibrant economy of the 1960s. Repeated oil crises frightened the public. Worse, "stagflation"—simultaneous high unemployment and high inflation—called into question the capacity of public officials to guarantee prosperity. By the late 1970s, taxpayers were in full-fledged revolt. As wage earners, especially blue-collar workers, struggled to hold on to their jobs, they lashed out not only at government but also at blacks. Their complaints ranged widely: black-incited riots had necessitated higher taxes so as to rebuild the cities; affirmative action guidelines and court-imposed "set-asides" discriminated against whites; "forced" busing increased the transportation costs of school budgets; detailed court-ordered desegregation plans, as critics of *Jefferson* had warned, were becoming extraordinarily complicated while doing little if anything to improve the quality of education.

Anger about policies such as these revealed that whites, especially working-class people, had become resistant to further activism on behalf of civil rights. The quest for racial justice, no longer cost free in the North, had led to backlash that no ambitious politician could ignore. Thus, neither Gerald Ford nor Jimmy Carter, who was elected on an anti-Washington platform in 1976, tried hard to reinvigorate governmental activism in domestic affairs. Ronald Reagan, president between 1981 and early 1989, insisted that government was not the "answer" to problems; it was itself the problem. His administration denounced court-ordered busing, sought to abolish the Department of Education (which had been established in the Carter years), and favored tax credits and vouchers to help people opt out of the public schools. Meanwhile, many black neighborhoods within the inner city could scarcely cope with serious social ills, among them—in some places—near-chaotic public schools.

Top officials in Reagan's Justice Department waged sporadic battles against affirmative action and various other policies that attempted to give special help to women and people of color. And the department did not pursue "color-blind" policies in an even-handed way. It virtually stopped supporting suits against segregated schools. In 1982 it backed a case brought by Bob Jones University against the Treasury Department, which (following established policy) had refused to grant the university tax-exempt status. Treasury officials, noting that Bob Jones had a rule prohibiting black students from dating or marrying white students, maintained that the university was engaging in racial discrimination. Although the Burger Court in 1983 rejected the Justice Department's effort eight to one (Rehnquist dissenting), the Reagan administration remained cool indeed to much of the civil rights agenda.[2]

The interracial coalition that had formed in the 1950s and 1960s behind the civil rights movement, meanwhile, remained fragmented along the racial lines that had developed in the mid-1960s. Nothing made this fragmentation more clear than a widely reported controversy that erupted when Jack Greenberg, Marshall's hand-picked successor as executive secretary of the Legal Defense Fund, was asked in 1982 to help teach a three-week winter-term course titled "Racial Discrimination and Civil Rights" at Harvard Law School. At that time he had spent thirty-three years with the Fund. When he arrived in Cambridge in January 1983, African-American law students picketed in protest. Harvard, they said, should employ black professors on a permanent basis (the school then had two black professors, one of them tenured, on its full-time faculty of sixty-six.) Whites, the students further emphasized, were not qualified by personal experience to teach such a subject.

Harvard stood firm, and Greenberg co-taught the course with Julius Chambers, a well-known black leader who was then president of the Defense Fund. But Chambers's presence (which had been assumed from the start in 1982) did nothing to settle the controversy. All forty-three students who enrolled in the course were white. Black students, who were one-tenth of the law school student body of approximately 1,500, stood united against participation in the course.[3]

No race-related issue evoked more passionate feelings in the 1970s and early 1980s than court orders and regulations by HEW to desegregate schools. By 1979 these interventions had become widespread, involving 1,505 school districts with more than 12 million children—28 percent of students overall. Many of these orders called for race-based busing.[4] President Ford exclaimed that busing "brought fear to both black students and white students—and to their parents. No child can learn in an atmosphere of fear. Better remedies to right constitutional wrongs must be found." President Carter, too, was cool to widespread busing. Most white parents heartily agreed, especially working-class people who could not afford to flee to suburbs or to pay for private education. Some white students were blunt. "Nobody's busing me just so some niggers can get a better deal," one white student cried. "I didn't set up the schools. . . . Niggers don't like their schools, let *them* change 'em, but they don't have the right to tell me what to do. Kids don't got any rights anyways. The only right we got is to go to school near where we live."[5]

Controversies over court-ordered busing often polarized urban politics in the 1970s. Nowhere was the battle more fiercely waged than in Boston. Starting in 1973, the struggle consumed the city for many years, generally (as in Little Rock in 1957 and in many other places) pitting working-class whites against wealthier white people—"limousine liberals," to their foes—and some blacks. Many of these liberals lived in white suburbs unaffected by busing within Boston. Among them were editors of the *Boston Globe*, which supported busing. Infuriated opponents of the *Globe* fired shots into its lobby. For a time the paper stationed police sharpshooters on the roof.

At one antibusing rally in the city, a speaker nominated Senator Ted Kennedy, a liberal, for "bus driver of the year—if he ever gets his driver's license back." (The reference, of course, was to the auto accident in Chappaquiddick where Kennedy had driven off a bridge, causing the death by drowning of a young female passenger.) Another white parent, father of seven children, shouted, "The question is: Am I going to send my young daughter, who is budding into the flower of her womanhood, into [black-dominated] Roxbury on a bus?" On the first day of busing in the fall of 1974 only ten of 525 whites assigned by the court to Roxbury High, previously a heavily black school, showed up. Buses carrying fifty-six black children from Roxbury (450 more dared not ride) to white South Boston High School were stoned.[6]

Many advocates of desegregation continued in the 1970s to give strong support to court-ordered busing. Ridiculing the claim of opponents that busing cost great sums of money, they pointed out that whites had long spent tax dollars to transport black children to faraway segregated schools. They also dismissed complaints from whites about long bus rides: an NAACP official retorted, "It's not the distance, it's the niggers." Supporters of busing, citing scattered statistics, also began to maintain that blacks transported to predominantly white schools did better on academic achievement tests than did blacks in mainly black schools.

Violence surrounding the struggle over busing in Boston in the 1970s, July 1975. *(Stanley J. Forman,* The Soiling of Old Glory—*Pulitzer Prize, 1977)*

White students who were bused, they added, did not fall back academically. Supporters stressed that busing was often the only way that black children could move out of ghetto schools and into the mainstream of American life. An eleven-year-old black student from Roxbury explained, "Busing's just got to be, man. Got to be. We got it coming to us. We got to open up ourselves, spread out. Get into the city. . . . Go to good schools, live in good places like white folks got. . . . That's why they're busing us."[7]

Some black parents, however, became increasingly ambivalent about busing, which was in fact an imperfect, emergency approach to coping with deep social problems, notably residential segregation. Too often, they reiterated, black children had to take the longest bus rides, where they ended up in white-dominated schools far from home. While poll data were inconclusive—much depended on the questions asked—it seemed that roughly 50 percent of blacks were cool to the practice. Some attending a National Black Political Convention in Gary in 1972 sided with Roy Innis, executive director of CORE, who rejected busing.

Blacks, Innis said, were "tired of being guinea pigs for social engineers and New York liberals." A year later the Atlanta branch of the NAACP backed a drastic reduction in busing in return for more black administrators and a black school superintendent. What they hoped to do was to give qualified African Americans a major say in educational policy making and perhaps to stem the flight of whites from the system. Atlanta, the local NAACP leader declared, should "get out of the court and move on to the more important business of educating kids." The strongly integrationist national NAACP in New York, reflecting divisions among blacks, countered by demanding busing across county lines. It suspended the Atlanta branch for its action.[8]

White flight led to impassioned arguments among social scientists who studied busing in the 1970s. One such expert was James Coleman, chief author of the Coleman Report in 1966. In 1975 he co-wrote a study, *Trends in School Segregation, 1968–1973*, which linked widespread flight of white parents to race-based busing plans. Court orders, he wrote, were "probably the worst instrument of social policy." He recommended instead various voluntary plans to promote school desegregation. In part because Coleman was a renowned social scientist and in part because he was a supporter of school desegregation, his findings created a considerable stir in academic circles. Some advocates of busing damned him as a racist. [9]

In the lengthy debates that followed, advocates of busing made a number of salient points. Large-scale population movements out of cities into predominantly white suburbs, they emphasized, had a long history predating court-ordered busing and occurred in cities without such orders—for instance New York, Chicago, and Houston. A host of socioeconomic forces since World War II—rising crime rates, deteriorating city services (including schools), crumbling infrastructure, the movement of jobs from central cities to suburbs—had even in the 1940s and 1950s predisposed people who could afford it (mainly middle-class whites) to leave the cities. Riots in the 1960s intensified such urges. Fear of busing, these scholars added, sometimes quickened the pace of out-migration, but only in some cities. White flight, they said, often accelerated during the first two or three years following court orders to bus, but then—when whites got used to change—slowed to prebusing rates.

Supporters of busing emphasized that the situation differed from city to city. In Charlotte, Seattle, and Austin, Texas, they said, busing worked all right. They stressed that substantial white flight was likely to follow court-mandated busing only under certain circumstances: when heavily white suburbs with very good schools were nearby; when white children in the city were assigned to schools that had relatively high percentages (a "tipping point" was often around 10 to 25 percent) of blacks, not when small percentages of blacks were assigned to predominantly white schools; when the busing involved elementary school children; when it affected whites with relatively high family incomes; and when bus rides were lengthy. The message of arguments such as these was that race-based busing per se need not cause panic or mammoth flight to suburbs. If crafted carefully and firmly supported by local leaders, busing could advance desegregation without disrupting good education or neighborhoods.[10]

Opponents of busing, however, fought back. Neighborhood schools, they said, were better for many reasons: parents were closer in case of emergencies and more able to take part in school functions; children could meet both during and after school and form closer friendships; students could more easily engage in after-school activities. Neighborhood schools, they added, were more likely to promote community cohesion. They advanced school spirit. Why would a bused-in student feel loyal to a school that was miles from his or her home?[11]

Foes of court-mandated busing were often willing to concede that long-standing social forces had impelled white flight. But they insisted that race-based busing considerably accelerated it. Their argument seemed valid in many large cities to which masses of southern blacks had migrated since the 1940s. By 1976, twenty-one of the nation's twenty-nine biggest city school districts had a black majority. Eight of these had lost their white majority between 1968, when busing began to spread, and 1976.[12] And the change in some cities was staggering. In Boston, for instance, 54 percent of public school students in 1974 were white; by 1985, only 27 percent were. By 1994, Boston was spending $30 million on busing, or $500 per student, to avert greater racial segregation.[13]

Whatever benefits court-ordered busing had in certain circumstances, it surely did not seem to be promoting interracial harmony in cities such as Boston or Denver, site of the decision in *Keyes* (1973). Although school desegregation moved slowly forward during the 1970s and 1980s in many rural areas and small towns and cities—it was surely inaccurate to see these years as an era of ubiquitous retrogression concerning segregation in schools—it got nowhere in many large cities of the Northeast and

Midwest, which were becoming holding pens for the poorest people of color in the country. A "white noose" of suburban development was encircling them. And residential segregation, as always, sharpened racial separation in the schools, which continued after 1970 to be more pronounced in most cities of the North than in the South.

What, if anything, could litigation or the Supreme Court do about this situation?

In March 1973 the Burger Court reached a decision on a highly important, contested matter that hinted at directions it would take. The case involved Demetrio Rodriguez and his neighbors in the relatively poor, mostly Mexican-American neighborhood of Edgewood in west San Antonio. Rodriguez, a veteran of World War II and Korea, had initiated the suit in 1968 because he was angry that his two boys had to attend a badly equipped, dilapidated elementary school, whereas children who lived in Alamo Heights, an affluent school district ten minutes away—within the city but financed separately by residents of that district—went to a much better facility. His complaint pointed to a fundamentally inegalitarian aspect of American educational practice: public schools were supported primarily by local property taxes and therefore differed greatly in the levels of their financing. Spending per student was more than twice as high in Alamo Heights as it was in Edgewood.

In January 1971 a three-judge federal panel agreed unanimously with Rodriguez and his fellow plaintiffs. The school financing system in Texas, they said, violated the equal protection clause of the Fourteenth Amendment. The decision, which cited Warren's emphasis in *Brown* on the importance of public education in modern life, delighted liberals. They foresaw the onset of a "new national standard" to be applied to America's public schools. Such a standard, they expected, would greatly assist central city minorities and other poor people attending ill-financed schools. If the Supreme Court backed the lower court, it would enable the reshaping of the financing of American education.

The Court, however, ruled five to four against Rodriguez. The five included Nixon's four appointees, plus Potter Stewart. Lewis Powell, writing for the majority, insisted that education must remain locally controlled. He found no proof that San Antonio's financing system disadvantaged any indentifiable group of poor people or that the poorest students lived only in the districts with the most badly financed schools.

"The Equal Protection Clause," he added, "does not require absolute equality or precisely equal advantages." He emphasized that education was not a "fundamental interest" under the Constitution and that levels of financing were only a part of what made good schools.

Potter Stewart, concurring, conceded that school financing arrangements in Texas were "chaotic and unjust." But he concluded that the Court must exercise judicial restraint, thereby leaving it to the state to improve its policies. Thurgood Marshall dissented sharply from *San Antonio Independent School District v. Rodriguez*, citing *Brown* in an opinion that dismissed as a "sham" Powell's argument for the virtues of educational localism. Rodriguez was outraged and told reporters, "I cannot avoid at this moment feeling deep and bitter resentment against the supreme jurists and the persons who nominated them to that position."[14]

In subsequent years most states expanded aid to schools and approved distributive formulas that helped to narrow the gaps between rich and poor school districts. But most large cities continued to confront losses in their tax bases. Many had to provide education for increasing numbers of poor people, including thousands of immigrants from the Caribbean and Central America. Despite the new formulas, cross-district differences persisted, thereby subverting the American dream of equality of opportunity of education. *Rodriguez*, however, remained the key constitutional test on the issue. The decision suggested that the four Nixon appointees had come together in 1973 and would maintain a conservative stance on such issues. Indeed, with few exceptions, the Burger Court thereafter avoided judicial activism on racial and educational matters.

Even more discouraging to liberal integrationists like Marshall was a landmark decision, *Milliken v. Bradley*, which the Court handed down in July 1974. This decision had been keenly awaited, for it involved a critical undecided issue concerning the very meaning of "desegregation." Did it mean, as Judge Parker's "Briggs Dictum" had said in 1955, only that states and municipalities must not deliberately segregate students by race, or did it mean, as *Green* and *Swann* had argued, that *results* of school actions—appropriate racial balance—were what really mattered? More specifically, the case addressed a key question: whether a city school district—in this case, Detroit—could be required to merge with suburban districts (as Charlotte had done voluntarily in 1960) to enable metropolitan-wide districting and busing for the purposes of promoting better racial balance. Detroit's public schools, which had long featured *de facto* segregation, had become 72 percent black as a result of white flight; surrounding suburban schools were overwhelmingly white. If the cities and suburbs were ordered to operate one metropolitan system, they might contain white flight and move toward desegregation.

Federal District Judge Stephen Roth agreed with Mrs. Verda Bradley, leader of a number of black parents in Detroit who secured the local NAACP to handle their litigation against state and local officials. Her son's virtually all-black school was badly overcrowded, necessitating the erection of portable classrooms that quickly fell into disrepair. Teachers at the school, it seemed, had stopped teaching. The judge declared that real progress toward desegregation could not be achieved within the boundaries of the city. Consolidation of school districts, he pointed out, had a long history. He therefore ordered a multidistrict remedy. "School district lines," he said, "are simply matters of political convenience and may not be used to deny constitutional rights." A court of appeals affirmed the order.[15]

Roth's decision alarmed many school officials. A city-suburban plan involving Detroit, they complained, would affect fifty-three suburbs and 780,000 students, of whom some 310,000 would have to be bused. That seemed to present an administrative and logistical nightmare. Some students would probably have to spend an hour and a half each way on a bus. White parents, too, were frightened. One exclaimed that he did not want his children going to "dirty, violent, undesirable Detroit." A white mother explained that she and her husband had moved to the suburbs because "my kids weren't going to go to that school down there." She added, "You've got your good colored and your bad, just like white. But if you could live down there and see those animals coming and going . . ." Another mother resisted the idea of busing her children long distances. She wanted her kids close by. Busing was expensive and unsafe. "No kid of mine is going to get on a bus. I'd go to jail first."[16]

They need not have worried, for Burger was determined to draw the line. He set one of his clerks to work on the case for months. Ultimately, the same five justices who had formed the majority in *Rodriguez*—Burger, Blackmun, Powell, Rehnquist, and Stewart—overruled the lower court. In *Milliken*, Burger wrote, "The notion that school district lines may be casually ignored or treated as a mere administrative convenience is contrary to the history of public education in our country." He continued by agreeing that "disparate treatment of white and Negro students" occurred within the Detroit system. If the suburbs had also practiced discrimination of that sort, an interdistrict remedy might be in order. But he found no intent to discriminate or segregate in the fifty-three suburban towns. The proposed interdistrict remedy was therefore "wholly impermissible." The Court sent the case back to the lower courts and told them to develop remedies to improve districting within city limits, an action that Marshall called a "solemn mockery" of *Brown*.

Top Michigan officials greeted the decision with great sighs of relief. Governor William Milliken (named as defendant in the case) said, "I feel very strongly that to deal with integrated schools by busing is very superficial and very counterproductive." Vice President Ford of Michigan, who was shortly to move into the White House, added, "I think it is a great step forward to finding another answer to quality education." A suburban mother was delighted. "I clapped my hands and said something like 'goodie.' My kids would have been bused into a bad neighborhood. I was worried. My school's here in the back yard. That's why we moved here."

Some black leaders, too, were not troubled by the result. Mayor Coleman Young of Detroit explained, "I shed no tears for cross-district busing. . . . I don't think there's any magic in putting little white kids alongside little black kids if the little white kids and little black kids over here have half a dollar for their education and the little black kids and little white kids over there are getting a dollar." A black woman on the Atlanta school board added, "I've always thought it was insulting to blacks to say that they would do better if they could just sit next to a white child in school. What we need are better schools." Derrick Bell, a professor at Harvard Law School, echoed such sentiment: "The insistence on integrating every public school that is black perpetuates the racially demeaning and unproven assumption that blacks must have a majority white presence in order to either teach or learn effectively."

Advocates of desegregation, however, denounced *Milliken*. Nathaniel Jones, a top NAACP attorney, commented, "The Court has said to black people; 'You have rights but you don't have a remedy.' We're back in the same position as we were before Dred Scott." Justice Douglas, in one of his last dissents, said that the decision would make Detroit's schools "not only separate but inferior." He added, "The wheel had come more than full circle since 1954."[17] Marshall, also dissenting, took the unusual step of speaking directly from the bench: "Our nation, I fear, will be ill-served by the Court's refusal to remedy separate and unequal education, for unless our children begin to learn together, there is little hope that our people will ever learn to live together." Lamenting the antigovernment mood that had descended on the nation, he added,

> Today's holding, I fear, is more a reflection of a perceived public mood that we have gone far enough in enforcing the Constitution's guarantee of equal justice than it is of neutral principles of law. In the short run, it may seem to be the easier course to allow our great metropolitan areas to be divided up each into two cities—one white and one black—but it is a course, I predict, our people will ultimately regret. I dissent.

Marshall's strong dissent came two weeks after the death in Washington of Earl Warren, who succumbed to heart troubles at Georgetown Hospital. The dissent attested to Marshall's long-held faith that desegregated schools were the best hope for the development of better race relations in America and that the state must enforce such desegregation. Indeed, his dissent took him well beyond where he and other liberals had stood in 1954, when the central issue had been *de jure* segregation in the South, not efforts to fight *de facto* segregation, as in Detroit, or to secure racial balance throughout the nation. The demands of Verda Bradley and her fellow plaintiffs showed how far the pendulum, once started by *Brown*, had swung toward affirmative efforts on behalf of racial justice. But Marshall had been outvoted. *Milliken*, the first key Supreme Court decision to back away from *Brown*, became—and remained—the law of the land.

Integrationists argued unhappily that *Milliken* had no end of deleterious long-term effects. Whites in Detroit, assured that suburban schools would remain predominantly white, continued to move out of the city. By 1986, Detroit's public schools were 89 percent black. More generally, the decision stymied efforts elsewhere for metropolitan desegregation and busing plans. Thereafter, no school districts voluntarily adopted city-suburban educational plans of such a kind, for *Milliken* said that none had to. In only a few places—notably Wilmington, Delaware; Louisville, Kentucky; and Indianapolis—were existing plans thereafter pursued. Wilmington, site of one of the five cases in 1954, struggled for many years, busing some 100,000 students in or out of the city until the courts declared in 1995 that it had achieved racial balance at last. This was forty-one years after *Brown*.[18]

We cannot conclude, however, that a decision the other way in *Milliken* would have transformed race relations or education in America's metropolitan regions. Thanks in part to the economic problems beset-

Justice Marshall in his Supreme Court chambers, August 1976. At the far right corner of his desk is a small bust of Frederick Douglass. (*Photo by Gerald Martineau. © 1976, The Washington Post. Reprinted with permission*)

ting the United States in the 1970s and early 1980s, cities and suburbs alike confronted deep fiscal problems that compounded existing class and cultural differences, among them the new mix caused by the arrival of a great many people of Hispanic background. There was often little political will to devise metropolitan solutions to these differences. If city-suburban school districting plans had been approved by the Court as a weapon against *de facto* segregation, racial mixing might have increased in small metropolitan areas where the percentages of minorities were relatively low (10 or 25 percent continued to be regarded as a "tipping point") and where leaders (as in Charlotte) steadfastly supported the plans. In large, minority-dominated cities, however, the logistical problems were formidable and the white opposition fierce. It also seemed likely that plans of this sort would have to be redrawn often—probably every year—in order to combat resegregation. Redistricting of this frequency would have created large discontinuities in the education of children and further incensed black as well as white opponents. There were surely no easy answers to racial hostilities of this magnitude.[19]

Concerns such as these lead us to a larger one: how far can courts move if they attempt to swim against the tides of majority opinion? Liberals like Brennan and Marshall insisted that the courts—and other agents of state authority—could change behavior: people who face a firmly enforced law will necessarily think and act differently. Passage and swift enforcement of the effective civil rights acts of the mid-1960s was convincing Exhibit A of their argument. Compliance in the South with firm orders from federal officials and with *Green* and *Alexander* was Exhibit B. Many advocates of desegregation have since kept this liberal faith.

Conservatives, including the majority of the Burger Court after 1973, thought otherwise. They asserted the virtues of judicial restraint in such hotly contested matters. And they normally commanded center stage through the 1980s and into the 1990s. Polls in these years, moreover, indicated that the majority of the American people did not wish to embark on arduous new treks in quest of broader civil rights. National political leaders seemed equally reluctant to fight for major changes in race relations. If the democratically elected Congress and president were not willing to press harder for desegregation, how could the courts accomplish it alone?

Warren Burger stayed on as Chief for another twelve years following *Milliken*, retiring in September 1986 (the Senate then confirmed President Reagan's nomination of Justice Rehnquist as Chief). During these years the Burger Court confronted a few more important cases relating to race and education. One of the most controversial, *University of California Regents v. Bakke* (1978), proved especially difficult for the Court, which finally ruled five to four (Marshall among the four) that the University of California at Davis medical school might not establish quotas of places in each class for minority group members. Softening this blow to advocates of strong affirmative action, which by then had joined busing as a contentious popular issue, a five-justice majority also held that admissions officers might include racial considerations, if managed benignly, among the criteria it used for judging applicants. Racial diversity, it said, was highly desirable. Lewis Powell, a swing man, made it possible for the Court to reach a majority of five in both conclusions.[20]

Bakke showed that even the "conservative" Burger Court was willing to move beyond *Brown*, which had implied (not said) that public education should operate as if color-blind. As Justice Blackmun wrote in a widely cited defense of his vote in *Bakke* to allow race as a criterion, "In order to get beyond racism we must first take account of race. There is no other way.... In order to treat persons equally, we must treat them differently." Most Americans seemed relieved at the Court's compromise, which remained the law of the land though it was seriously challenged by lower courts in the 1990s. But some on the left, like Marshall, were bitter. After *Bakke* he grew depressed and choleric, even addressing some of his colleagues as "Massa" in a deep slave dialect. And some on the right damned the justices for approving "reverse discrimination." The decision showed that the Court, like the country, remained deeply divided concerning issues such as affirmative action.[21]

The Court's ruling, however, affected universities, not public schools. And most of the key affirmative action cases that occupied the Burger Court from 1974 to 1986 concerned employment, not education. To be sure, the Legal Defense Fund remained active in the quest for desegregated schools. But much of its litigation concerned ancillary educational issues, such as the depiction of blacks in textbooks, the hiring and firing of black teachers, and—increasingly—the impact of resegregation.[22] The Supreme Court made no more major public school decisions in these years. The justices, having demanded progress toward racial balance in the previously *de jure* systems of the South (*Green* and *Alexander*), having approved intradistrict busing (*Swann*) and having discouraged interdistrict plans (*Milliken*), for the most part stood aside until the 1990s. The main stories of the mid-1970s and 1980s played themselves out in the school districts. How did local leaders manage in a conservative era of lowered expectations about the ability of public officials to improve race relations?

In some ways, encouragingly for integrationists. By many measures of desegregation, progress toward racial balance in schools was visible, though far less dramatic than it had been between 1968 and 1973. The

Cartoon by Mike Peters, Dayton Daily News, December 1997. *(Tribune Media Services)*

percentage of black students in public schools that were 90 percent or more minority (for the most part, "black" schools) declined from 62.9 percent in 1968 to 34.8 percent in 1980, and to 34.1 percent in 1992. As these numbers indicate, most of the change occurred between 1968 and 1980.[23]

As had been the case since decisions such as *Green* and *Alexander* forced southern districts to hasten their all-too-deliberate speed, change in many (not all) areas of the South was especially large. In 1968, for instance, 77.5 percent of black students went to "black" schools in the South, as defined above. This percentage fell dramatically to 24.6 percent in 1980 and rose a little to 26.5 percent by 1992. By contrast, the percentage of blacks who went to "black" schools in the Northeast rose in these years, from 42.7 percent in 1968 to 48.7 percent in 1980 and to 49.9 percent in 1992. The percentages of blacks in black schools in the Midwest declined steadily between 1968 and 1992, but these, too, were higher throughout this period than they were in the South. Only in the West, where desegregation made strides both in the 1970s and 1980s, did the percentage of black students in black schools fall to levels close to those in the South in 1992.

The extent of change in many areas of the South, indeed, can scarcely be exaggerated. Dismiss nostalgia and recall the handicaps of most black schools prior to *Brown*: crowded, often leaky tarpaper buildings; awful facilities; poorly educated, badly paid black teachers. Thousands of black children across the South, like those of Summerton, South Carolina, had to walk miles to school. By the late 1980s, most of the heavily black schools in the South were much better funded and much closer to having equal facilities than earlier. Black teachers generally received salaries equal to those of white teachers with similar qualifications and experience. Some blacks taught white students in the mostly white schools and vice versa. Many schools went so far as to introduce aspects of black history and culture into their curricula. Here and there, whites perceived improvement in mixed public schools and pulled their children out of the private academies.[24] In all these respects, public education in many parts of the South had been revolutionized, in part because of demands by the courts.

In large northern cities, the comparatively low levels of desegregation reflected the size of black in-migrations, the extent of white flight, the intractability of residential segregation, and as the Court discovered in the *Keyes* case involving Denver, deliberate public policies aimed at preventing or inhibiting the growth of racially mixed schools. *De facto* segregation, as before, was purposeful, not accidental.[25] Big cities like New York, Philadelphia, and Washington, with huge black populations, had schools that had become overwhelmingly black (and by the late 1980s, increasingly Hispanic as well). So did cities such as Detroit and Chicago in the Midwest. Because of overall population growth among African Americans and because so many blacks had moved to such cities in the 1940s, '50s, and '60s, the *number* (as opposed to the percentage) of black children who attended all- or predominantly black schools in America was higher in 1980 than it had been in 1954.[26]

Even in these large cities, however, real spending per student for the heavily black schools (as in the white schools) increased considerably in the 1980s, a trend that reflected growing national demands for better, more achievement-oriented schools. Most of these cities also began to offer various "choice" plans, including "magnet" schools, many of them involving tax-supported busing to promote racial mixing. Some of these magnet schools were elitist "islands" of quality education that failed to enroll many inner-city minorities and that perpetuated school segregation by class as well as by race. Still, those that prompted more racial mixing were welcomed by integrationists.[27]

Another heartening sign for integrationists had to do with the experiences of *white* students in these years. In 1968, 77.8 percent of white pupils attended public schools that were more than 90 percent white. By 1980 this percentage had fallen to 60.9, and it kept dropping in the 1980s—to 48.9 percent in 1992. Again, southern states led the way toward this kind of mixing: 68.8 percent of white students attended such schools in the South in 1968, 32.2 percent in 1980, and 26 percent in 1992. By contrast, the percentage of whites in "white" schools dropped more slowly in the Northeast, from 82.5 percent in 1968 to 66.7 percent in 1992. Modest decreases in the Midwest approximated those in the Northeast—from 89.4 percent to 71.9 percent between 1968 and 1992. In the West, the percentages fell almost as fast as they did in the South: from 61.4 percent in 1968 to 26.7 percent in 1992. Nationally, this trend was significant: three-quarters of white students had gone to heavily white schools in 1968, compared to slightly fewer than half twenty-four years later.[28]

Whether mixed schools promoted more amicable race relations in the 1970s and 1980s remained, as in the past, a near-impossible question to answer. In some places, perhaps yes. At Little Rock's Central High, 57 percent of the students in 1981 were black. While few of them were placed in the honors classes, their morale was thought to be fairly good. The reading scores of black students at Central were higher than the national average for blacks. In other places, perhaps no. Louisville, which fashioned an initially promising metropolitan desegregation plan in the mid-1970s, encountered serious difficulties within a few years. There, as in many other cities, blacks continued to complain that they were bused for more years than whites were, and for longer distances. Tensions rose, and many observers came to doubt that interracial relations had changed for the better if at all. Large generalizations about the impact of desegregation on interracial understanding in schools could not stand careful scrutiny. As of the late 1980s, variations were endless, and the jury remained out.[29]

It also remained difficult by that time to know whether increased levels of racial mixing greatly improved the academic achievement of blacks. To be sure, other educational trends, following in the wake of the rising public concern about schools, seemed highly encouraging. Per pupil spending in constant dollars was growing enormously—by 122 percent between 1965 and 1994. Student-teacher ratios were improving dramatically—from twenty-five students per class to seventeen over the same period. And blacks were staying in school longer than earlier: by the mid-1990s, they were almost exactly as likely to complete high school as whites. This considerable change accompanied other noteworthy developments after 1960: the expansion of a significant black middle class and a rapid rise in the number of blacks who attended college. By 1997, more than half of black high school graduates went on to college (compared to two-thirds of white high school graduates). These trends had scarcely been visible in the days of Jim Crow.[30]

But did nonsegregated schools do better than primarily black schools to improve academic achievement? Here one reenters a debate that had first erupted in the 1960s and early 1970s. Derrick Bell of the Harvard Law School was hardly the only person at the time who doubted the academic virtues of racial mixing in all circumstances. But if there was a consensus by 1990, it was that the average achievement scores of black students in well integrated schools had risen in these years. Because the scores of whites in most of these schools improved little if at all, the once substantial black-white gap narrowed slowly. Given more time, reformers said, the gap would close still more. Some optimists, moreover, thought that the scores of black students in fairly well mixed schools tended to increase more than did the scores of black students in predominantly black schools. It was generally (though not universally) believed that blacks in these mixed schools were more likely than other blacks to stay out of trouble with the law, to avoid out-of-wedlock pregnancy, to go on to college, and to get good jobs.[31]

It was still hard to say, however, how much racial mixing per se accounted for these developments. James Coleman, after all, had long ago stressed that the socioeconomic background of students, the educational level of parents, the nature of neighborhoods, and the ambitions of peer groups were keys to the academic success of children. After 1970, as before, black children from middle-class backgrounds were more likely to attend significantly mixed schools—and classrooms—than were the poorer black children who lived in central city ghettos, whose scores were abysmally low. Rising scores of black children in racially mixed schools might reflect advances in the socioeconomic or educational status of their parents. The independent effect of mixing, therefore, remained debated.[32]

There were also voices in the 1970s and 1980s—as well as later—that questioned the emphasis of reformers on the independent virtues of school desegregation. Was a focus on racial mixing in the schools a highly promising strategy for improving the life chances of black children, especially the hordes of poverty-stricken blacks in the inner cities? There, the most powerful trends since World War II had reflected social change—massive in-migrations of blacks, white flight, deteriorating urban services, and the loss of jobs to suburbs. Would it have been better, some asked, for reformers to concentrate on coping with these and other structural and familial problems instead of expending time and resources on busing and other strategies to mix children in classrooms?

One such reform, these critics often added, would have been to focus less on school desegregation and more on expanding the availability of preschools that emphasized cognitive development and on improving the academic quality of inner-city schools. Advocates of this persuasion stressed two obvious points: first, that since *Milliken* it was virtually impossible to achieve extensive racial mixing within cities from which most white families had fled; and second, that many central city schools for minorities—even when funded equally with white schools—were struggling and turbulent places where little serious learning went on. Moreover, many lower-class black children at these inner-city schools arrived in the first grade with very low cognitive skills; from a very early age they needed much more sustained and thoughtful academic attention than they tended to receive.[33]

These inner-city black schools were hardly the only ones that seemed in trouble in the 1970s and 1980s. In 1979, the twenty-fifth anniversary of *Brown*, the public schools in Summerton, South Carolina—where the saga of litigation for school desegregation had begun in the late 1940s—were almost entirely black: one white student went to classes with 2,029 blacks. Observers gave these schools low marks. Whites went to Clarendon Academy and other schools outside the town. Harry Briggs, whose name was featured in *Briggs v. Elliott*, was asked in 1979 what he had accomplished. He replied, "Nothing!" He then reflected a minute and reconsidered, but only slightly. His effort had been necessary, he admitted, "for the younger generation, even if they don't know what it was all about." He concluded, "It's still separate, the whites they got the private school. But at least the children can ride the buses to school, and they couldn't do that before. You got to take some pride, it's better."[34]

Linda Brown-Thompson, like Briggs, had once held high expectations. By the 1980s, however, she, too, was becoming ambivalent about the cause that had greatly affected her life. In 1984, on the thirtieth anniversary of *Brown*, she was asked what she thought about her struggles. At the time she was still participating in the long-running suit against school segregation in Topeka. She replied that she was "dismayed at school integration today." She added, "It was not the quick fix we thought it would be."[35]

Indeed it was not.

9

RESEGREGATION?

We do not have to look far to find blacks who expressed doubts about progress in race relations—and about the special virtues of desegregation—in the early 1990s. Three comments will do:

"There's a moving violation that many African Americans know as D. W. B.: Driving While Black" (street wisdom).

"THE BLACKER THE COLLEGE, THE SWEETER THE KNOWL-EDGE" (T-shirt worn by students at Jackson State University in Mississippi, which had an overwhelmingly black student body).

A cartoon strip: black students, having taken over an administration building, are pressing the university president. When asked what they want, they send out a note. Its demand: separate water fountains for whites and blacks (Garry Trudeau's "Doonesbury").

A widely reported controversy that erupted in Selma at the very start of the decade helped to account for the apparent ubiquity of gloomy black attitudes such as these. There, where Jo Anne Bland's father had punched her high school principal in 1970, tense interracial struggles over school management had persisted. In 1990 they exploded when Norward Roussell, a recently appointed black superintendent of schools, called for honors courses to be opened up to more African-American students at Selma High School. A white-dominated school board (which had earlier dared to appoint him) responded to parental protests by refusing to renew his contract, which was to expire in six months. Roussell, however, remained on the job and stood by his decision.

In the struggles that followed, some 200 white children were pulled by their parents from the school and enrolled in nearby white academies. Black students demonstrated their backing of Roussell by picketing and sitting in at the school, whereupon some white students engaged them in fights. The fighting stopped only when state police and the Alabama National Guard were called to the scene. Americans could watch these struggles on television. Selma, site of dramatic demonstrations for voting rights in 1965, had again become a focus of national news. In 1965 the events had inspired activists for civil rights; in 1990 they prompted disillusion.[1]

Many subsequent racial controversies broke out in the early and mid-1990s, some of which stimulated separatist urges, notably the bloody riot in Los Angeles in 1992 and the murder trial of O. J. Simpson in 1995. African-American authors wrote books with despairing titles: *Faces at the Bottom of the Well: The Permanence of Racism* (1992), *American Apartheid* (1993), and *The Coming Race War* (1996).[2]

Hear especially Derrick Bell, who often told audiences in the early 1990s a story about a group of aliens who land in the United States on a trade mission and offer white Americans sums of gold to pay off national debts, chemicals to cleanse pollution, and a safe nuclear engine and fuel. In return, the aliens promise to fly all blacks off to their home star. Bell said that African-American audiences were certain that whites would accept the deal. Many thought that whites would send away blacks for nothing.[3]

Even the NAACP, long-time force for racial desegregation, betrayed occasional uncertainty about its mission. In 1997 it went so far as to hold a formal debate over the virtues of nonsegregated versus black-run schools for black students. At the same time a Gallup Poll revealed that 76 percent of black college graduates thought that race relations would always be troublesome for the country. Fifty-six percent of blacks who had not earned a college degree felt the same way. The poll conveyed further bad news about the future: young African Americans were more pessimistic about race relations than their elders, 65 percent of whom said that conflicts could be worked out.[4]

The pessimists offered familiar statistics. Unemployment rates among African Americans continued to be much higher than they were among whites. Poverty rates among African Americans, at roughly 30 percent

Black students occupied Selma High School in protest over racial issues in February 1990. *(AP/Wide World photo)*

until they declined considerably late in the decade, nonetheless remained three times as high as among whites in 1998. The median family income of African Americans was roughly 55 percent of that for non-Hispanic whites. Many black ghettos remained frightening places.

Not all observers, however, were so pessimistic. Orlando Patterson, a leading scholar of race relations, dismissed the dourest prophets of doom and gloom. White attitudes, he wrote in 1997, had grown considerably more tolerant since the 1950s. Contacts between whites and blacks had increased: "A portrait of a separate America for blacks is no longer valid." He concluded, "The record of the past half century, especially the past thirty years, has been one of progress, in some cases considerable progress. The positive progress made toward social, political, and cultural inclusion has been phenomenal, reflected in the impressive growth of the middle class and the not insignificant penetration of the nation's upper class by Afro-Americans."[5]

Faced with such conflicting views about race relations in the United States, what are we to believe? First, that scholars who wrote about race in the 1990s continued to disagree sharply about the extent of change. Second, that a dose of historical perspective can be helpful: progress for African Americans, especially legal progress, had indeed been impressive, particularly between 1960 and the early 1970s. Jim Crow, including *de jure* segregation of schools, had become history. Blacks were no longer prevented from voting. Organized white violence against minorities was far less frequent. Racial discrimination in many areas of life, such as workplaces, was less common than it used to be. Gunnar Myrdal, although a little too optimistic about improvement in race relations over time, had been correct in 1944 about a good many long-range trends.[6]

Separatist nostalgia about the blessings of all-black institutions during the Jim Crow era, moreover, was simply fatuous—a poor reading of history and the product of disillusion with the stalemates that had stymied progress in many aspects of race relations since the 1960s. An NAACP leader was one of many who properly dismissed such nostalgia:

> What gets me now is that so many people are asking, "Was integration the right thing to do? Was it worth it? Was *Brown* a good decision?" It's asinine. To this day, I can remember bus drivers pulling off and blowing smoke in my mother's face. I can remember the back of the bus, colored water fountains. . . . I can hear a cop telling me, "Take your black butt back to nigger town." What I tell folk . . . is that there are a lot of romanticists now who want to take this trip down Memory Lane, and they want to go back, and I tell the young people that anybody who wants to take you back to segregation, make sure you get a round-trip ticket because you won't stay. Like Michael J. Fox in *Back to the Future*, the minute you get back [to the past], you will say, "Take me back to the future."[7]

Third, expectations of many African Americans had risen faster, especially in the 1960s, than later efforts were able to meet, thereby leaving frustration in their trail. Recall again the agenda of civil rights activists such as Thurgood Marshall as late as 1964: it demanded equal rights and the abolition of legal distinctions based on race or color. The Civil Rights Act of 1964 responded well to these goals. Thereafter, the civil rights agenda quickly expanded to include demands such as affirmative action, racial balance, and (for some) racial quotas, which many whites stoutly resisted. Hence the many stalemates that characterized the era after 1970. Marshall himself, having succeeded with *Brown*, endorsed a good deal of this new agenda. But this effort engaged him in a tougher fight, and he became very frustrated by the early 1990s. Retiring in 1991 after nearly twenty-four years on the Court, he reflected, "I don't know what legacy I left. It's up to the people. . . . I have given fifty years to it, and if that is not enough, God bless them."[8]

In 1998 James Q. Wilson, a leading student of race relations, thoughtfully evaluated downbeat attitudes such as Marshall's. After conceding that economic growth, which was remarkable in the late 1990s, was contributing to a general sense of material well-being, he concluded that concerns about race would always loom large in the thinking of African Americans, regardless of their socioeconomic standing. "For many middle-class blacks . . . race remains a constant reminder of their difficulty in being judged solely as individuals, and for many low-income (and young) blacks, race is an explanation for the gains they have not made." Wilson concluded by citing W. E. B. Du Bois, who had described his conflicted feelings in *Souls of Black Folk* (1903):

> One feels his two-ness, an American, a Negro, two souls, two thoughts, two unreconciled strivings, two warring ideals in one dark body.

In the 1990s most African Americans still felt strongly their "two-ness."[9]

Amid these debates about the future of race relations, legal fights concerning desegregation in schools again aroused controversy. Much of this fighting centered on decisions of the Supreme Court, which in the 1990s reentered battles over school districting.

Liberals had of course been unhappy since the mid-1970s about the Court's decisions concerning race relations. After all, Nixon's appointees had turned the Court to the right as early as 1973, when the *Rodriguez* decision had allowed unequal cross-district school financing to stand. *Milliken* in 1974 had discouraged efforts for metropolitan-based desegregation of schools. After William Douglas retired in 1975, replaced by John Paul Stevens, only William Brennan and Thurgood Marshall remained as liberal stalwarts on the Court. President Jimmy Carter, who might have named a liberal, never had the opportunity; no retirement occurred during his administration. President Ronald Reagan then appointed three justices: Sandra Day O'Connor (the first female justice in American history), who replaced Potter Stewart in 1981; Antonin Scalia, who became an associate justice when William Rehnquist was confirmed to succeed Warren Burger as Chief Justice in 1986; and Anthony Kennedy, chosen when Lewis Powell left the Court in 1987. Like Stevens, all three of Reagan's new nominees had judicial experience and were unanimously confirmed.

Some of the new justices, notably O'Connor and Kennedy, appeared to be moderates. Replacing centrists like Stewart and Powell, they did not obviously tip the Court's ideological balance. Scalia, however, was an outspoken conservative on virtually all issues that came before the Court. And Rehnquist proved to be a forceful leader of a conservative majority that became slowly but steadily self-assured, especially on cases involving affirmative action, by the end of the 1980s. *New York Times* Court correspondent Linda Greenhouse dubbed 1989, "The Year the Court Turned Right." The term, she wrote, "was a watershed in the Court's modern history. For the first time in a generation, a conservative majority was in a position to control the outcome on most important issues."[10]

The Court's movement to the right accelerated when Brennan, a justice since 1956, stepped down in 1990 and Marshall, on the Court since 1967, followed him in 1991. President George Bush replaced Brennan with David Souter, a New Hampshire native who took moderately liberal stands on many issues. Still, Souter displayed none of the liberal zeal that had marked Brennan's long and influential career on the Court. And Clarence Thomas, Bush's nominee to take the seat of Marshall, held decidedly conservative views. Confirmed only after a vicious battle in the Senate, Thomas joined Scalia on the right wing of the Court. Liberals prepared for the worst.[11]

Sometimes, the liberals were pleasantly surprised; the Court, for instance, refused in the 1990s to overturn *Roe v. Wade*, the still controversial decision that had legalized abortion in 1973. In affirmative action and race-related voting rights cases, however, the Court continued to take a conservative view. And in a series of cases involving schools, it greatly alarmed advocates of desegregation. Four in particular, decided between 1991 and 1995, stood out. Three of these concerned a key long-term development: white flight. As earlier, ongoing movement of this sort was provoking widespread "resegregation" and raising havoc with the painstakingly crafted, often extraordinarily detailed court-ordered districting and busing plans that courts had been trying since the 1960s to monitor. Struggles over these issues posed a basic question that the Court had partially addressed in its decision concerning Pasadena in 1976: how much must a school district do in order to satisfy judges that it has seriously tried to desegregate its schools?[12]

The first of these four cases, decided while Marshall still sat on the Court in 1991, set the tone. It involved Oklahoma City, which had responded to a federal court order by establishing a race-based busing plan in 1972. White flight had followed, necessitating more busing. In 1985, the city's school board introduced a student reassignment plan that did away with busing for elementary schoolchildren. The change, said the board, was necessary because the existing system had come to impose special busing burdens on black children. The Urban League, a predominantly African-American organization, initially supported the board. It emphasized that many black parents preferred neighborhood schools, even if these schools were virtually all black. Other black parents were tired of litigating and resigned themselves to an apparent fact of life: *de facto* segregation of housing, and therefore of schools, was here to stay.[13]

The NAACP, however, opposed the reassignment plan, which would have meant that eleven elementary schools would remain all black. The federal district court backed the city, which insisted that private decisions by residents, not deliberately racist actions by the school board, had caused resegregation. The court of appeals then held for the black plaintiffs, and the case finally landed at the Supreme Court.

During the hearings that followed, an angry, frustrated Marshall clashed with Bush's solicitor general, Kenneth Starr, who supported the city's position. When Starr asserted that a racially segregated school had merely reflected residential changes, not the intent of the school board, Marshall said sharply, "But it still remains a segregated school." Starr replied, "By virtue of residential segregation." Marshall thundered, "You don't think segregation is unconstitutional?" Starr had some precedent on his side: in *Keyes*, a highly relevant case, Brennan had been careful to insist that plaintiffs must prove that *de facto* school segregation stemmed from intentional public policies. To Marshall, as to others who shared his position, however, demographic change leading to resegregation was no excuse to back away from desegregation decrees of a court.[14]

Rehnquist, writing for a five-justice majority, mainly sided with Starr.[15] Court-ordered busing plans, he said, could be dropped when school districts became resegregated because of private choices, were not themselves "vestiges" of the era of Jim Crow, and had taken all "practicable" steps to eliminate segregation. The courts, the Chief added, should not "condemn a school district . . . to judicial tutelage for the indefinite future." Federal supervision of school districts had always been "intended as a temporary measure to remedy past discrimination."

The decision, *Board of Education of Oklahoma City v. Dowell*, sent the case back to the district court and was not expected to have great practical effect. Observers recognized that more precise definitions of "vestiges" and "practicable" needed to be developed by the Court, and they predicted that courts would continue to validate court-ordered desegregation plans. Still, the decision indicated that a resegregated city might be released from court-ordered busing. The Court, it seemed, was backsliding.

Marshall's dissent was his last opinion in a school case. It showed that some of his core beliefs remained rooted in conclusions that he had reached in the early 1950s. Citing *Brown*, *Green*, and *Swann*, he quoted what Earl Warren, following Kenneth Clark, had written in 1954: state-sponsored segregation conveyed a message of "inferiority as to the status [of African-American schoolchildren] in the community that may affect their hearts and minds in a way unlikely ever to be undone." Racially identifiable schools, Marshall added, inflicted "stigmatic injury" on black students who had to attend them.

The Court's next major school decision, *Freeman v. Pitts* in 1992, considered similar circumstances, this time involving De Kalb County, a suburb of Atlanta. Thanks to white flight and resegregation, more than 50 percent of black students in the county were by then attending schools that were 90 percent or more black. County officials, like their counterparts in Oklahoma City, argued that private decisions by people, not public policies, had caused the resegregation. The Court agreed with them, this time unanimously (Clarence Thomas, new to the Court, did not vote). Justice Kennedy wrote, "Where resegregation is a product not of state action but of private choices, it does not have constitutional implications." He continued, "It is beyond the authority and beyond the practical ability of the federal courts to try to counteract these kinds of continuous and massive demographic shifts."[16]

As with *Dowell*, it was unclear how much *Freeman* would matter in practice. Kennedy qualified his ruling in various ways, suggesting that even a school district that had erased the "vestiges" of *de jure* segregation in its assignment of students might have to remain under court supervision until it made progress in desegregating other aspects of its operations. Still, liberals worried that the decision could ultimately affect the more than 500 school systems still under court orders to desegregate. If these districts showed good faith to comply with efforts to abolish the vestiges of *de jure* segregation, they might be released bit-by-bit from court orders.

Reactions to *Freeman*, like those to *Dowell*, exposed the ambivalent feelings that many black people were then expressing openly—and more loudly than in the 1980s—about the long and fatiguing business of litigation. Kenneth Clark, still holding the old integrationist faith, exclaimed in protest, "We are now not only whittling down *Brown v. Board*, we are moving back to the 'separate-but-equal' doctrine of *Plessy v. Ferguson*." But a black parent, Brenda Jackson, disagreed. "I'm a firm believer," she said, "that you support the school that's within your community." She added,

> I'm from the segregation time, back in the '50s and '60s, so coming from that background I felt that my children would have a better opportunity to interact socially in an integrated situation. That's where it turned out to be a mirage. It proved to me that educationally and socially your children can learn just as much in a predominantly black situation as opposed to an integrated situation.[17]

A High Court decision two months later, in June 1992, further revealed the complexity of contemporary attitudes concerning race and education. This decision, *United States v. Fordice*, involved higher education in Mississippi, which had been desegregated following governmental pressure in the 1960s. Still, the state in 1992 maintained five predominantly white institutions and three overwhelmingly black ones at that level. (Ninety-nine percent of white college and university students in the state attended the white institutions; 71 percent of black students went to the black ones.) By a vote of eight to one, Scalia dissenting, the Court declared that the system sustained racially discriminatory features. It sent the case back to a lower court and insisted that the state take "affirmative steps" to dismantle vestiges of discrimination in its system of higher education.

The Legal Defense Fund, which litigated the case against the state, was delighted with the ruling, which was expected to promote greater racial mixing in the state's higher educational system. Solicitor General Starr also hailed the result, which he said would require that the state eliminate unnecessarily duplicated programs in the black and white institutions. Some African Americans, however, disagreed. Frank Matthews, publisher of the journal *Black Issues in Higher Education*, complained, "What will happen is that the black colleges will eventually be merged out of existence or will be closed in the name of integration."[18]

The third public school case, *Missouri v. Jenkins*, was decided in June 1995, by which time Justices White and Blackmun had left the Court, replaced by Clinton appointees Ruth Bader Ginsburg and Stephen Breyer, both of whom were expected to maintain fairly liberal views. The case concerned Kansas City, which had tried to comply with court orders to desegregate by creating magnet schools. The most elaborate of these, Central High, had a six-lane indoor track, a $5 million Olympic-sized swimming pool, a 2,000-square-foot planetarium, radio and TV studios, and a host of special academic and job training programs. Teachers who agreed to work there received raises. The city, however, had trouble inducing white students to attend the school, which had a large black majority: even public payment of student taxi fares failed to attract the whites.[19]

State authorities estimated by 1995 that efforts to comply with the court orders had cost some $800 million since 1985, but without significant gains. Academic performance of African Americans had not improved. The effort, white officials insisted, was unfair to the taxpayers of Missouri. "The state has been writing the checks and we have no control over how the money is spent," Attorney General Jeremiah Nixon complained. "We want to return control of the district to parents and teachers." Nixon and other state officials objected also to a requirement of the federal court overseeing the plan—that student academic achievement must improve before the court might step aside. Such a standard, state officials protested, was unprecedented.

The Court's five to four decision, written by Rehnquist, showed how divided the justices had become on the issue.[20] Rehnquist stopped short of ordering the city's plan dismantled, observing that vestiges of segregation had not been erased "to the extent practicable" (the standard set in *Dowell*). But he ruled that lower court decisions had improperly ordered the State of Missouri to help pay for it. Rehnquist's decision left the fate of the program very much in doubt and incensed liberal backers of bold efforts, such as Kansas City's, to lessen segregation in the schools.

The most striking statements concerning the case came from Justice Thomas, an African American. Cool to integration, he had long been critical of many arguments on behalf of *Brown*. Those who supported Kansas City's plan, he now complained, seemed to believe that "any school that is black is inferior, and that blacks cannot succeed without the company of whites." He then fired a shot at psychological theories, such as Kenneth Clark's, that Warren had used in *Brown*: "The theory that black students suffer an unspecified psychological harm from segregation that retards their mental and educational development . . . not only relies upon questionable social science research rather than constitutional principle, but it also rests on an assumption of black inferiority."[21]

Many liberal African Americans strongly opposed Thomas's presence on the Court. Mayor Willie Brown of San Francisco later called him a shill for white racism and compared him to a leader of the Ku Klux Klan. Still, Thomas was hardly the only black person to express doubts in the 1990s about the presumed superiority of desegregated schools. Glenn Loury, a prominent black social scientist, reiterated these doubts in a widely noted opinion piece in 1997, "Integration Has Had Its Day." Blacks, he said, needed better schools, not condescension.[22] Complaints such as this, by Thomas on the right, Loury (who was moving at the time from the right toward the center), and Derrick Bell on the left could not easily be ignored. They challenged Thurgood Marshall, Kenneth Clark, Earl Warren, and others who in a half-century of struggle had stressed the blessings—academic, social, and economic—of desegregation.[23]

Integrationists who backed Marshall's point of view in the early and mid-1990s responded, as they had done earlier, that blacks who went to predominantly white schools profited in many ways. By then, these arguments were familiar: the performance of African-American students in reading and math improved in nonsegregated schools, slowly narrowing the gaps in achievement scores between blacks and whites. The earlier that black students were exposed to nonsegregated settings, the better their scores. Liberal integrationists further asserted, as the Clarks had done in the 1950s, that desegregation helped white people: most whites who went to school with minorities became more tolerant. *Brown* and subsequent decisions, they added, had prodded white Southerners into the modern world and guided the region into a racially more harmonious national mainstream—southern whites, like blacks, were liberated by the change. These liberals emphasized that school desegregation was imperative if whites were ever to become more understanding of blacks—and vice versa. Julius Chambers, long-time advocate on the Legal Defense

Fund, concluded in 1993, "Integrated education remains the best way to prepare all students—black and white—for the complex, multicultural, multiracial society which they'll soon be joining."[24]

A journalistic exploration of race relations in Montclair, New Jersey, reached similar if guarded conclusions in 1999. In the 1960s and early 1970s, racial tensions in Montclair, a suburban enclave of 36,000 people twelve miles west of New York City, had become serious, leading finally to a state-levied school desegregation order in 1976. By 1999, thanks to steady in-migrations of blacks, 53 percent of the students at Montclair High School were African Americans. When teachers stopped academic tracking in some subjects in 1993, a significant number of white parents (and a few black parents) removed their children from the public schools. Opponents of these parents deplored these actions as "bright flight," or "I-can-afford-it flight."

Interracial tensions, moreover, persisted in Montclair's schools, where students tended to separate along class and racial lines in the cafeteria. "We want to sit with our friends," a white girl explained. "I'm not saying this racistly, but black people are brought up different, because of persecutions and slavery and stuff—they're brought up to feel different things than white kids, which makes their personalities different. I don't get along with the black kids in my school. I get along with my friends, who are mostly white. . . . And it's just like that."

Montclair's struggle for interracial understanding, in short, was on-going, revealing not only divisions between blacks and whites but also class cleavages within each racial group. Nothing like absolute integration was in sight. But advocates of racial mixing remembered the bad old days, and they remained hopeful. "I don't think [integration] happens in your lifetime," one white mother said, but "the long and short of it is the contribution you make along the way and the fervor you bring to it. The fact that a lot of things around here are wrong doesn't mean for a minute you change doing your best to do right." A white teacher added, "Young people need to know that they can produce history, and hopefully that's the legacy of this town. It's not just about raising kids to be good citizens or good boys and girls, it's actually a town committed to raising young people who know how to live in a multiracial, multi-ethnic community." [25]

Liberal activists, finally, kept up the fight to advance equality of schools. In Texas, Demetrio Rodriguez, whose suit on behalf of equal educational spending had failed in the Supreme Court in 1973, was still making himself heard on the subject almost twenty years later. He told reporters in 1992 that his six-year-old grandson was enjoying a very well equipped school. His classroom was spacious and had lots of books and computers. There was one teacher for every six children. But his grandson was lucky, Rodriguez said, for he was in a specially funded pilot program available to only fifty-four children. Persistent inequities across districts made a mockery of the American dream. "If money is not necessary," he asked, "why is it people have been fighting us over it for twenty-two years?"[26]

Thurgood Marshall, aged eighty-four, died in Bethesda Hospital on January 21, 1993. Three days later some 20,000 people—most of them blacks—endured winds and twenty-degree temperatures while standing in line to pay tribute at his flag-draped coffin in the Supreme Court building. So many had to wait that Chief Justice Rehnquist ordered the

Thousands of mourners came to pay their respects to Thurgood Marshall as he lay in state at the Supreme Court after his death in January 1993. *(AP/Wide World photo)*

building to be kept open into the night. Some of the mourners stopped to lay copies of the Court's decision in *Brown* next to the coffin. A retired government clerk remembered living in the city when it had been segregated by law and rejoiced that her grandchildren "won't see colored fountains, colored restaurants. No sir, Justice Marshall saw to that." Another black mourner said, "He stood for so many things he helped me learn to stand for, to do what you can, and that color of skin really should not make any difference, and that you have to fight for what you believe in."[27]

The outpouring of affection for Marshall indicated two important truths: first, notwithstanding the frustrations of his final years, his efforts and those of many fellow crusaders for civil rights had indeed helped to better the legal status of black people. Second, most African Americans still hoped for progress toward integration; they were not separatists. Still, pessimism about the future of race relations accompanied celebrations of Marshall's accomplishments. It reflected the fact that in the early 1990s, as in the previous fifteen-odd years, African Americans had lost a number of legal struggles. These losses underlined a sobering reality: as many activists had long argued, legal fights such as those that had occupied all of Marshall's adult life were often time-consuming and difficult to manage. The capacity of litigation alone to transform racial patterns was limited. At Marshall's death, moreover, schools remained especially embattled institutions—still the hardest to desegregate in many places. So it was that Kenneth Clark, Marshall's compatriot, despaired in 1993, "I am forced to recognize that my life has been, in fact, a series of glorious defeats."

Clark's pessimism, reflecting disillusion in the wake of his once-high expectations, was understandable. He had been realistic enough to understand that black and white children would not always get along well in desegregated schools, and that many whites would resist strongly. Like Marshall, however, he had thought that with pain could come progress. And if blacks and whites did not go to school together, what chance was there that they would come together as adults? Clark, like Marshall, had worked for desegregated schools because he believed in equality and because he hoped for greater interracial harmony in society at large. These were noble dreams.

Were such dreams realistic? The most ambitious goals of many civil rights activists, especially since the rise of grand expectations during the peak of the civil rights movement, had been to go beyond the establishment of legal equality so as to achieve greater social and economic equality for black people and then to move toward racial integration. But these were very difficult goals to reach. Striking down Jim Crow, thereby ending *de jure* segregation of schools and enabling legal equality, had required great effort and had been largely achieved by the early 1970s. These were stunning accomplishments. But driving toward social and economic equality has never been easy in any nation or culture. And it was surely difficult for Americans after 1970. Expecting greater progress, Clark and many others—especially young people—became embittered.

Moving toward integration was equally difficult. For there is a difference, however imprecise, between desegregation and integration. To desegregate is to break down separation of the races and to promote greater equality of opportunity. To integrate is to reach further: to bring together people of different colors and ethnic backgrounds so that they associate not only on an equal basis but also make a real effort to respect the autonomy of other people and to appreciate the virtues of cultural diversity. This was a part of the dream of Martin Luther King, Jr. Alas, as Diane Ravitch has put it, "A successful multiethnic society is a rare and wondrous achievement in the world."[28]

That the high expectations raised by *Brown*, and especially by the civil rights victories of the 1960s, had subsequently been stalled helps to account for the pessimism that gripped men like Marshall and Clark late in their lives. Given the magnitude of their goals, their disillusion is hardly surprising.

10

LEGACIES AND LESSONS

Anyone who reads this far will be aware of the many disappointments and triumphs surrounding *Brown*. A few examples still stand out in the twenty-first century.

One involves race and legal education. Thurgood Marshall had celebrated in 1950 when the Supreme Court ordered the all-white Texas Law School to admit Heman Sweatt, a black mail carrier. By the 1980s, the University of Texas (UT) was educating more minorities than any law school in the United States. In March 1996, however, the Fifth Circuit Court of Appeals prohibited the UT Law School from enforcing affirmative action guidelines that had reserved places for African Americans and other minorities. Enrollment of blacks plummeted from thirty-one in 1996 to four in 1997.[1]

Ted Shaw, associate director of the still combative Legal Defense Fund, complained that the court's decision was "disturbing" and "troubling." Like other advocates of desegregation, he feared that it would harm the quest for racial diversity in higher education that Justice Blackmun had espoused in the *Bakke* case of 1978. But conservatives applauded. Clint Bolick, director of the Institute for Justice in Washington, exulted that the court had "banged another nail in the coffin of racial preferences." Bolick insisted that *Brown* had established color-blindness as a constitutional principle. This was inaccurate but ironic: *Brown*, which many conservatives had deplored in the 1950s, had become a guiding light for some on the right by the 1990s.[2]

The situation in Summerton, South Carolina, where Marshall had begun a struggle against racial discrimination in the late 1940s, revealed other legacies discouraging to desegregationists in the 1990s. School District No. 1 of Summerton still had an overwhelmingly black population. Its schools received more funding per pupil than the state average. Yet student achievement scores lagged badly, and only a few white students went there in the mid-1990s. Other whites still attended all-white private academies or predominantly white public schools in nearby Manning, where parents with money had bought land so that their children might enroll. Race relations at Manning High were said to be calm. But academic tracking was common, with few African Americans in college prep courses. Reporters observed that white and black students rarely socialized. Self-segregation seemed to be the norm.[3]

Summerton's high level of segregation was not typical of towns in South Carolina, which like many southern states continued in the 1990s to have a larger percentage of black students attending schools with white majority enrollments than most states in the union. Who would have expected in 1954 that the South would climb out of the abyss of Jim Crow to stand tall in this way? Yet it was surely discouraging to proponents of desegregation that some of Summerton's schools, like many others in heavily black areas of the South, were just about as segregated in the 1990s, though not *de jure*, as they had been in 1954.

The legacy of *Brown* in Topeka also remained unsettling. In 1994 a federal district court finally approved a new city plan to desegregate the schools. The plan featured magnet schools, voluntary transfers of white and black students, and the closing of some heavily black schools. The courts, however, continued to oversee the plan. And Linda Brown-Thompson, whose children had gone to segregated schools in Topeka, remained pessimistic. She said, "Sometimes I wonder if we really did the children and the nation a favor by taking this case to the Supreme Court. I know it was the right thing for my father and others to do then. But after nearly forty years we find the Court's ruling unfulfilled."[4]

A happier legacy of *Brown* could be found at the University of Alabama, from which Autherine Lucy had been expelled in 1956. Federal muscle had finally forced token integration of 'Bama in 1963, and desegregation inched ahead there—as at other white universities in the South—in the next two decades. Lucy reenrolled at Alabama in 1989 and graduated in 1992 with a master's degree in elementary education. Her daughter received an undergraduate degree at the same time. She was one of 1,755 African Americans at a campus of 18,096 students. George Wallace, who had tried to bar black students in 1963, had been crippled by a would-be assassin's bullet in 1972 but lived until 1998. By then he had long since claimed to rue his racist past. Recognizing the power of blacks at the polls, he had wooed African Americans in political campaigns.[5]

In Little Rock, where troops had patrolled Central High School for all of the 1957–58 school year, the legacy of *Brown* was mixed in the 1990s. By then the school was approximately 60 percent black. Some 50 percent of whites of school age in the district fled to academies outside the city. Although some students at Central—blacks as well as whites— thrived academically (twenty-three students became National Merit Scholarship semifinalists in 1997), 70 percent of the black students and 30 percent of the whites read below grade level. Whites and blacks did not socialize much at Central, but advocates of racial diversity remembered the bad old days when *de jure* segregation had prevented black and white students from associating at all.

Central High's only African-American senior in 1958—of the nine who had dared to desegregate the school—had been Ernest Green. He had gone on to earn a master's degree at Michigan State and to become a managing director of Lehman Brothers, a major investments firm. He had contributed to the Democratic party and become acquainted with President Bill Clinton, who flew to Little Rock in 1997 for ceremonies commemorating the forty years since Governor Faubus had tried to stop desegregation. Green rode with Clinton on *Air Force One*.

Green's eight black schoolmates had also attended colleges and universities. All but one had left Little Rock and said in 1997 that they were glad they had challenged racial segregation. Their experiences, while bruising, had not left scars. Elizabeth Eckford appeared to be an exception. In 1997, she was unemployed and lived in Little Rock. When asked if she felt good about what she had done, she said, "Absolutely not. Positively not." She complained that her oldest child had had to be bused ten miles so as to promote better racial balance in the district. She added, "There was a time when I thought integration was one of the most desired things. . . . I appreciate blackness more than I did then."[6]

In New Orleans, where Ruby Bridges had braved abusive crowds in 1960 in order to attend a white school, race relations were calmer in the 1990s. Bridges had graduated from the city's increasingly black public schools and gone on to take business courses and work as a travel agent.

Forty years after the struggles over integration at Little Rock, President Bill Clinton greeted members of the "Little Rock Nine," at an anniversary ceremony in September 1997. Pictured (*l. to r.*) are Terrence Roberts, Jefferson Thomas, Minnijean Brown Trickey, and Thelma Mothershed Wair. *(AP/WideWorld photo)*

By 1992, as Ruby Bridges-Hall, she was the mother of four children. Using royalties from a book about her experience, she set up the Ruby Bridges Educational Foundation, which gave grants to inner-city schools for art education. She also returned to her old elementary school—all-black by 1992—as a volunteer. Bridges-Hall, too, seemed proud of her efforts and unscarred by her travails. The city's school board, meanwhile, decided to rechristen any school that had been named after a slaveowner or after someone who had not supported equal opportunity for all. Two dozen schools were to receive new names, including one that had been called George Washington.[7]

Anecdotal examples such as these highlight a few legacies of judicial decisions concerning race and schools in the decades since *Brown* in 1954. Some of these outcomes suggested progress toward desegregation in public education; others obviously did not.

A number of scholars kept the faith in court action that optimists had expressed immediately after *Brown* and had reiterated following decisions such as *Green* in 1968 and *Swann* in 1971. In 1975, for instance, Richard Kluger, who wrote a magisterial book about *Brown*, said that the decision "represented nothing short of a reconsecration of American ideals." It showed, he said, that the United States stood for more than anticommunism or material abundance. Four years later, J. Harvie Wilkinson, author of another thoughtful book on the subject, wrote that *Brown* had been the "catalyst that shook up Congress and culminated in the two major Civil Rights acts of the century." Glowing appraisals such as these were harder to find in the more dispirited 1990s, but Aldon Morris, a historian of civil rights, concluded in 1993 that with *Brown* "a significant chunk of the symbolic pillar of white supremacy crumbled." The decision, he said, enabled blacks to believe that it was possible to bring down the "entire edifice of Jim Crow."[8]

Many Americans in the 1990s, however, shared the gloom of Linda Brown-Thompson and Elizabeth Eckford. Robert Carter, Marshall's one-time aide, wrote in 1994 that "for most black children, *Brown*'s constitutional guarantee of equal educational opportunity has been an arid abstraction, having no effect whatever on the educational offerings black children are given or the deteriorating schools they attend." A still bitter Kenneth Clark, when asked in 1995, "what is the best thing for blacks to call themselves?" answered, "white." Four years later Gary Orfield, a prominent scholar concerned with segregation in schools, lamented, "We are clearly in a period when many policy makers, courts, and opinion makers assume that desegregation is no longer necessary, or that it will be accomplished somehow without need of any deliberate planning."[9]

As earlier, there was ample reason for liberal laments like these. The civil rights movement continued to be weak and fragmented in the 1990s. In 1996 California voters approved Proposition 209, which barred affirmative action in state university admissions, hiring, or public contracting. Voters in the state of Washington favored a similar referendum in 1998. Then and later, race-based admissions procedures faced serious court challenges in many other states. Most liberals, of course, still asserted the virtues of affirmative action. Undaunted, they managed to pass laws and devise procedures that minimized the impact, at least in the short run, of these conservative court decisions and referenda. Their moves in turn, unsettled many whites and Asian Americans whose academic test scores were generally superior to those of blacks and Hispanics. Overall, however, proponents of affirmative action remained on the defensive at the turn of the century.[10]

Advocates of desegregation especially deplored the continuing conservatism of the Supreme Court under Chief Justice Rehnquist. As in the 1980s and early 1990s, a narrow majority of the justices chipped away at affirmative action. And the justices did little to promote integration in the offices where they worked. The nine on the bench in 1998 had hired a total of 394 clerks during their time on the court. Of these clerks, seven had been black, four Hispanic, and eighteen Asian-American. Rehnquist and three of his colleagues had never taken on an African-American clerk. Only one graduate of Howard University Law School, where Thurgood Marshall and many of his fellow attorneys on the Defense Fund had learned their craft, had ever been named as a clerk. There were no black clerks in October 1998, when more than 1,000 protestors massed outside the Court building. Chanting "No Justice, No Peace," they struggled to deliver the resumés of minority lawyers. Nineteen demonstrators, including NAACP head Kweisi Mfume, were arrested.[11]

Robert Carter's pessimism about the education of blacks was also understandable, in part because the resources of America's schools still differed greatly across districts. As in the past, wealthy suburban areas— most of them overwhelmingly white in makeup—tended to offer far more in the way of facilities and quality instruction than did poorer districts, many of which were heavily populated by minorities. The persistence of such inequality, rooted in class as well as racial cleavages, revealed the chasm that often separated the rhetoric of equality of educational opportunity in America from the reality of it.[12]

America's inability to desegregate many of its neighborhoods and schools, moreover, stood out in the early twenty-first century as the largest failure among efforts—most of them more successful—to move toward greater interracial mixing. Classrooms in many big cities, notably in the Northeast and Midwest, were still overwhelmingly black and Hispanic. In 1998–99, 90 percent of public school students in Chicago were African American or Latino; 83 percent lived in poverty-stricken households. In Detroit, 90 percent of public school students were black and 70 percent were poor enough to qualify for free school lunches; more than one-half of the city's students did not graduate from high school. Mayors in both cities despaired of their school boards, which seemed unable to promote academic progress (or in some schools, to ensure discipline or safety), and assumed control of public education. Many other cities considered the same therapy, even though there was little strong evidence to suggest that mayoral doctoring would cure the ills of their schools.

By the beginning of the new century there was special reason for civil rights activists to worry about resegregation. The trend encouraged by decisions such as *Dowell* (1991) and *Jenkins* (1995) seemed to accelerate in the late 1990s, to affect Latinos as well as blacks, and to involve southern as well as northern areas. Some of the larger school districts—including Cleveland, Dallas, Denver, Minneapolis, Buffalo, Nashville, Grand Rapids, Jacksonville, Mobile as well as Prince George County, Virginia, and Wilmington, Delaware—were allowed by judges in the late 1990s to phase out or terminate court supervision.

For this and other reasons, notably white flight and segregation of housing, racial mixing in schools was showing an overall national decline by the late 1990s. In 1999 Gary Orfield and his colleagues estimated that in 1972–73 (following the encouraging burst of desegregation after *Swann*), 63.6 percent of black public school pupils had gone to schools where less than half the student body was white. Similar percentages had persisted until the late 1980s. By 1996–97, however, this percentage had increased to 68.8. Many suburbs, among the fastest growing areas in the nation, also seemed to be breaking apart along racial lines: in 1996–97 the typical African-American child residing in the suburbs of a large metropolitan region went to a school in which 60 percent of students were nonwhite. The luminous star of racial mixing in schools had dimmed.[13]

Lawsuits in the late 1990s further troubled proponents of desegregation. In San Francisco, a Chinese-American parent threatened legal action when his fourteen-year-old son was denied admission to Lowell High, an academically well-regarded school. His lawyers turned the tables on Marshall's arguments in *Brown* by maintaining that the use of racial classifications in assignment of students to public schools violated the equal protection clause of the Fourteenth Amendment. The city's school board managed to avoid the suit in 1999 when it agreed to drop race-based admissions procedures. Though the board said that it would seek racial diversity through other means, it seemed clear that efforts by liberals to achieve considerable racial balance had a dim future in the city.[14]

Litigation also exposed racial divisions in Boston, which was still try-ing to recover from the battles over busing that had bruised the city twenty-five years earlier. A white parent accused the school board of racial discrimination when the prestigious Boston Latin School did not admit his daughter. Her test scores were higher than those of many minority students who were accepted. A host of people—not all of them conservatives—rallied to her side, asking in effect whether Earl Warren and his colleagues had intended a legacy such as this. In November 1998 a federal court agreed with them and struck down the Latin School's affirmative action procedures. City school officials, fearing to invite an adverse Supreme Court ruling that would be binding nationwide, de-cided not to appeal. In July 1999 the school board voted to drop racial considerations in pupil placements. The mayor, meanwhile, said that he would try to build more schools in heavily minority neighborhoods. No one imagined that nonsegregated education had much promise in the Hub, an increasingly nonwhite city.[15]

Integrationists found litigation in Charlotte particularly disturbing. The Charlotte-Mecklenburg district, after all, had complied with the *Swann* decision in 1971, which had sanctioned busing to achieve better racial balance. To many people, the city thereafter seemed to be a model community. As in San Francisco and Boston, however, a white parent complained that the city had discriminated against his daughter by de-nying her admittance (via lottery) to a magnet school. Other white par-ents joined him. In September 1999 a federal judge concluded that local school officials had done all they could to abolish the vestiges of *de jure* segregation and ordered an end to race-based busing in the city. Inte-grationists, maintaining that discrimination persisted, lamented that the court was dismantling nearly thirty years of effort.[16]

What especially troubled advocates of desegregated education at the turn of the century was their sense that federal court decisions, including those from the Supreme Court, were closing the door to virtually all strategies aimed at elevating the value of racial balance in the schools. What quest for racial diversity, if any, might pass constitutional muster? Feeling vulnerable, desegregationists often feared to go to court or to appeal when they lost.

Widely noted ligitation involving Montgomery County, Maryland greatly intensified these feelings of vulnerability in 2000. Hoping to preserve racial balance at an elementary school where white enrollment was declining, county officials adopted a policy in 1998 that no student could transfer out of a school if the transfer would adversely affect racial diversity, unless the student could prove some sort of unique "personal hardship." A white parent who sought to send his kindergartener to a magnet school complained, whereupon the federal court of appeals for the fourth circuit in Virginia struck down the county's policy. The Constitution, said the court, prohibited "racial balancing" from being used as the decisive factor in school assignments.

The county then appealed to the Supreme Court, which in March 2000 let the decision stand. The National School Boards Association (which had filed a brief supporting the county) said it was "profoundly disappointed" that the justices would not hear the case. It added that "education attorneys advising the 15,000 school districts across the country still remain in the dark as to what constitutional standard applies when dealing with this issue."[17]

The dismay of descgregationists was fully understandable. For the Court's refusal to intervene indicated that it tended to value parental choice over strategies that seriously tried to ensure racial diversity. As in *Dowell* (1991) and *Jenkins* (1995), its most recent statements on the subject, the Rehnquist Court remained cool indeed toward tougher enforcement of desegregation of America's schools.

Results of various standardized educational test scores further discouraged proponents of educational desegregation in the new century.[18] As was well known by then, scores for blacks had risen slowly between 1970 and the late 1980s, and gaps in scores that separated blacks and whites had narrowed. These were heartening results. But the gaps remained huge. And they widened again in the 1990s, when scores for whites grew faster than those for blacks.[19] The gaps, moreover, seemed mystifyingly intractable as of the new century. They did not seem to be narrowing within districts where compensatory education programs (still receiving $7.7 billion in 1999–2000) were important to funding. Nor did they appear to stem from differences in the physical resources available to predominantly black and predominantly white schools within given districts: as James Coleman had discovered as early as 1966, intradistrict funding per pupil, white or black, did not differ significantly in most places. Even the extent of racial mixing within schools also did not seem to affect the gaps—blacks in schools with fairly well-mixed student populations tended to read a little better at age nine than blacks in more segregated schools, but to do no better in math, and they lost the small gains they had made in reading by the time they reached junior high school. [20]

Social class and parental educational levels also did not do much to explain the gaps in scores. Most black students from relatively well-off families, like blacks from poorer families, continued (*vis-à-vis* whites from families with comparable incomes and educational backgrounds) to score poorly on many of these tests. Black children from families in the top income bracket ($70,000 and up) actually did a little worse on Scholastic Aptitude Test (SAT) verbals, and considerably worse on SAT mathematics tests, in 1994 than white students from the poorest income brackets. And family structures did not seem to matter: black children from single-parent homes scored no lower on the average than black children in two-parent families of comparable class standing.

The conclusions from data like these were sobering indeed. As of the new century it seemed depressingly clear that the considerable increases in educational levels and income among blacks since World War II and *Brown* had not brought about the degree of relative improvement in black academic achievement that many optimists had expected would occur among younger generations of African Americans.[21]

Why, then, do these gaps persist? Some observers think that they stem in part from flaws in the tests. They say accurately that many of the widely used standardized tests measure a relatively narrow range of talents, rewarding students who are quick readers and problem solvers. [22] Critics of these tests further maintain (although unconvincingly) that questions measuring verbal skills tend to be greatly biased against minorities. Critics, finally, point out that many wealthy students pay for prep courses that help them do better on SATs, thereby widening the gap between their scores and those of poorer students, including African Americans. SATs continue to be used, many critics lament, mainly because admissions officers at many of the most selective colleges and universities—a small minority of higher education institutions in the United States—seek additional guidance to help them choose among the hordes of applicants who appear qualified.[23]

Other people who try to account for test score gaps take a historical view that emphasizes the power of racist oppression. Some blame the dark shadow of slavery, when most blacks were forbidden to learn to read, as well as racial and social class isolation stemming from long-standing discrimination and residential segregation.[24] The poverty rate for blacks, continues to be three times as high as that for whites. Average black incomes still hover at around two-thirds of white incomes.[25] Anticipating dim futures such as these, why would black students, especially lower-class students, strive hard for academic excellence? Many observers also deplore the persistence (though in somewhat weakened form) of a historically powerful racist preconception among many whites—that blacks are fit for brawn work, whites for brain work. This stereotype, it is plausibly believed, continues to appeal to a number of whites, including teachers, who expect too little academic achievement from blacks, and to damage blacks, some of whom are said to absorb these low expectations and give up trying.

Students of the gaps suggest a range of specific remedies. One rests on the obvious fact that a number of predominantly black schools, while generally equal in financial resources to predominantly white schools within a given district, are far from equal to many wealthy schools in middle-class, white-dominated towns and suburbs. Because relatively few black students go to these white schools, they are at a competitive disadvantage. Stuck in unequal schools, they are likely to score less well, on the average, on standardized tests. A remedy, therefore, would be to reconfigure state and federal aid to education formulas so as to provide still more compensatory education and other forms of academic assistance to schools in low-income towns and cities. Such an effort would lessen the cross-district inequality of educational resources that the decision in *Rodriguez* (1973) had refused to challenge.

Other proposed remedies also stem from this same assumption: that the key to narrowing gaps in academic achievement is to upgrade schools that are heavily attended by minorities. One calls for considerable reassignment of teachers within districts: predominantly black schools, critics point out, are still less likely than largely white schools to have teachers with strong educational backgrounds and high test scores. Another recommendation is to fight for still smaller classes for black students; learning in small groups is generally thought to make a considerable difference.[26] Reformers also urge other efforts to improve the schools: battling against peer pressures, which have led some black students to accuse their academically ambitious black classmates of "acting white"; expanding mentoring groups, in which bright high schoolers tutor minority junior high school students; developing test preparation courses for minorities; "clustering" minorities in advanced courses so as to reduce their feelings of racial isolation; offering greater support for after-school and summer programs that focus on cognitive development; and—a key—doing everything possible to raise academic standards.[27]

Helpful though some of these school-based reforms would be, scholars are surely correct to emphasize that the gaps start when children are very young—before they get to school. Black children, for instance, are more likely than white children to bring severe academic and behavioral problems with them to the first grade. They have far smaller vocabularies, on the average, than white children do at that age. It follows, these reformers maintain, that schools with pupils such as these need more than equality of resources. They require considerably greater support per child than do other schools.

It also follows, however—as Coleman had emphasized in 1966—that better financed schools alone may not go far to close the gaps, which stem from deeper social and cultural forces that badly affect the cognitive development of very young black children. For this reason, America would very probably do well to strengthen the cognitive content of programs such as Head Start and to invest heavily in day-long, year-long child care and *pre*school programs that would concentrate on stimulating the cognitive development of all children—or at least of all poor children—beginning at age three.[28]

None of these explanations for test score gaps, however, fully satisfies scholars who have studied the question. Stephan and Abigail Thernstrom, who explored the issue, speculated in 1997 that rising levels of urban violence associated with the spread of crack cocaine in central cities may have depressed black scores in the early 1990s. They also thought that many educators of black children, especially those of an Afrocentric persuasion, were guilty of "dumbing down" the curriculum. But the Thernstroms did not really know what was happening to scores in the 1990s. They conceded, "We're stumped."[29]

A year later, Christopher Jencks and Meredith Phillips edited a book of essays on the problem, in which they argued that the gaps—environmental, not genetic in origin—could be narrowed, perhaps significantly. More desegregation of schools, they speculated, might help a little to close the gulf. They also called for smaller classes and for assignment to minority schools of teachers with high test scores. Like Coleman three decades earlier, they looked primarily to parental and community efforts, not to better financed school resources, for improvement in the cognitive skills of black children. But they, too, conceded that they did not fully understand the reasons for the gaps. In 1999 they confessed that they had "hardly more than hunches about the causes of the black/white test gap."[30]

Why dwell on these gaps? One answer is that they have large and long-range social and economic consequences, because academic achievement and credentials have become vitally important in modern American society. So long as these gaps persist they will slow the mobility of African Americans who yearn to do well in school, go to college, and advance in life. Jencks and Phillips argue cogently that "reducing the black-white test score gap would do more to move America toward racial equality than any politically plausible alternative."[31]

A second answer is that parents are deeply aware of the gaps. Until the gaps close, a number of white people will continue to believe that blacks are less intelligent. Many people (including some African Americans) will remain cool to school desegregation, let alone of strategies like busing, if these approaches do not seem to have beneficial academic effects. Like Thurgood Marshall, like the parents who embarked on "bright flight" from Montclair, they will send their kids to schools— that is, heavily white schools—that promise to give their children a competitive edge in life.

Deeply concerned about these problems, proponents of school desegregation continue to fight their good fight. The gaps, they predict, will narrow as more and educated parents come to emphasize the value of imparting strong cognitive skills to their very young children. Significant academic progress among marginalized groups, they remind us, takes time. They insist also that desegregation involves more than *academic* issues. Americans, they declare, have a moral obligation to fight against racial segregation and inequality in public education. These advocates especially celebrate the *social* virtues of racial mixing and diversity. As Thurgood Marshall had done, they argue that desegregation, especially of such formative influences as schools, can help to break down ugly stereotypes, to promote interracial understanding, and—in time—to nudge the nation toward integration. Backsliding from the goal of racial mixing in schools would therefore be catastrophic. As Jencks wrote in 1998, segregation and resegregation "lead to the general erosion of social ties in society. The more you let society pull itself apart, the less commitment the haves have to the have-nots."[32]

Advocates such as these accurately emphasize that racial discrimination in housing, which reflects class as well as racial divisions, still feeds the roots of school segregation. It is vital, therefore, to combat such discrimination, which as in the past stems from public policies as well as from private actions. Orfield, for instance, has applauded activists who take minority families on trips to suburbs so as to encourage them to move out of the inner city. Like others, he has praised the Gautreaux experiment in the Chicago area, which has subsidized interracial public housing in white suburbs. The key to advancing desegregation in schools, he points out, is to promote and preserve stable, desegregated communities. Once parents and children feel secure in such surroundings, they will rally—as some have done in Montclair, New Jersey, and other places—behind their neighborhoods and their schools. Proposals such as these assert two important truths: school desegregation requires vigilant, unending community commitment from whites as well as blacks, and it depends on larger structural reforms, especially in housing arrangements.[33]

But how to implement these various ideas for reform? In what ways, for instance, can well-meaning "outsiders" get parents, especially those who are poor and over-burdened, to engage more consistently in those key activities—reading regularly to their children, seriously encouraging their creative tendencies, taking them on intellectually liberating excursions—that are vital to early cognitive development? How many white people can be mobilized to storm the barricades of housing segregation? How can school superintendents move their teachers to demand more of students? What would induce white taxpayers to support a vast and expensive preschool and summer school network that would primarily benefit minorities?[34] And why would taxpayers agree to reconfigured formulas of school aid that would direct more of their money to controversial federal programs such as compensatory education? Many Americans, indeed, continue to believe strongly that education must be a local matter. Like Justice Powell in his *Rodriguez* decision, they are convinced that faraway federal and state bureaucrats cannot understand the needs of communities.

Since the 1960s, moreover, no substantial lead for change in race relations has come from the federal government. In the 1990s neither Congress nor the Clinton administration did much to combat segregation in schools or housing. And a majority of the American people, as skeptical as ever since the late 1960s about the capacity of government to do good things, still seem content with the "benign neglect" of the civil rights agenda that President Nixon had agreed to in the early 1970s. They have not applied strong pressure on public officials.[35]

So it is that many African Americans, resenting these attitudes, understandably blame whites for the persistence of racially segregated and unequal schools. They feel no guilt—no great responsibility—for the barriers that since the 1960s have blocked their once grand expectations. Many therefore conclude that further fights for desegregated schools, especially those that depend on complicated, expensive, and slow-moving litigation, are no longer worth the effort. With varying degrees of resignation, resentment, and rage, they live with a good deal of separate-but-equal within districts, so long as it is truly equal and not *de jure*, especially if they can have a major hand in running their own schools.[36]

For blacks like these—and many others—the "wonderful world of possibilities" that Ralph Ellison had dared to anticipate in 1954 has seemed to become an all-too-distant dream by the onset of the twenty-first century.

These, then, were some of the reasons that advocates of racial justice such as Carter and Clark had grown pessimistic. They were valid reasons, for stalemates that had developed since the brighter years of the 1960s still stymied the lengthy agendas of most civil rights leaders at the turn of the century.[37] But Clark and others like him, their expectations dashed, tended to downplay the extent of changes in race relations since *Brown*. These, to repeat, have been large. The many developments promoting progress for blacks since the 1950s—mass migrations out of the poverty-stricken rural South, the inspiring civil rights movement, strong and well-enforced federal civil rights laws, significant economic growth, wide expansion of public education, more liberal white attitudes, memorable court decisions—vastly improved the legal and socioeconomic status of black people, including millions who by the 1960s were moving into the middle classes and sending their children to colleges and universities. Many of these impressive gains remained real—apparently permanent—at the turn of the twenty-first century.[38] Moreover, few people in this new century would abandon the goals of *Brown*, let alone endorse the return of state-sponsored racial segregation.[39] As if rooted in sand, the ugly institutions of Jim Crow had finally collapsed.

Robert Carter and others nonetheless ask: to what extent was *Brown* responsible for these considerable improvements? The answer to this question remains impossible to pin down. On the one hand, we can agree that the decision did not quickly transform race relations in public education. For many years, *Brown* promoted little change in schools outside some of the border regions. Only in the late 1960s, when the Civil Rights Act of 1964; court decisions like *Jefferson*, *Green*, and *Alexander*; and firm federal enforcement attacked evasion that had persisted under the guise of "all deliberate speed," did white Southerners begin to comply. Potentially explosive racial tensions nonetheless simmered thereafter in cities like Selma, and highly segregated schools persisted in heavily black areas such as Summerton. *De facto* segregation thrived in many cities, especially large metropolitan areas with substantial African-American populations. It survived also in thousands of towns and suburbs, in the North as well as in the South. Court decisions and other governmental efforts finally did destroy *de jure* segregation—a huge achievement—but *de facto* segregation was, and is, another story.

We also need to qualify claims, such as Wilkinson's, that *Brown* touched off the spark that ignited the more militant civil rights movement of the 1960s. To be sure, the decision aroused feelings of guilt and responsibility among many liberally inclined whites. The ruling also spurred a number of activists to demonstrate—activists such as the four students who launched the electrifying sit-ins in Greensboro. Blacks who accelerated the movement took heart from knowing that the High Court, at last, was bravely on their side. But the expanding civil rights movement of the 1960s also depended on the many other powerful social and economic sources noted above, most of which had helped to inspire *Brown* itself. A more militant civil rights movement, even in the absence of a decision such as *Brown*, seems in retrospect to have been highly likely by the 1960s.

Yet *Brown* is far more than a footnote to the history of race relations in the postwar era. After all, the decision took aim at the heart of constitutionally sanctioned Jim Crow—segregated public education. Once enforced at last, Warren's ruling did help to desegregate many American schools, especially in the border states and the South. And it greatly stimulated the transformation of the Court. Energized by their boldness in 1954, the justices pursued a liberal, activist course, especially in the 1960s, that profoundly affected American jurisprudence. The Burger Court, too, briefly felt obliged to protect and to extend the Warren Court's rulings regarding race and schools. And passionately committed liberal bureaucrats and judges, inspired by the civil rights revolution and the Court, ensured that these rulings would continue to make a difference. Even in the 1980s and 1990s, when conservative Court rulings began to proliferate, the liberal jurisprudence set in motion by the Warren Court—especially by the example of *Brown*—still mattered to many of these judges and officials. Their responses sustained a larger rights-consciousness that deeply influenced American law and life throughout much of the late twentieth century.[40]

Some of these responses, of course, called for major reforms—not only of race relations, but also of criminal justice, welfare administration, and management of civil liberties, among many other matters—that majorities of democratically elected congressmen and state legislators normally opposed. Court-ordered busing, never popular, often aroused furious controversy. Was it appropriate that nonelected, life-tenured justices and judges—or appointed federal bureaucrats—should so greatly affect the lives of a democratic people? Apostles of judicial restraint generally thought not. From Felix Frankfurter and John Marshall Harlan in the 1950s to Potter Stewart and Byron White in the 1970s and 1980s, and to the conservatives on the Rehnquist Court at the turn of the century, they often assailed the "judge-made law" of Earl Warren, William Brennan, Thurgood Marshall, and their interventionist ilk on the lower courts. But advocates of judicial restraint, too, sometimes concluded that the courts—comparatively isolated as they are from popular attitudes— had to challenge oppressive racial practices. Thus it was in 1954 that the Supreme Court, acting alone, unanimously took the bold and fateful step of assailing *de jure* segregation in the public schools.

Richard Kluger, finally, was on target when he wrote that *Brown* enabled a "reconsecration of American ideals"—ideals of justice and equality that outshone contemporary goals such as anticommunism and material prosperity. This reconsecration by the highest court in the land had considerable, though incalculable, symbolic value, for liberal whites as well as for many hopeful blacks. To be sure, *Brown* called for changes that the Court by itself could not enforce. In time, however, some of these changes came to pass, even in schools, those most highly sensitive of institutions. And it was the courts, aided powerfully by civil rights activists, civil rights acts, and federal officials, that stepped forward to give these changes constitutional standing.

Jack Greenberg, a thoughtful observer of the role of law in American life, has come as close as anyone to assessing the influence of *Brown*, and by extension the capacity of the Court to affect American society. It is a cautiously positive appraisal that credits the role of the judiciary but that also recognizes the necessity of greater popular and governmental engagement on behalf of racial justice if the grand expectations of 1954 and the 1960s are ever to be realized. In 1994 he wrote, "Altogether, school desegregation has been a story of conspicuous achievements, flawed by marked failures, the causes of which lie beyond the capacity of lawyers to correct. Lawyers can do right, they can do good, but they have their limits. The rest of the job is up to society."[41]

Appendix I
KEY CASES

Below is a chronological list of the most important Supreme Court decisions discussed in this book. They may be found in *United States Reports* (Washington, 1790–). The first number in each case listed below is the volume number of these reports; the second number is the page in that volume on which the decision begins.

Plessy v. Ferguson, 163 U.S. 537 (1896)
Cumming v. Richmond County Board of Education, 175 U.S. 528 (1899)
Gong Lum v. Rice, 275 U.S. 78 (1927)
Missouri ex rel. Gaines v. Canada, 305 U.S. 337 (1938)
Sweatt v. Painter, 339 U.S. 629 (1950)
McLaurin v. Oklahoma State Regents for Higher Education, 339 U.S. 637 (1950)
Henderson v. United States, 339 U.S. 816 (1950)
Brown v. Board of Education of Topeka, 347 U.S. 483 (1954)
Bolling v. Sharpe, 347 U.S. 497 (1954)
Brown v. Board of Education of Topeka, 349 U.S. 294 (1955)—"*Brown II*"
Naim v. Naim, 350 U.S. 891 (1955)
NAACP v. Alabama ex rel. Patterson, 357 U.S. 449 (1958)
Cooper v. Aaron, 358 U.S. 1 (1958)
Shuttlesworth v. Birmingham Board of Education, 358 U.S. 101 (1958)
Griffin v. County School Board of Prince Edward Co., 377 U.S. 218 (1964)
Loving v. Virginia, 388 U.S. 1 (1967)
Green v. County School Board of New Kent County, Va., 391 U.S. 430 (1968)
Alexander v. Holmes County Board of Education, 396 U.S. 19 (1969)
Swann v. Charlotte-Mecklenburg County Board of Education, 402 U.S. 1 (1971)
San Antonio Independent School District v. Rodriguez, 411 U.S. 1 (1973)
Keyes v. Denver School District No. 1, 413 U.S. 921 (1973)
Milliken v. Bradley, 418 U.S. 717 (1974)
Pasadena City Board of Education v. Spangler, 427 U.S. 424 (1976)

University of California Regents v. Bakke, 438 U.S. 265 (1978)
Board of Education of Oklahoma City v. Dowell, 489 U.S. 237 (1991)
Freeman v. Pitts, 503 U.S. 467 (1992)
United States v. Fordice, Governor of Mississippi, 505 U.S. 717 (1992)
Missouri v. Jenkins, 515 U.S. 1139 (1995)

Appendix II
TABLES AND FIGURES

TABLE 1
Percentage of Whites Giving Pro-Integration Responses, 1942–1963

"White students and Negro students should go to the same schools."

	Total	South	North
1942	30	2	40
1956	49	15	61
1963	62	31	73

There should not be "separate sections for Negroes on streetcars and buses."

1942	44	4	57
1956	60	27	73
1963	79	52	89

Would not make any difference to them if
"a Negro with the same income and education as you moved into your block."

1942	35	12	42
1956	51	38	58
1963	64	51	70

Source: From Stephan Thernstrom and Abigail Thernstrom, *America in Black and White: One Nation, Indivisible* (New York, 1997), 141.

FIGURE 1

Percentage of Black Students in 50-100% Minority* Schools and 90-100% Minority Schools, 1968-1996

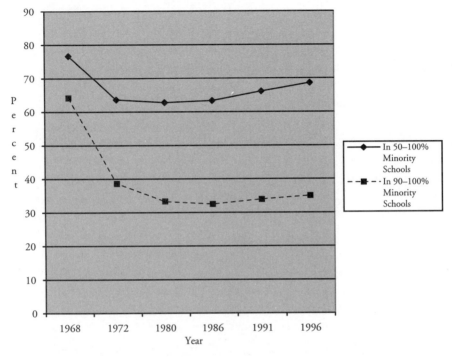

*Includes Latinos, Asian Americans, and Native Americans, as well as African Americans.

Source: Adapted from Gary Orfield and John Yun, Civil Rights Project, Harvard University, *Resegregation in American Schools* (Cambridge, Mass., 1999), 31.

FIGURE 2

Percentage of Black Students Attending Majority White Schools in the South, 1954–1996

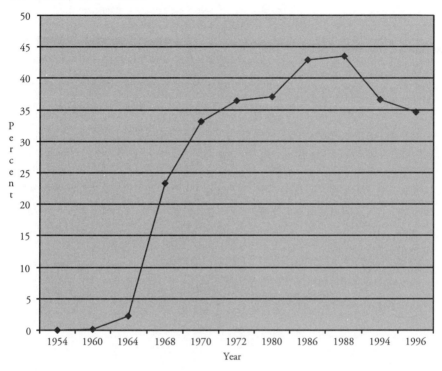

Source: Adapted from Gary Orfield and John Yun, Civil Rights Project, Harvard University, *Resegregation in American Schools* (Cambridge, Mass., 1999), 29.

TABLE 2
Measures of Desegregation, 1968–1992

	U.S.	South	Northeast	Midwest	West
Percentage of black students in schools more than 90 percent minority					
1968	62.9	77.5	42.7	58.0	50.9
1980	34.8	24.6	48.7	43.6	33.9
1992	34.1	26.5	49.9	39.4	26.6
Percentage of white students in schools 90 percent white					
1968	77.8	68.8	82.5	89.4	61.4
1980	60.9	32.2	79.5	81.0	40.0
1992	48.9	26.0	66.7	71.9	26.7

Source: From Stephan Thernstrom and Abigail Thernstrom, *America in Black and White: One Nation, Indivisible* (New York, 1997), 341.

TABLE 3
College Attendance and Completion Rates for Persons 25–29 Years of Age, by Race, 1965–1995

	Black	White	B/W Ratio	Black	White	B/W Ratio
	Percentage who had attended college			*Percentage who had completed 4 or more years*		
1965	15.2	26.2	58	6.8	13.0	52
1970	17.2	32.8	52	7.3	17.3	42
1975	27.6	42.8	64	10.7	22.8	47
1980	32.8	46.2	71	11.7	23.7	49
1985	34.4	44.5	77	11.5	23.2	50
1990	36.0	45.3	79	13.4	24.2	55
1995	44.9	55.4	81	15.3	26.0	59

Source: From Stephan Thernstrom and Abigail Thernstrom, *America in Black and White: One Nation, Indivisible* (New York, 1997), 391.

TABLE 4
Racial Patterns in Enrollment of the Largest Central City School Districts by Race and Ethnicity, 1996–97

City	Enrollment	% White	% Black	% Latino	% Asian
New York	1,062,016	16.1	36.1	37.3	10.0
Los Angeles	667,305	11.0	14.0	68.0	6.7
Chicago	421,334	10.5	54.1	32.1	3.2
Miami-Dade	341,090	13.5	33.6	51.5	1.3
Philadelphia	212,150	19.8	64.0	11.6	4.7
Houston	209,375	11.1	34.3	51.8	2.8
Detroit	187,590	5.2	90.1	2.8	1.0
Dallas	154,847	11.0	41.5	45.5	1.7
San Diego	133,687	29.3	16.9	34.4	18.7
Memphis	111,140	15.1	86.6	0.7	1.4
Baltimore	108,759	13.4	85.1	0.4	0.5
Milwaukee	101,007	22.2	60.1	12.5	3.6
Albuquerque	88,886	44.2	3.6	46.2	1.8
New Orleans	85,064	5.5	90.7	1.3	2.5
Washington, D.C.	78,553	3.9	87.3	7.2	1.4
Fresno	78,470	22.8	11.1	43.6	21.7
Austin	76,054	37.7	18.0	41.7	2.2
Fort Worth	75,813	25.9	33.2	38.4	2.3
Cleveland	74,026	20.6	70.4	7.7	1.0

Source: From Gary Orfield and John Yun, Civil Rights Project, Harvard University, *Resegregation in American Schools* (Cambridge, Mass., 1999), 9.

TABLE 5
Percentages of a Typical Black Student's Classmates that are Likely to be White 1989–90 and 1997–98

	1997-98	1989-90	Change		1997-98	1989-90	Change
U.S. average	32.4%	34.7%	-2.3	New Mexico	42.4%	46.0%	-3.6
Northeast	25.2	26.4	-1.2	Virginia	43.7	—	—
Midwest	29.8	31.7	-1.9	Arizona	44.3	49.8	-5.5
South	35.4	38.7	-3.3	Oklahoma	45.0	50.9	-5.9
West	31.7	35.2	-3.5	Rhode Island	45.0	53.8	-8.8
New York	18.4	20.4	-2.0	Indiana	45.0	46.7	-1.7
Michigan	19.5	21.2	-1.7	Colorado	45.8	53.8	-8.0
Illinois	19.7	20.0	-0.3	Nevada	46.0	64.0	-18.1
California	24.5	28.0	-3.5	Minnesota	46.0	61.2	-15.2
Maryland	25.5	30.2	-4.8	North Carolina	46.3	51.2	-4.8
New Jersey	26.1	25.9	+0.2	Kansas	53.5	58.7	-5.2
Mississippi	27.2	30.2	-3.0	Nebraska	57.0	63.7	-6.7
Louisiana	28.4	33.1	-4.8	Delaware	58.2	65.6	-7.4
Pennsylvania	30.2	31.6	-1.4	Washington	59.1	63.8	-4.7
Texas	30.9	35.7	-4.8	Oregon	59.7	61.3	-1.6

State			
Wisconsin	31.0	40.9	−9.9
Alabama	31.6	35.1	−3.5
Georgia	32.3	—	—
Connecticut	33.6	35.5	−1.9
Hawaii	35.1	37.7	−2.6
Ohio	35.6	42.2	−6.6
Missouri	36.8	—	—
Florida	37.8	43.9	−6.1
Arkansas	39.4	45.0	−5.6
South Carolina	40.0	42.0	−2.0
Tennessee	41.1	35.8	+5.4
Massachusetts	41.2	45.9	−4.7
Alaska	60.5	68.0	−7.5
Kentucky	67.7	72.2	−4.5
Iowa	72.7	77.1	−4.3
Utah	77.2	82.9	−5.8
West Virginia	78.4	78.7	−0.3
Wyoming	81.2	—	—
South Dakota	84.2	—	—
Montana	87.4	—	—
North Dakota	87.7	86.8	+0.8
New Hampshire	91.8	93.0	−1.2
Maine	92.9	—	—
Vermont	94.1	97.8	−3.6

Source: New York Times, April 2, 2000

TABLE 6

Mean Scores of 17-Year-Olds by Race, and the Racial
Gap Between Blacks and Whites in Years, National
Assessment of Educational Progress, 1970–1994

	Black	White	Gap in Years
Reading			
1971	239	291	5.9
1980	243	293	6.0
1988	274	295	2.5
1990	267	297	3.4
1994	266	296	3.9
Mathematics			
1973	270	310	4.3
1982	272	304	4.1
1986	279	308	3.4
1990	289	310	2.5
1994	286	312	3.4
Science			
1970	258	312	4.7
1982	235	293	7.1
1986	253	298	4.4
1990	253	301	5.7
1994	257	306	5.4
Writing			
1984	270	297	3.1
1988	275	296	2.1
1990	268	293	2.3
1994	267	291	3.3

Source: From Stephan Thernstrom and Abigail Thernstrom, *America in Black and White: One Nation, Indivisible* (New York, 1997), 355.

TABLE 7

Current Expenditure per Pupil in Public
Elementary and Secondary Schools:
1919-20 to 1996-97[1]

School year	Expenditure per pupil in average daily attendance (constant 1996-97 dollars)[2]
1919–20	$445
1929–30	805
1939–40	1,002
1949–50	1,411
1959–60	2,029
1965–66	2,678
1971–72	3,822
1976–77	4,434
1981–82	4,603
1986–87	5,672
1991–92	6,233
1996–97	6,564

Source: Adapted from National Center for Education Statistics, U.S. Department of Education, *Digest of Education Statistics, 1997* (Washington, D.C., 1998), 172.

[1]The term "current expenditures" excludes public funding for adult education, community colleges, private school programs funded by local and state education agencies, and community services.

[2]Constant dollars are based on the Consumer Price Index, prepared by the Bureau of Labor Statistics, U.S. Department of Labor, adjusted to a school-year basis.

NOTES

Preface

1   Jack Slater, "1954 Revisited," *Ebony*, 29 (May 1974), 126.
2   *Time*, Sept. 19, 1955, 27. Marshall headed the Legal Defense and Educational Fund, which was an autonomous ally of the National Association for the Advancement of Colored People (NAACP).
3   *New York Times*, May 18, 1954. For many reactions see also John Howard, *The Shifting Wind: The Supreme Court and Civil Rights from Reconstruction to Brown* (Albany, 1999), 328–29. For Ellison's letter of May 19, 1954, see John Callahan, "American Culture Is of a Whole," *New Republic*, March 1, 1999, 38–39. Emphasis mine.
4   Richard Kluger, *Simple Justice: The History of Brown v. Board of Education and Black America's Struggle for Equality* (New York, 1975), 326–28; Diane Ravitch, *The Troubled Crusade: American Education, 1945–1980* (New York, 1983), 127. Quotation from Stephan Thernstrom and Abigail Thernstrom, *America in Black and White: One Nation, Indivisible* (New York, 1997), 97. Wyoming had no segregated schools in 1954. Until 1949 Indiana permitted local school districts to segregate.

The case number of *Brown* is 347 U.S. 483 (1954), which means that its text may be found in volume 347 of U.S. Supreme Court, *U.S. Reports*, starting on page 483. I will use this common system of citation for all Supreme Court cases mentioned in the pages that follow. See my Appendix of Key Cases for the *U.S. Reports* numbers of many of these cases.
5   The Census of 1950 enumerated 15,042,286 "Negroes," or 10 percent of a total population of 150,697,361. Of these Negroes, 10.2 million lived in the eleven states of the Confederacy and in Delaware, Maryland, the District of Columbia, West Virginia, Kentucky, and Oklahoma. Unless indicated otherwise, statistics in this book are taken from Bureau of the Census, *Statistical History of the United States, Colonial Times to the Present* (New York, 1976). Statistics here are on pages 14–18, 22–37.
6   Tom Dent, *Southern Journey: A Return to the Civil Rights Movement* (New York, 1997), 332–33.
7   Cited in Robert Wiebe, "White Attitudes and Black Rights from *Brown* to *Bakke*," in ed. *Have We Overcome? Race Relations Since Brown*, Michael Namorato (Jackson, Miss., 1979), 156–57.
8   David Garrow, "From *Brown* to *Casey*: The U.S. Supreme Court and the Burdens of History," in *Race, Law, and Culture: Reflections on Brown v. Board of Education*, ed. Austin Sarat (New York, 1997), 74; Carter cited in Herbert Hill and James Jones, Jr., eds., *Race in America:*

The Struggle for Equality (Madison, 1993), 93; John Salmond, *"My Mind Set on Freedom": A History of the Civil Rights Movement* (Chicago, 1997), 25–26.

9 Brady, *Black Monday* (Brookhaven, Miss., 1954). Quote cited in Thernstroms, *America in Black and White*, 106; Bowles quoted in *Newsweek*, Oct. 18, 1954, 32.

10 Eastland cited in Richard Fried, *Nightmare in Red: The McCarthy Era in Perspective* (New York, 1990), 176; Talmadge, in *Newsweek*, May 31, 1954, 31.

11 Cited in Kluger, *Simple Justice*, 461.

12 Michael Klarman, "How *Brown* Changed Race Relations: The Backlash Thesis," *Journal of American History*, 81 (June 1994), 91; Gerald Rosenberg, *The Hollow Hope: Can Courts Bring About Social Change?* (Chicago, 1991), 70–71.

13 *Plessy v. Ferguson*, 163 U.S. 537 (1896).

14 *Brown v. Board of Education of Topeka*, 347 U.S. 483 (1954). In the late 1940s, all southern states, as well as nineteen northern states, had laws on their books banning marriages between whites and blacks. Laws that were not repealed continued to be enforceable until the Court ruled against them in 1967. The Court's position in *Brown* also meant that future policies recognizing race-based classifications, such as affirmative action, could be established. That is a later story, to be discussed in subsequent chapters.

15 Diane Ravitch, "Desegregation: Varieties of Meaning," in Derrick Bell, ed., *Shades of Brown: New Perspectives on School Desegregation* (New York, 1980), 31–47.

16 Three other state suits—concerning schools in Delaware, Virginia, and South Carolina— were combined with Brown's. A fifth case concerned segregated schools in the District of Columbia. All five cases were decided in favor of plaintiffs on May 17, 1954.

17 Kluger, *Simple Justice*, 3–26.

18 *Ibid.*, 479.

19 Cited in Jack Greenberg, *Crusaders in the Courts: How a Dedicated Band of Lawyers Fought for the Civil Rights Revolution* (New York, 1994), 129.

20 Thernstroms, *America in Black and White*, 103–4.

21 Cited in Hill and Jones, eds., *Race in America*, 185–86.

22 Hurston, "Court Order Can't Make Races Mix," *Orlando Sentinel*, Aug. 11, 1955, reprinted in Cheryl Wall, ed., *Folklore, Memoirs, and Other Writings* (New York, 1995), 956–58.

23 J. Harvie Wilkinson III, *From Brown to Bakke: The Supreme Court and School Integration: 1954–1978* (New York, 1979), 3, 6.

24 Cited in Hill and Jones, eds., *Race in America*, 18.

25 Franklin, *The Color Line: Legacy for the Twenty-First Century* (Columbia, Mo., 1993), 5.

Chapter 1

1 Quotes, in order, from Joseph Goulden, *The Best Years, 1945–1950* (New York, 1976), 353; Gunner Myrdal, *An American Dilemma: The Negro Problem and American Democracy* (New York, 1944), lxi; Richard Kluger, *Simple Justice* (New York, 1975), 250–51; and Mark Tushnet, *Making Civil Rights Law: Thurgood Marshall and the Supreme Court, 1936–1961* (New York, 1994), 232.

2 For race relations early in the century, see Leon Litwack, *Trouble in Mind: Black Southerners in the Age of Jim Crow* (New York, 1998). For forces propelling change in the 1940s, see John Higham, "Introduction," in *Civil Rights and Social Wrongs: Black-White Relations since*

World War II, ed. John Higham (University Park., Pa., 1997), 3–30; Stephan Thernstrom and Abigail Thernstrom, *America in Black and White* (New York, 1997), 69–96; Kluger, *Simple Justice*, 238–55.

3 Tushnet, *Making Civil Rights Law*, 135–36; Kenneth Jackson, *Crabgrass Frontier: The Sub-urbanization of the United States* (New York, 1985), 279.

4 Kenneth Kusmer, "African Americans in the City Since World War II: From the Industrial to the Post-Industrial Era," *Journal of Urban History*, 21 (May 1995), 458–504; Charles Payne, *I've Got the Light of Freedom: The Organizing Tradition and the Mississippi Freedom Struggle* (Berkeley, 1995), 22–25, 431.

5 Alonzo Hamby, *Beyond the New Deal: Harry S. Truman and American Liberalism* (New York, 1973), 188–90.

6 Arnold Hirsch, *Making the Second Ghetto: Race and Housing in Chicago, 1940–1960* (New York, 1983), 30–31, 175–79; Kluger, *Simple Justice*, 237–38, 251–55. See my Appendix I, which identifies key cases covered in this book.

7 Thernstroms, *America in Black and White*, 131–33; Michael Klarman, "How *Brown* Changed Race Relations: The Backlash Thesis," *Journal of American History*, 81 (June 1994), 81–118.

8 James Cobb, "World War II and the Mind of the Modern South," in *Remaking Dixie: The Impact of World War II on the American South,* ed. Neil McMillen (Jackson, Miss., 1997), 3–20 (quote on 10).

9 Tushnet, *Making Civil Rights Law*, 152–53.

10 Thomas Sugrue, *The Origins of the Urban Crisis: Race and Inequality in Postwar Detroit* (Princeton, 1996), 8–12, 267; Orlando Patterson, *The Ordeal of Integration: Progress and Resentment in America's "Racial" Crisis* (Washington, D.C., 1997), 21–22.

11 Gary Orfield and Susan Eaton, *Dismantling Desegregation: The Quiet Reversal of Brown v. Board of Education* (New York, 1996), 303–8; Michelle Foster, *Black Teachers on Teaching* (New York, 1997), xxv–xxix.

12 Myrdal, *An American Dilemma*, 660–62.

13 There had been eighty-four officially recorded lynchings (seventy-five of blacks) between 1931 and 1935, and thirty (twenty-eight of blacks) between 1936 and 1940. There were no lynchings of whites between 1941 and 1945, and two (of twelve in all) between 1946 and 1950. *Historical Statistics of the United States* (New York, 1976), 422.

14 The Reverend James P. Dees, cited in Thernstroms, *America in Black and White*, 42.

15 *Henderson v. United States*, 339 U.S. 816 (1950). Jack Greenberg, *Crusaders in the Courts* (New York, 1994), 72–73.

16 Sass, "Mixed Schools and Mixed Blood," *Atlantic Monthly* (Nov. 1956), 49.

17 For an article that emphasizes the potential for the development of an interracial working-class alliance in the late 1940s, see Robert Korstad and Nelson Lichtenstein, "Opportunities Found and Lost: Labor, Radicals, and the Early Civil Rights Movement," *Journal of American History*, 75 (Dec. 1988), 786–811.

18 McMillen, "Fighting for What We Didn't Have: How Mississippi's Black Voters Remember World War II," in *Remaking Dixie*, ed. McMillen, 98–99. Harvard Sitkoff, "African American Militancy in the World War II South: Another Perspective," ibid., 70–92, stresses the severe constraints on African-American militancy in the South during and after the war. For sources emphasizing the early roots of civil rights activity, see Patricia Sullivan, *Days of Hope: Race and Democracy in the New Deal Era* (Chapel Hill, 1996), and John Egerton, *Speak Now*

against the Day: The Generation before the Civil Rights Movement in the South (New York, 1994).

19 Tushnet, *Making Civil Rights Law*, 102–4, 148–50.

20 Thernstroms, *America in Black and White*, 531–35; Herbert Hyman and Paul Sheatsley, "Attitudes toward Desegregation," *Scientific American*, 211 (July 1964), 16–23. See my Appendix II, Table 1.

21 Hurston, *Dust Tracks on a Road: An Autobiography* (2d. ed., Urbana, 1984), xxix–xxx; Baldwin cited in Hinton Als, "The Enemy Within," *New Yorker*, Feb. 16, 1998, 74.

22 Du Bois, "Does the Negro Need Separate Schools?" *Journal of Negro Education*, 4 (July 1935), 328–35. John W. Davis, lead attorney for the state of South Carolina, later used Du Bois's argument in summing up his case for segregation before the Supreme Court in 1952.

23 Among the many other black writers who have subsequently stressed the virtues of all-black schools are Vanessa Siddle Walker, *Their Highest Potential: An African American Community in the Segregated South* (Chapel Hill, 1996); and Thomas Sowell, "Black Excellence: The Case of Dunbar High School," *The Public Interest*, No. 35 (Spring 1974), 1–12.

24 In 1950, 22.5 percent of the southern population was black, compared with 10 percent in the United States as a whole. Mississippi's population was almost 50 percent black.

25 Thernstroms, *America in Black and White*, 36. For other accounts of inequality in schools see Robert Margo, *Race and Schooling in the South, 1880–1950* (Chicago, 1990); and Greenberg, *Crusaders in the Courts*, 40, 78–79, 116.

26 Cited in Thernstroms, *America in Black and White*, 39.

27 Constance Curry, *Silver Rights* (Algonquin Books, Chapel Hill, 1995), 10–33. Later chapters will say more about the Carter family's efforts for good schooling.

28 Ronald Bayor, *Race and the Shaping of Twentieth-Century Atlanta* (Chapel Hill, 1996), 198–219.

29 George Kateb, "*Brown* and the Harm of Legal Segregation," in *Race, Law, and Culture*, ed. Austin Sarat (New York, 1997), 91–109; Patterson, *Ordeal of Integration*, 64–65, 185.

30 For portraits of Marshall, see Juan Williams, *Thurgood Marshall: American Revolutionary* (New York, 1998); Kluger, *Simple Justice*, esp. 173–94, 272–74, 642–44; Greenberg, *Crusaders in the Courts*, 29–32; Tushnet, *The NAACP's Legal Strategy against Segregated Education, 1925–1950* (Chapel Hill, 1987), 34–48; and *Time*, Sept. 19, 1955, 23–27.

31 For Marshall and Houston, see Greenberg, *Crusaders in the Courts*, 5–6; and Kluger, *Simple Justice*, 186–87, 197–99. For the founding of the LDF see Tushnet, *NAACP's Legal Strategy*, 100; and Benjamin Hooks, "Birth and Separation of the Legal Defense and Educational Fund," *Crisis*, June 7, 1979, 218–20.

32 Williams and Kelly, cited in Kluger, *Simple Justice*, 273, 643.

33 Kluger, *Simple Justice*, 325.

34 Greenberg, *Crusaders in the Courts*, 81.

35 Williams, *Thurgood Marshall*, 174–75.

36 *Missouri ex rel. Gaines v. Canada*, 305 U.S. 337 (1938). For this case, see Lucille Bluford, "The Lloyd Gaines Story," *Journal of Educational Sociology*, (Feb. 1959), 242–46; Constance Baker Motley, *Equal Justice . . . Under Law* (New York, 1998), 34, 62; Tushnet, *NAACP's Legal Strategy*, 70–81; Williams, *Thurgood Marshall*, 96–98; and Kluger, *Simple Justice*, 212–13. Many southern states at that time employed ruses like Missouri's out-of-state-tuition plan.

37 *Sweatt v. Painter*, 339 U.S. 629 (1950) and *McLaurin v. Oklahoma State Regents for Higher Education*, 339 U.S. 637 (1950). In 1948 the Court had also gratified Marshall, in the case of *Sipuel v. Oklahoma State Board of Regents* 332 U.S. 631. Echoing its decision in *Gaines*, it ruled that Oklahoma, which had no law school for blacks, must provide Ada Lois Sipuel, a black women who sought admittance to the state law school, with equal facilities. State officials, however, made a mockery of the ruling, and the Court did not intervene to enforce its stand. See Motley, *Equal Justice*, 64–65; Tushnet, *NAACP's Legal Strategy*, 25–50; and Paul Wilson, *A Time to Lose: Representing Kansas in Brown v. Board of Education* (Lawrence, 1995), 11–12.

38 For *Sweatt* and *McLaurin* see *New York Times*, June 6, 7, 1950; Kluger, *Simple Justice*, 260–69; Tushnet, *NAACP's Legal Strategy*, 125–37; and Williams, *Thurgood Marshall*, 175–76.

39 Tushnet, *NAACP's Legal Strategy*, 134. See also John Howard, *The Shifting Wind: The Supreme Court and Civil Rights from Reconstruction to Brown* (Albany, 1999), 292–97.

40 For informed commentary on *Sweatt* and its impact on legal strategies after 1950 see Morton Horwitz, *The Warren Court and the Pursuit of Justice* (New York, 1998), 21–22; Andrew Kull, *The Color-Blind Constitution* (Cambridge, Mass., 1992), 161; Alfred Kelly, "The School Case," in *Quarrels That Have Shaped the Constitution*, ed. John Garraty (rev. ed., New York, 1987), 307–44; Peggy Cooper Davis, "Performing Interpretation: A Legacy of Civil Rights Lawyering in *Brown v. Board of Education*," in *Race, Law, and Culture*, ed. Sarat, 23–48; Greenberg, "Racial Integration of Teachers—A Growing Problem," *Journal of Negro Education*, 20 (Fall 1951), 584–87; and Kluger, *Simple Justice*, 291–92.

Chapter 2

1 Mark Tushnet, *Making Civil Rights Law* (New York, 1994), 155. The decision of the Fund to focus on desegregation, thereby downplaying fights for equality, caused rifts and resignations within the organization.

2 Robert Carter, "A Reassessment of *Brown v. Board*," in *Shades of Brown: New Perspectives on School Desegregation*, ed. Derrick Bell, (New York, 1980), 20–28.

3 For black activism prior to the 1950s see Charles Payne, *I've Got the Light of Freedom: The Organizing Tradition and the Mississippi Freedom Struggle* (Berkeley, 1995).

4 For the South Carolina story that follows, see Richard Kluger, *Simple Justice* (New York, 1975), 3–26 and passim.

5 For Whitehead's report, see Kluger, *Simple Justice*, 331–33.

6 For the troubles of Briggs and others, see ibid., 24–26.

7 Woodward, "*Strange Career* Critics: Long May They Persevere," *Journal of American History*, 75 (Dec. 1988), 865.

8 Juan Williams, *Thurgood Marshall* (New York, 1998), 195–200.

9 For the Farmville story, see Robert Pratt, *The Color of Their Skin: Education and Race in Richmond, Virginia, 1954–1989* (Charlottesville, 1992), 3–79; Taylor Branch, *Parting the Waters: Martin Luther King and the Civil Rights Movement, 1954–63* (New York, 1988), 19–24; and Kluger, *Simple Justice*, 451–79. Moton High was named after Booker T. Washington's aide and successor at Tuskegee Institute in Alabama.

10 In 1954 the twenty-seven-year-old Reverend Martin Luther King, Jr., became pastor of the

church from which Johns resigned in 1952. For a vivid portrait of the Reverend Johns, see the opening chapter of Branch, *Parting the Waters*, 1–26.

11 For the D.C. case, see Kluger, *Simple Justice*, 508–40.

12 Because the Fourteenth Amendment sought to prevent *states* from discriminating, Nabrit did not rely on it in the *Bolling* case. Instead he relied on the Fifth Amendment, which stated that no person should be deprived of "life, liberty, or property without due process of law."

13 For Delaware, see Kluger, *Simple Justice*, 425–50.

14 For Topeka, see Paul Wilson, *A Time to Lose: Representing Kansas in Brown v. Board of Education* (Lawrence, 1995), 60–61 and passim. Wilson was the somewhat reluctant attorney handling the case against desegregation. Also see Quintard Taylor, *In Search of the Racial Frontier: African Americans in the American West, 1528–1990* (New York, 1998), 280–83; and Kluger, *Simple Justice*, 396–424.

15 Named after Charles Sumner of Massachusetts, who had argued against segregated schools in the first important case on the issue, in 1849.

16 By the time the Supreme Court issued *Brown* in 1954, Linda (a third-grader in the 1950–51 school year) was set to begin the city's nonsegregated junior high school in the fall; ironically, the decision did not directly affect her. Oliver Brown died in 1961, without leaving a full account of his reasons for participating as a plaintiff.

17 Huxman and Greenberg cited in Kluger, *Simple Justice*, 424. See also Tushnet, *Making Civil Rights Law*, 161–62.

18 For Ashmore, see Kluger, *Simple Justice*, 535. Byrnes had had a distinguished political career before becoming governor of South Carolina in 1951: U.S. Congressman, U.S. Senator, Supreme Court justice (a Roosevelt appointee), and Secretary of State.

19 For Nabrit's role, see ibid.

20 For key studies of the actions and intentions of political leaders in the 1860s see Alfred Kelly, "The School Desegregation Case," in *Quarrels That Have Shaped the Constitution*, ed. John Garraty (rev. ed., New York, 1987), 307–34; and Alexander Bickel, "The Original Understanding and the Segregation Decision," *Harvard Law Review*, 69 (Nov. 1955), 1–65.

21 David Donald, *Charles Sumner and the Coming of the Civil War* (New York, 1981), 180–81.

22 *Cumming v. Richmond (Ga.) County Board of Education*, 175 U.S. 528 (1899).

23 *Gong Lum v. Rice*, 275 U.S. 78 (1927).

24 Kluger, *Simple Justice*, 73–83, 121–22, and passim offers the fullest accounts of these cases. See also J. Harvie Wilkinson III, *From Brown to Bakke: The Supreme Court and School Integration: 1954–1978* (New York, 1979), 11–25; J. Morgan Kousser, "Separate but *Not* Equal: The Supreme Court's First Decision on Racial Discrimination in Schools," *Journal of Southern History*, 46 (Feb. 1980), 17–44; Lawrence Friedman, "*Brown* in Context," in *Race, Law, and Culture*, ed. Austin Sarat (New York, 1997), 49–73; and Kelly, "School Segregation Case."

25 Kluger, *Simple Justice*, 533–34; Stephan Thernstrom and Abigail Thernstrom, *America in Black and White* (New York, 1997), 316–19. For commentary on this issue see Andrew Kull, *The Color-Blind Constitution* (Cambridge, Mass., 1992), 175 and passim.

26 Kluger, *Simple Justice*, 529–31.

27 Du Bois and Truman's Commission cited in Daryl Scott, *Contempt and Pity: Social Policy*

and the Image of the Damaged Black Psyche, 1880–1996 (Chapel Hill, 1997), 13, 48. As Scott's title indicates, his book focuses on ideas such as the Clarks' in American social science writing.

28 Clark and Clark, "Racial Identification and Preference in Negro Children," in *Readings in Social Psychology*, ed. Eleanor Maccoby et al. (New York, 1952), 602–11; Jack Greenberg, *Crusaders in the Courts* (New York, 1994), 124.

29 Coleman cited in Kluger, *Simple Justice*, 321. Marshall's role in Williams, *Thurgood Marshall*, 209–10.

30 A powerful early critique is Edmond Cahn, "Jurisprudence," *New York University Law Review*, 30 (Jan. 1955), 150–69. For criticisms see also Kluger, *Simple Justice*, 317–21, 353–56.

Chapter 3

1 Quoted in Richard Kluger, *Simple Justice* (New York, 1975), 246.

2 For some of the many scholarly criticisms of the Vinson Court, see Melvin Urofsky's aptly titled, *Division and Discord: The Supreme Court under Stone and Vinson, 1941–1953* (Columbia, S.C., 1997); Mark Tushnet, with Katya Levin, "What Really Happened in *Brown v. Board of Education*," *Columbia Law Review*, 91 (Dec. 1991), 1867–1930; Bernard Schwartz, *Super Chief: Earl Warren and His Supreme Court* (New York, 1983), 72–73; and Kluger, *Simple Justice*, 243–46, 582–91. For biographical portraits of key justices such as Black and Douglas see James Simon, "William O. Douglas," and Schwartz, "Hugo L. Black" in *The Warren Court: A Retrospective*, ed. Bernard Schwartz (New York, 1996), 195–210, 211–23; Ed Cray, *Chief Justice: A Biography of Earl Warren* (New York, 1997), 262–67; and Morton Horwitz, *The Warren Court and the Pursuit of Justice* (New York, 1998), 4–6.

3 Cited in Simon, "William O. Douglas," 217–18.

4 Douglas and Frankfurter cited in Schwartz, "Hugo L. Black," 196.

5 Urofsky, *Division and Discord*, 143–45.

6 Jack Greenberg, *Crusaders in the Courts* (New York, 1994), 72; Kluger, *Simple Justice*, 567–68, 596–603; William Brennan, "A Personal Remembrance," in *Warren Court*, ed. Schwartz, 8–11.

7 William Harbaugh, *Lawyer's Lawyer: The Life of John W. Davis* (New York, 1973), 483–519; Juan Williams, *Thurgood Marshall* (New York, 1998), 214–15.

8 For informed research concerning the views of the justices in 1952–53, see Kluger, *Simple Justice*, 582–613.

9 Roger Newman, *Hugo Black: A Biography* (New York, 1994), 429–44.

10 No justice on the Court in 1952—or at any earlier time in American history—had a black person as a law clerk. The first black page was taken on in July 1954. A virtually all-black staff served the justices in more menial ways at the Court building, notably as waiters, custodians, and elevator operators. See Cray, *Chief Justice*, 261.

11 Kluger, *Simple Justice*, 595.

12 Mark Tushnet, *Making Civil Rights Law* (New York, 1994), 195–96.

13 Kluger, *Simple Justice*, 613–16.

14 Schwartz, "Chief Justice Rehnquist, Justice Jackson, and the *Brown* Case," *Supreme Court Review* (1988), 267.

15 Among the many sources on Warren, several stand out, including Schwartz, *Super Chief,* and Cray, *Chief Justice.* See also Kluger, *Simple Justice,* 664–67; and *Newsweek,* May 11, 1964, 24–33.

16 Cray, *Chief Justice* 246–47; Michael Mayer, "With Much Deliberation and Some Speed: Eisenhower and the *Brown* Decision," *Journal of Southern History,* 52 (Feb. 1986), 43–76.

17 Kluger, *Simple Justice,* 672. Jack Greenberg later told a friend about Davis's tears. The friend replied that a colleague had whispered to him at the time, "That sonofabitch [Davis] cries in every case he argues." Cited in Greenberg, *Crusaders in the Courts,* 190.

18 Davis's comment on "fluff," in Daryl Scott, *Contempt and Pity: Social Policy and the Image of the Damaged Black Psyche, 1880–1996* (Chapel Hill, 1997), 35. Other comments by Davis cited in Kluger, *Simple Justice,* 672. See also Harbaugh, *Lawyer's Lawyer,* 499–500.

19 Kluger, *Simple Justice,* 676.

20 For Warren and this conference, see Schwartz, "Earl Warren," in *Warren Court,* ed. Schwartz, 256–75; Kluger, *Simple Justice,* 677–85.

21 For Reed, see Schwartz, *Super Chief,* 88–90; Cray, *Chief Justice,* 283–84; and Newman, *Hugo Black,* 438.

22 For a dramatic narrative of Warren's decision, see Kluger, *Simple Justice,* 700–9. An appendix to his book, 779–875, reprints the *Brown* and *Bolling v. Sharpe* decisions. See also *New York Times,* May 18, 1954. The *Brown* case is 347 U.S. 483; *Bolling v. Sharpe* is 347 U.S. 497.

23 J. Harvie Wilkinson III, *From Brown to Bakke: The Supreme Court and School Integration: 1954–1978* (New York, 1979), 29.

24 Andrew Kull, *The Color-Blind Constitution* (Cambridge, Mass., 1992), 2–6, 153–61. In 1955 and again in 1956 the Court declined to consider a judicial challenge to Virginia's law against interracial marriage. See *Naim v. Naim,* 350 U.S. 891 (1955). In 1967 it unanimously struck down such a law, in *Loving v. Virginia,* 388 U.S. 1 (1967).

25 Wilkinson, *From Brown to Bakke,* 31–33. See also Scott, *Contempt and Pity,* 121–36, 184–85; Waldo Martin, Jr., *Brown v. Board of Education: A Brief History with Documents* (New York, 1998), 29, 36–37; and David Garrow, "From *Brown* to *Casey:* The U.S. Supreme Court and the Burdens of History," in *Race, Law, and Culture,* ed. Austin Sarat (New York, 1997), 74–88.

26 Newman, *Hugo Black,* 437.

27 Sources stressing these positive points about *Brown*—among a very large number—include Lawrence Friedman, "*Brown* in Context," in *Race, Law, and Culture,* ed. Sarat 49–73; Horwitz, *Warren Court,* 85–88; and Kluger, *Simple Justice,* 714.

Chapter 4

1 Sources for these reactions, in order: Julius Chambers, "*Brown v. Board of Education,*" in *Race in America,* ed. Herbert Hill and James Jones, Jr. (Madison, 1993), 184–85; Lightfoot, in Patricia Edwards, "Before and After School Desegregation: African American Parents' Involvement in Schools," in *Beyond Segregation: The Politics of Quality in Afro American Schooling,* ed. Mwalimu Shujaa (Thousand Oaks, Calif., 1996), 139; Johnson in Robert Pratt, *The Color of their Skin: Education and Race in Richmond, Virginia, 1954–89* (Charlottesville, 1992), 3; NAACP, in Gerald Rosenberg, *The Hollow Hope: Can Courts Bring About Social*

Change? (Chicago, 1991), 145–46; Marshall in ibid., 43; Johnson in C. S. Johnson, "Some Significant Social and Educational Implications of the U.S. Supreme Court's Decision," *Journal of Negro Education*, 23 (Summer 1954), 364–71.

2 Elman cited in Mark Tushnet, *Making Civil Rights Law* (New York, 1994), 216; Greenberg quoted in Rosenberg, *Hollow Hope*, 169.

3 William Chafe, *Civilities and Civil Rights: Greensboro, North Carolina, and the Black Struggle for Freedom* (New York, 1980), 6–7, 60–66.

4 The plan proposed that the tenth grade in 1955–56 would also include some blacks, and so forth, so that by 1956–57 all three high school grades would include black students.

5 The story of Milford is well told in Ed Kee, "The *Brown* Decision and Milford, Delaware, 1954–1965," *Delaware History*, 27 (Fall–Winter 1997), 205–44.

6 Neil McMillen, *The Citizens' Councils: Organized Resistance to the Second Reconstruction, 1954–1964* (Urbana, 1971), 7–9; J. W. Peltason, *Fifty-Eight Lonely Men: Southern Federal Judges and School Desegregation* (New York, 1961), 31–32, 114–15.

7 For the Baltimore story, see Elinor Pancoast and others, *The Report of a Study on Desegregation in the Baltimore City Schools* (Baltimore, 1956), for the Maryland Commission on Interracial Problems and Relations.

8 Philip Brown, *A Century of "Separate but Equal": Education in Anne Arundel County* (New York, 1988), 131–39. Three Maryland counties did not totally desegregate their schools until the early 1970s.

9 McMillen, *Citizens' Councils*, 8–9.

10 *New York Times*, May 18 and 28, 1954; *Newsweek*, May 24, 1954, 25.

11 Pratt, *The Color of Their Skin*, 1–13.

12 This is a main theme in Tony Badger, "Fatalism, not Gradualism: The Crisis of Southern Liberalism, 1945–1965," in Brian Ward and Tony Badger, eds., *The Making of Martin Luther King and the Civil Rights Movement* (London, 1996), 67–95. See also Chafe, *Civilities*, 60–82.

13 The main theme of Chafe, *Civilities*, passim.

14 Herbert Hyman and Paul Sheatsley, "Attitudes toward Segregation," *Scientific American*, 195 (Dec. 1956), 35–39; Lawrence Bobo, "The Color Line, the Dilemma, and the Dream," in *Civil Rights and Social Wrongs*, ed. John Higham (University Park, Pa., 1997), 31–55. See also my Appendix II, Table 1.

15 Quotes in Diane Ravitch, *The Troubled Crusade: American Education, 1945–1980* (New York, 1983), 135; and Robert Griffith, "Dwight D. Eisenhower and the Corporate Commonwealth," *American Historical Review*, 87 (Feb. 1982), 116.

16 Quotes in Stephen Ambrose, *Eisenhower: Soldier and President* (New York, 1990), 367–68; and Emmet John Hughes, *The Ordeal of Power: A Political Memoir of the Eisenhower Years* (New York, 1963), 201.

17 Cited in Rosenberg, *Hollow Hope*, 76. For other criticisms of Ike and civil rights see Michael Mayer, "With Much Deliberation and Some Speed: Eisenhower and the *Brown* Decision," *Journal of Southern History*, 52 (Feb. 1986), 43–76; Peltason, *Fifty-Eight Lonely Men*, 45–55; and Jack Bass, *Unlikely Heroes: The Dramatic Story of the Southern Judges of the Fifth Circuit Who Translated the Supreme Court's Brown Decision into a Revolution for Equality* (New York, 1981), 150–52.

18 Cited in Roger Newman, *Hugo Black: A Biography* (New York, 1994), 439–40. Prohibition, of course, was not "issued" by the Supreme Court, but suffered from problems of enforcement.

19 For the Court and deliberations concerning *Brown II*, see Tushnet, *Making Civil Rights Law*, 228–31; Richard Kluger, *Simple Justice* (New York, 1975), 729–47; Jack Greenberg, *Crusaders in the Courts* (New York, 1994), 389–90; J. Harvie Wilkinson III, *From Brown to Bakke* (New York, 1979), 66–67; Bernard Schwartz, *Super Chief: Earl Warren and His Supreme Court* (New York, 1983), 113–24; and Ed Cray, *Chief Justice: A Biography of Earl Warren* (New York, 1997), 292–94.

20 *Brown v. Board of Education of Topeka*, 349 U.S. 294 (1955).

21 Cited in Kluger, *Simple Justice*, 746–47.

22 For Parker's key decision, see Wilkinson, *From Brown to Bakke*, 81–85. The emphasis is mine.

Chapter 5

1 Stephen Whitfield, *A Death in the Delta: The Story of Emmett Till* (Baltimore, 1988); John Dittmer, *Local People: The Struggle for Civil Rights in Mississippi* (Urbana, 1994), 54–58.

2 Randall Kennedy, *Race, Crime, and the Law* (New York, 1997), 63.

3 Key sources for southern reactions described in this chapter include Numan Bartley, *The Rise of Massive Resistance* (Baton Rouge, 1969), 3–120 and passim; and J. Harvie Wilkinson, *From Brown to Bakke* (New York, 1979), 61–127.

4 *Time*, Dec. 20, 1954, 54; Sass, "Mixed Schools and Mixed Blood," *Atlantic Monthly*, Nov. 1956, 45–48.

5 For Eastland, see *Newsweek*, June 13, 1955, 30; Dan Wakefield, "Respectable Racism: Dixie's Citizens Councils," *Nation*, Oct. 22, 1955, 339; and (for this speech) Bartley, *Massive Resistance*, 119–20.

6 Charles Payne, *I've Got the Light of Freedom: The Organizing Tradition and the Mississippi Freedom Struggle* (Berkeley, 1995), 110–14.

7 Bartley, *Massive Resistance*, 19. Georgia had 159 counties.

8 J. W. Peltason, *Fifty-Eight Lonely Men* (New York, 1961), 4–6, 43–45. Quotes from Gerald Rosenberg, *The Hollow Hope: Can Courts Bring about Social Change?* (Chicago, 1991), 90. In 1960 one of the circuit court judges (William Hastie) was black, and one was a woman (Florence Allen).

9 Richard Kluger, *Simple Justice* (New York, 1975), 295–301, 366.

10 *New York Times*, July 24, 1999. Johnson, like fifteen other federal district court judges in the South in 1960, was a Republican. Eisenhower had appointed most of them.

11 For quotes from Griffin and the Richmond editorial, see *Time*, June 13, 1955, 22.

12 Cited in Peter Applebome, *Dixie Rising: How the South Is Shaping American Values* (San Diego, 1996), 99. A fine study of Wallace's career is Dan Carter, *The Politics of Rage: George Wallace, the Origins of the New Conservatism, and the Transformation of American Politics* (New York, 1995).

13 Peltason, *Fifty-Eight Lonely Men*, 93–96.

14 Juan Williams, *Thurgood Marshall* (New York, 1998), 253–74; Constance Baker Motley, *Equal Justice . . . Under Law* (New York, 1998), 125–29, 150–55. The case was *NAACP v. Alabama*

ex rel. Patterson, 357 U.S. 449 (1958). Other southern states followed Alabama's example, requiring further legal efforts by NAACP attorneys under Carter after 1956.

15 Peltason, *Fifty-Eight Lonely Men*, 116–22. The federal circuit court later rejected Davidson's plan and reordered implementation of the stair-step plan.

16 Peltason, *Fifty-Eight Lonely Men*, 132.

17 Neil McMillen, *The Citizens' Councils: Organized Resistance to the Second Reconstruction, 1954–1964* (Urbana, 1971), 17–19, passim; Bartley, *Massive Resistance*, 82–85; Payne, *I've Got the Light of Freedom*, 34–36; Dittmer, *Local People*, 80–83, 378–79. Quote from Payne, 35.

18 McMillen, *Citizens' Councils*, 27.

19 Randall Woods, *Fulbright: A Biography* (Cambridge, Eng., 1995), 207–11; Tony Badger, "The Forerunner of Our Opposition: Arkansas and the Southern Manifesto of 1956," *Arkansas History Quarterly*, 56 (No. 3, 1997), 353–60.

20 Bartley, *Massive Resistance*, 116–17, 148; Mark Tushnet, *Making Civil Rights Law* (New York, 1994), 240–45. In all, Texas sent twenty-one representatives to Washington.

21 Tony Badger, "Southerners Who Refused to Sign the Southern Manifesto," *The Historical Journal*, 42 (No. 2, 1999), 517–34

22 Bartley, *Massive Resistance*, 75–77; Peltason, *Fifty-Eight Lonely Men*, 93–96; Stephan Thernstrom and Abigail Thernstrom, *America in Black and White* (New York, 1997), 114–15; Rosenberg, *Hollow Hope*, 79–83.

23 Amy Murrell, "The 'Impossible' Prince Edward Case: The Endurance of Resistance in a Southside County, 1959–1964," in *The Moderates' Dilemma: Massive Resistance to School Desegregation in Virginia*, Matthew Lassiter and Andrew Lewis, (Charlottesville, 1998), 134–67; Lassiter and Lewis, "Massive Resistance Revisited: Virginia's White Moderates and the Byrd Organization," in ibid., 1–21; Peltason, *Fifty-Eight Lonely Men*, 208–18; and Tushnet, *Making Civil Rights Law*, 247–49. For the *Griffin* case, see my chapter 6.

24 The case involved the efforts of the Reverend Fred Shuttlesworth of Birmingham, a leading civil rights activist who struggled for two years to help black people, including his two daughters, gain admission to white schools. Opponents attacked him and bombed his home. See Peltason, *Fifty-Eight Lonely Men*, 60, 83–85. The case is *Shuttlesworth v. Birmingham Board of Education*, 358 U.S. 101 (1958).

25 For pupil placement and freedom of choice laws see Bartley, *Massive Resistance*, 77–80; Thernstroms, *America in Black and White*, 316–19; Wilkinson, *From Brown to Bakke*, 109–11; McMillen, *Citizens' Councils*, 267–69; and Andrew Kull, *The Color-Blind Constitution* (Cambridge, Mass., 1992), 176.

26 Stanley Trent, "School Choice for African-American Children Who Live in Poverty: A Commitment to Equity or More of the Same?" *Urban Education*, 27 (Oct. 1992), 291–92.

27 Peltason, *Fifty-Eight Lonely Men*, 149–50.

28 William Kellar, *Make Haste Slowly: Moderates, Conservatives, and School Desegregation in Houston* (College Station, Tex., 1999), 85; Peltason, *Fifty-Eight Lonely Men*, 151–54. Eisenhower did not wish to antagonize Shivers, who though a Democrat, was supporting him in the upcoming presidential election.

29 Ibid.

30 Peltason, *Fifty-Eight Lonely Men*, 143–46.

31 Ronald Bayor, *Race and the Shaping of Twentieth-Century Atlanta* (Chapel Hill, 1996), 226–32.

32 *New York Times*, Feb. 2–29, March 1–11, 1956; Tushnet, *Making Civil Rights Law*, 238–40; Tony Badger, "Fatalism, not Gradualism: The Crisis of Southern Liberalism, 1945–1965," in *The Making of Martin Luther King and the Civil Rights Movement*, ed. Brian Ward and Tony Badger (London, 1996), 67–95; John Salmond, *"My Mind Set on Freedom": A History of the Civil Rights Movement, 1954–1968* (Chicago, 1997), 32.

33 *New York Times*, July 22, Aug. 28, Sept. 5, 13, 16, 1957; Davison Douglas, *Reading, Writing, and Race: The Desegregation of the Charlotte Schools* (Chapel Hill, 1995), 72–73; Frye Gaillard, *The Dream Long Deferred* (Chapel Hill, 1988), 4–9.

34 Adam Fairclough, *Race and Democracy: The Civil Rights Struggle in Louisiana, 1915–1970* (Athens, Ga., 1995), 248–49.

35 *New York Times*, Nov. 15–19, Dec. 1–4, 28, 1960, and Jan. 28–30, Feb. 2, 9, 1961; Fairclough, *Race and Democracy*, 234–64; Liva Baker, *The Second Battle of New Orleans: The Hundred-Year Struggle to Integrate the Schools* (New York, 1996), 2–4, 396–453, 472–73; Jack Bass, *Unlikely Heroes: The Dramatic Story of the Southern Judges of the Fifth Circuit Who Translated the Supreme Court's Brown Decision into a Revolution for Equality* (New York, 1981), 114–15, 129–36, 157; and McMillen, *Citizens' Councils*, 289–96. Three black girls managed to desegregate a second elementary school in November 1960 without experiencing the turmoil that surrounded Ruby Bridges.

36 Among the many sources concerning Little Rock, see Bartley, *Massive Resistance*, 147; Salmond, *"My Mind Set on Freedom,"* 35–38; Jack Greenberg, *Crusaders in the Courts* (New York, 1994), 238–42; Wilkinson, *From Brown to Bakke*, 87–95; McMillen, *Citizens' Councils*, 269–82; Tony Badger, "The White Reaction to *Brown*: Arkansas, the Southern Manifesto, and Massive Resistance," in *Understanding the Little Rock Crisis: An Exercise in Remembrance and Reconciliation*, ed. Elizabeth Jacoway and C. Fred Williams, (1999), 83–97; and Tony Freyer, *The Little Rock Crisis: A Constitutional Interpretation* (Westport, Conn., 1984).

37 For Faubus, see Roy Reed, *Faubus: The Life and Times of an American Prodigal* (Fayetteville, Ark., 1997), esp. 85–127, 356–57.

38 Eyewitness memoirs concerning these events are Melba Pattillo Beals, *Warriors Don't Cry: A Searing Memoir of the Battle to Integrate Little Rock's Central High* (New York, 1994), esp. 48–52; and Elizabeth Huckaby, *Crisis at Central High: Little Rock, 1957–58* (Baton Rouge, 1980), esp. 51–53, 161. Beals was one of the nine black students; Huckaby was a top school teacher/administrator.

39 See Bernard Schwartz, *Super Chief* (New York, 1983), 288–93.

40 Walter Gellhorn, cited in Wilkinson, *From Brown to Bakke*, 102; statistic in Rosenberg, *Hollow Hope*, 52.

41 See especially Jennifer Hochschild, *The New American Dilemma: Liberal Democracy and School Desegregation* (New Haven, 1984), 1–12, 90–91, 146–205. A summary of such critiques can also be found in Rosenberg, *Hollow Hope*, 49–51.

42 Cited in Wilkinson, *From Brown to Bakke*, 67. Clark issued warnings along these lines even before *Brown* was decided. See Clark, "Desegregation: An Appraisal of the Evidence," *Journal of Social Issues*, 9 (No. 4), 2–76.

43 Michael Klarman, "How *Brown* Changed Race Relations: The Backlash Thesis," *Journal of American History*, 81 (June 1994), 81–118.

Chapter 6

1   *New York Times*, Jan. 3, 1960.

2   Jack Greenberg, *Crusaders in the Courts* (New York, 1994), 254–55, 304, 391; Gerald Rosenberg, *The Hollow Hope* (Chicago, 1991), 90–93; Mark Tushnet, *Making Civil Rights Law* (New York, 1994), 234–35, 268, 305–6. For Topeka, see Paul Wilson, *A Time to Lose: Representing Kansas in Brown v. Board of Education* (Lawrence, 1995), 224–30.

3   For activities of older civil rights leaders see Charles Payne, *I've Got the Light of Freedom* (Berkeley, 1995), 29–76; and Taylor Branch, *Parting the Waters: America in the King Years, 1954–63* (New York, 1988).

4   Among the many scholars who stress the great legacy of *Brown* are J. Harvie Wilkinson III, *From Brown to Bakke* (New York, 1979), 48–49; Richard Kluger, *Simple Justice* (New York, 1975), 710; and Aldon Morris, "Centuries of Black Protest: Its Significance for America and the World," in *Race in America*, ed. Herbert Hill and James Jones, Jr. (Madison, 1993), 46.

5   Stephan and Abigail Thernstrom, *America in Black and White* (New York, 1997), 136; Lawrence Bobo, "The Color Line, the Dilemma, and the Dream," in *Civil Rights and Social Wrongs*, ed. John Higham, (University Park, Pa., 1997), 37.

6   Rosenberg, *Hollow Hope*, 17, 131–38, 151–57.

7   Branch, *Parting the Waters*, 143–205.

8   William Chafe, *Civilities and Civil Rights* (New York, 1980), 98–141; Robert Weisbrot, *Freedom Bound: A History of America's Civil Rights Movement* (New York, 1990), 1–3, 19–42; Clayborne Carson, *In Struggle: SNCC and the Black Awakening of the 1960s* (Cambridge, Mass., 1981), 10–18; Branch, *Parting the Waters*, 271–312.

9   Among them, the sources cited above.

10 Juan Williams, *Thurgood Marshall* (New York, 1998), 286–89; Tushnet, *Making Civil Rights Law*, 305–10.

11 For the tense relations between the Fund and the NAACP—and between Marshall and Carter—see Constance Baker Motley, *Equal Justice . . . Under Law: An Autobiography* (New York, 1998), 125–29, 150–55.

12 Williams, *Thurgood Marshall*, 296–310.

13 Robert Dallek, *Flawed Giant: Lyndon Johnson and His Times, 1961–1973* (New York, 1998), 112–13.

14 Constance Curry, *Silver Rights* (Chapel Hill, 1995).

15 The theme of James Patterson, *Grand Expectations: The United States, 1945–1974* (New York, 1996).

16 *New York Times*, May 17, 1964.

17 For Black, see Roger Newman, *Hugo Black* (New York, 1994), 470–71; and Morton Horwitz, *The Warren Court and the Pursuit of Justice* (New York, 1998), 39–43. For Brennan, see Bernard Schwartz, ed., *The Warren Court* (New York, 1996), 20; Ed Cray, *Chief Justice* (New York, 1997), 324; and Horwitz, *Warren Court*, 24–26.

18 For Fortas see Laura Kalman, *Abe Fortas* (New Haven, 1990), 240–48, 277–82.

19 Quotes from Johnson in Bob Woodward and Scott Armstrong, *The Brethren: Inside the Supreme Court* (New York, 1979), 47; and Randall Kennedy, " 'Mr. Civil Rights,' " *New*

Republic, April 5, 1999, 38–39. For the confirmation process see also Williams, *Thurgood Marshall*, 3–14, 332; and Tushnet, *Making Civil Rights Law*, 25–26.

20 White replaced Charles Whittaker, whom Eisenhower had named in 1957 to fill the seat of Stanley Reed. Thus, by the end of 1962, five of the justices who had decided *Brown*— Jackson, Minton, Reed, Burton, and Frankfurter—had left the Court. Four—Warren, Black, Douglas, and Clark—remained, joining the newer justices: Harlan, Brennan, Stewart, Goldberg, and White. These nine (except Goldberg and Clark) stayed together on the "Warren Court" until early 1969.

21 *Loving v. Virginia*, 388 U.S. 1 (1967). Warren wrote the decision.

22 Rosenberg, *Hollow Hope*, 82.

23 Rosenberg, *Hollow Hope*, 95.

24 One of the riots that followed the assassination in April 1968 of King occurred in Wilmington, Delaware, site of one of the five school cases decided by the Court in 1954. The riot, which caused the burning of seventeen buildings, featured forty-nine firebombings, 411 arrests, forty-five injuries, and two deaths. It led to a nine-month occupation of the city by the National Guard, the longest occupation by troops in peacetime American history.

25 For rapid changes in white attitudes during the early 1960s, see Howard Schuman et al., *Racial Attitudes in America: Trends and Interpretations* (rev. ed., Cambridge, Mass., 1997), 103–5, 126; and Robert Wiebe, "White Attitudes and Black Rights from *Brown* to *Bakke*," in Michael Namorato, ed., *Have We Overcome?* (Jackson, Miss., 1979), 147–71.

26 Peter Applebome, *Dixie Rising* (San Diego, 1996), 102.

27 For the report and rejoinders see Lee Rainwater and William Yancey, *The Moynihan Report and the Politics of Controversy* (Cambridge, Mass., 1967). For Johnson see Allen Matusow, *The Unraveling of America: A History of Liberalism in the 1960s* (New York, 1984), 195–97.

28 James Patterson, *America's Struggle against Poverty, 1900–1994* (Cambridge, Mass., 1995), 102.

29 Hugh Davis Graham, *The Uncertain Triumph: Federal Education Policy in the Kennedy and Johnson Years* (Chapel Hill, 1984), esp. 203–25.

30 Coleman et al., *Equality of Educational Opportunity* (Washington, 1966), 302–25. Quote on 325. The report was 737 pages long and was accompanied by a second volume including 548 pages of statistics.

31 James Traub, "What No School Can Do," *New York Times Magazine*, Jan. 16, 2000, 52ff; Nicholas Lemann, *The Big Test: The Secret History of the American Meritocracy* (New York, 1999), 159–62.

32 For some of the many writings on the Coleman Report, see Andrew Kull, *The Color-Blind Constitution* (Cambridge, Mass., 1992), 283; Diane Ravitch, *The Troubled Crusade* (New York, 1983), 167–74; Patricia Albjerg Graham, "Educational Dilemmas for Americans," *Daedalus*, 127 (Winter 1998), 225–36; and David Armor, "Why Is Black Educational Achievement Rising?" *The Public Interest*, No. 108 (Summer 1992), 77; and especially Daniel Moynihan, "A Pathbreaking Report," and Christopher Jencks, "The Coleman Report and Conventional Wisdom," in *On Equality of Educational Opportunity*, ed. Frederick Mosteller and Daniel Moynihan, (New York, 1972), 3–66, 69–115. Most of the excellent essays in this book, written by leading social scientists, backed the major findings of the report.

33 A summary of such views is in Daryl Scott, *Contempt and Pity* (Chapel Hill, 1997), 170–72. See also Patricia Edwards, "Before and After School Desegregation: African American Parents' Involvement in Schools," in *Beyond Segregation*, ed. Mwamilu Shujaa (Thousand Oaks,

Calif., 1996), 138–61. See also George Wright, "Growing Up Segregated," in *Understanding the Little Rock Crisis: An Exercise in Remembrance and Reconciliation*, ed. Elizabeth Jacoway and C. Fred Williams (Fayetteville, Ark., 1999), 45–55. Wright has fond memories of the quality of black schools in Louisville in the 1950s.

34   For the shift toward affirmative action in the late 1960s see Hugh Davis Graham, *The Civil Rights Era: Origins and Development of National Policy* (New York, 1990), 368–69, 382–89, 459–75; Kull, *Color-Blind Constitution*, 187–89, 207–10, 221–22; and Lawrence Fuchs, "The Changing Meaning of Civil Rights, 1954–1994," in *Civil Rights and Social Wrongs*, ed. Higham, 59–85.

35   Emphasis mine, because this clause became so widely cited in the future by opponents of affirmative action.

36   See Kull, *Color-Blind Constitution*, 174–87, 192–93, 281. Quote on 281.

37   Matusow, *Unraveling of America*, 189–94; Rosenberg, *Hollow Hope*, 48. The doubling was supposed to occur in districts where 8 to 9 percent of black students were attending schools with whites, the tripling in schools where the percentages were from 4 to 5 percent. Schools where no desegregation existed were expected to make a "very significant start" toward mixing. By the fall of 1966, HEW had often made good on threats to defer aid, by doing so in 122 school districts, most of which had 2 percent or less of black students in schools with whites. See Leon Panetta, *Bring Us Together: The Nixon Administration and the Civil Rights Retreat* (Philadelphia 1971), esp. 89–112, 130–47, for an informative memoir.

38   Among the many descriptions and evaluations of this law are Wilkinson, *From Brown to Bakke*, 103–7; Ravitch, *Troubled Crusade*, 153–67; and especially Graham, *Uncertain Triumph*, 150–51, 203–26, 369–90.

39   Hugh Davis Graham, "The Transformation of Federal Education Policy," in *Exploring the Johnson Years*, ed. Robert Divine (Austin, 1981), 155–84.

40   For statistics on blacks in schools, see Gary Orfield and John Yun, Civil Rights Project, Harvard University, *Resegregation in American Schools* (Cambridge, Mass., 1999), 13; Greenberg, *Crusaders in the Courts*, 380–81; and appendices to this book. For seventeen-year-olds, see Susan Mayer and Christopher Jencks, "War on Poverty: No Apologies, Please," *New York Times*, Nov. 9, 1995.

41   Gary Orfield, *The Reconstruction of Southern Education: The Schools and the 1964 Civil Rights Act* (New York, 1969), 181–207; Tom Dent, *Southern Journey: A Return to the Civil Rights Movement* (New York, 1997), 302–7.

42   Matusow, *Unraveling of America*, 200–3.

43   Kaestle and Smith, "The Federal Role in Elementary and Secondary Education, 1940–1980," *Harvard Educational Review*, 52 (Nov. 1982), 400.

44   For the 10 percent estimate see Armor, "Why Is Black Educational Achievement Rising?" 77; Ravitch, *Troubled Crusade*, 153. For a later estimate, that compensatory education had no effect on academic achievement, see Traub, "What No School Can Do," 55.

45   Gerald Bracey, "What Happened to America's Public Schools? Not What You Think," *American Heritage* (Nov. 1997), 39–52.

46   *Griffin v. County School Board of Prince Edward County*, 377 U.S. 218 (1964); Carter in *New York Times*, May 26, 1964.

47   Wilkinson, *From Brown to Bakke*, 111–14; Kull, *Color-Blind Constitution*, 177–79; Greenberg, *Crusaders in the Courts*, 382.

48 *Green v. County School Board of New Kent County, Va.*, 391 U.S. 430 (1968). For commentary see *New York Times*, May 28, 1968; Greenberg, *Crusaders in the Courts*, 383; Wilkinson, *From Brown to Bakke*, 116–17; Hugh Davis Graham, *Civil Rights Era*, 374; and Kull, *Color-Blind Constitution*, 194–95.

49 Tushnet, *Making Civil Rights Law*, 69–70; Bernard Schwartz, *Super Chief* (New York, 1993), 703–6.

50 Along with further toughening of HEW guidelines for integration, *Green* led to a rapid increase in the percentage of black students who attended schools in the South that were predominantly white—from 13.9 percent in 1967–68 to 23.4 percent in 1968–69. See Orfield and Yun, *Resegregation*, 13, and appendices to this book.

Chapter 7

1 A sign of the expanding role of the Court was its docketing of cases: 1,453 cases in the 1953–54 term, and 4,172 by 1969–70. Ed Cray, *Chief Justice* (New York, 1997), 517.

2 Cray, *Chief Justice*, 498–503.

3 Scholar's quote from Bernard Schwartz, *Super Chief* (New York, 1983), 31. For other accounts of Burger, see Bob Woodward and Scott Armstrong, *The Brethren* (New York, 1979), 65–88, passim; Mark Tushnet, *Making Constitutional Law* (New York, 1997), 72–77; Robert Henry, "The Players and the Play," in *The Burger Court: Counterrevolution or Confirmation?* ed. Schwartz (New York, 1998), 26; and Charles Lamb and Stephen Halpern, eds., *The Burger Court: Political and Judicial Profiles* (Urbana, 1991), 131.

4 Woodward and Armstrong, *The Brethren*, 23–24.

5 Stephen Wasby, "Justice Harry A. Blackmun: Transformation from 'Minnesota Twin' to Independent Voice," in Lamb and Halpern, eds., *The Burger Court*, 63–99.

6 *New York Times*, Aug. 26, 1998; Henry, "The Players," 23.

7 Lamb and Halpern, eds., *The Burger Court*, 437.

8 Schwartz, *Super Chief*, 678–89. An equally negative view is Woodward and Armstrong, *The Brethren*, 47–59. A slightly more favorable evaluation of Marshall's role on the Court is Juan Williams, *Thurgood Marshall* (New York, 1998), esp. 325–30, 347–56. Tushnet, *Making Constitutional Law*, esp. 68, has a generally high opinion of Marshall's judicial career.

9 Howard Schuman et al., *Racial Attitudes in America* (rev. ed., Cambridge, Mass., 1997), 126–27, 286–88; J. Harvie Wilkinson III, *From Brown to Bakke* (New York, 1979), 236–41.

10 Hugh Davis Graham, *The Civil Rights Era* (New York, 1990), 383–89, and works cited above on the Burger Court.

11 *Alexander v. Holmes County Board of Education*, 396 U.S. 19 (1969). See also Roger Newman, *Hugo Black* (New York, 1994), 601–2; Wilkinson, *From Brown to Bakke*, 119–22; Woodward and Armstrong, *The Brethren*, 36–61; and Jack Greenberg, *Crusaders in the Courts* (New York, 1994), 384–86.

12 Quotes, in order, from Woodward and Armstrong, *The Brethren*, 56; *New York Times*, Oct. 31, 1969; ibid.; *Crisis*, Nov. 1969, 387; *New York Times*, Oct. 31, 1969.

13 Wilkinson, *From Brown to Bakke*, 121.

14 Constance Curry, *Silver Rights* (Algonquin Books, Chapel Hill, 1995), 173–76. In 1973 the Court unanimously rejected Mississippi's effort to subsidize these "private" schools by lend-

ing them textbooks. *Norwood v. Harrison*, 413 U.S. 455 (1973). But whites found other ways to maintain these academies.

15 For Nixon's shrewd policies, see Graham, *The Civil Rights Era*, 320; and Gareth Davies, "Nixon and the Desegregation of Southern Schools," paper delivered at University of Cambridge, Oct. 1999.

16 Gary Orfield and John Yun, Civil Rights Project, Harvard University, *Resegregation in American Schools* (Cambridge, Mass., 1999), 13. See also my Appendix II, Figures 1 and 2, and Tables 2 and 3. Allen Matusow, *Unraveling of America* (New York, 1984), 193, offers slightly different statistics, concluding that 39 percent of black public school students in the South attended majority-white schools in the 1970–71 school year, and 46 percent by the 1972–73 school year. He writes that the percentage of blacks in such schools in the North and West was only 28 percent in 1972–73.

17 *Swann v. Charlotte-Mecklenburg County Board of Education*, 402 U.S. 1 (1971). For some of the many accounts of the case, see Davison Douglas, *Reading, Writing, and Race: The Desegregation of the Charlotte Schools* (Chapel Hill, 1995), 111–12; Bernard Schwartz, *Swann's Way: The School Busing Case and the Supreme Court* (New York, 1986), esp. 7–14, 186–90; Frye Gaillard, *The Dream Long Deferred* (Chapel Hill, 1988), 60–95; Wilkinson, *From Brown to Bakke*, 137–51; Gary Orfield and Susan Eaton, *Dismantling Desegregation: The Quiet Reversal of Brown v. Board of Education* (New York, 1996), 14; and William Chafe, *Civilities and Civil Rights* (New York, 1980), 312–15.

18 Newman, *Hugo Black*, 602.

19 Carter in *Time*, May 3, 1971, 14; Ribicoff in *Newsweek*, May 3, 1971, 27.

20 Woodward and Armstrong, *The Brethren*, 156.

21 Wilkins in *New York Times*, April 21, 1971. For southern cities, see David Armor, "Why Is Black Educational Achievement Rising?" *The Public Interest*, no. 108 (Summer 1992), 65–80.

22 For test scores, see Douglas, *Reading, Writing, and Race*, 245–47. Reagan's visit is remembered in *Charlotte Observer*, April 5, 1997.

23 *Keyes v. Denver School District #1*, 413 U.S. 921 (1973). For commentary on the case, see *New York Times*, June 23–26, 1973; Wilkinson, *From Brown to Bakke*, 193–200; Greenberg, *Crusaders in the Courts*, 392–93; and Woodward and Armstrong, *The Brethren*, 260ff.

24 Douglas cited in Tushnet, *Making Constitutional Law*, 83.

25 Jennifer Hochschild, *The New American Dilemma: Liberal Democracy and School Desegregation* (New Haven, 1984), 31–32.

26 For Powell comment, see *Newsweek*, July 2, 1973, 47.

27 *New York Times*, May 12, 1974. Gary Orfield, a tireless scholarly advocate of desegregation, called southern progress toward racial balance, late 1960s, a "remarkable achievement" and a "revolution." Orfield, *Reconstruction of Southern Education* (New York, 1969), 355.

28 *New York Times*, Nov. 10, 1969.

29 *Boston Globe*, Jan. 5, 1992.

30 *New York Times*, March 14, 1971, May 13, 1974; Marian Clayton, "Desegregating Public Schools," *Crisis*, May 1984, 20–23; Douglas, *Reading, Writing, and Race*, 4–5, 240–42.

31 Ronald Bayor, *Race and the Shaping of Twentieth Century Atlanta* (Chapel Hill, 1996), 236–60; *New York Times*, May 13, 1974.

32 For Clark, ibid. For Topeka, see Paul Wilson, *A Time to Lose* (Lawrence, 1995), 224–30.

33 Tom Dent, *Southern Journey: A Return to the Civil Rights Movement* (New York, 1997), 299.

34 Quotes in this and next paragraph from *New York Times*, Nov. 10, 1969.

35 Dent, *Southern Journey*, 332–33. For more on the long-range tensions aroused in Selma, see the beginning of my Chapter 9.

36 *New York Times*, May 13, 1974.

37 *New York Times*, Nov. 10, 1969.

38 David Cecelski, *Along Freedom Road: Hyde County, North Carolina and the Fate of Black Schools in the South* (Chapel Hill, 1994), 8. See also Michelle Foster, *Black Teachers on Teaching* (New York, 1997), xxxiv–xxxix.

39 For black power advocacy in Greensboro, see Chafe, *Civilities and Civil Rights*, 324–30. For Hyde County, see Cecelski, *Along Freedom Road*, 168.

40 *New York Times*, May 13, 1974.

41 Robert Foster, "A Reassessment of *Brown v. Board*," in Derrick Bell, ed., *Shades of Brown* (New York, 1980), 26.

42 Peter Applebome, *Dixie Rising* (San Diego, 1996), 210–36. Quote on 214.

Chapter 8

1 Robert Wiebe, "White Attitudes and Black Rights from *Brown* to *Bakke*," in *Have We Overcome?* ed. Michael Namorato, (Jackson, Miss., 1979), 147–71; J. Harvie Wilkinson III, *From Brown to Bakke* (New York, 1979), 152–53, 246–47.

2 Reagan, however, stopped short of issuing an executive order against affirmative action. Like President George Bush, who also rejected advice to take such a step, he feared the political repercussions. See Jack Greenberg, *Crusaders in the Courts* (New York, 1994), 397–98; Nathan Glazer, "Multiculturalism and a New America," in *Civil Rights and Social Wrongs*, ed. John Higham (University Park, Pa., 1997), 120–33; Hugh Davis Graham, *The Civil Rights Era* (New York, 1990), 213–26; and Orlando Patterson, *The Ordeal of Integration* (Washington, 1997), 9–11, 66–67, 192–93.

3 *New York Times*, Sept. 15, 1982, Jan. 6 and 13, 1983; *Newsweek*, Aug. 23, 1982, 71.

4 *U.S. News and World Report*, May 14, 1979, 51; Howard Schuman, et al., *Racial Attitudes in America* (rev. ed., Cambridge, Mass., 1997), 128–29; Wilkinson, *From Brown to Bakke*, 163–68, 190–92.

5 For Ford, *U.S. News and World Report*, July 5, 1976, 18; Wilkinson, *From Brown to Bakke*, 132.

6 For these quotes, see *Time*, Sept. 23, 1974, 29. For other accounts of the battles in Boston, see Ronald Formisano, *Boston against Busing: Race, Class, and Ethnicity in the 1960s and 1970s* (Chapel Hill, 1991); and J. Anthony Lukas, *Common Ground: A Turbulent Decade in the Lives of Three American Families* (New York, 1986).

7 Quotes, in order, from Christine Rossell, "Is It the Busing or the Blacks?" *Urban Affairs Quarterly*, 24 (Sept. 1988), 146; and Wilkinson, *From Brown to Bakke*, 173.

8 On busing see Orlando Patterson, "What to Do When Busing Becomes Irrelevant," *New York Times*, July 18, 1999. Quote from Wilkinson, *From Brown to Bakke*, 233. For Atlanta, see Ronald Bayor, *Race and the Shaping of Twentieth Century Atlanta* (Chapel Hill, 1996), 247–51. The quote concerning Atlanta is from David Plank and Marcia Turner, "Changing

Patterns in Black School Politics: Atlanta, 1872–1973," *American Journal of Education* (Aug. 1987), 601.

9 James Coleman et al., *Trends in School Segregation, 1968–1973* (Washington, 1975).

10 Gary Orfield, "School Desegregation after Two Generations: Race, Schools, and Opportunity in Urban Society," in *Race in America*, ed. Herbert Hill and James Jones, Jr. (Madison, 1993), 234–62; Orfield and Susan Eaton, *Dismantling Desegregation* (New York, 1996), 62–63, 314–16; Christine Rossell, "School Desegregation and White Flight," *Political Science Quarterly*, 90 (Winter 1975–76), 675–95.

11 Diane Ravitch, "The 'White Flight' Controversy," *The Public Interest*, no. 51 (Spring 1978), 135–49; Stephan Thernstrom and Abigail Thernstrom, *America in Black and White* (New York, 1997), 329–36.

12 Ravitch, " 'White Flight' Controversy"; Harvey Kantor and Barbara Brenzel, "Urban Education and the 'Truly Disadvantaged': The Historical Roots of the Contemporary Crisis, 1945–1990," in *The "Underclass" Debate: Views from History*, ed. Michael Katz, (Princeton, 1993), 366–402. These eight cities were Los Angeles, Houston, Miami, Dallas, Denver, Boston, Cincinnati, and Kansas City. The eight large cities that still had a white majority of school children in 1976 were Milwaukee, Jacksonville, Columbus, Indianapolis, San Diego, Seattle, Nashville, and Pittsburgh. Three of these—Milwaukee, Indianapolis, and Pittsburgh—soon had black majorities.

13 Thernstroms, *America in Black and White*, 334. For patterns of school segregation in American cities. See Appendix II, Table 4.

14 *San Antonio Independent School District v. Rodriguez*, 411 U.S. 1 (1973); *New York Times*, March 22, 1973.

15 Denton Watson, "The Detroit School Challenge," *Crisis*, June-July 1974, 188–93.

16 *Milliken v. Bradley*, 418 U.S. 717 (1974); quotes here and in the following four paragraphs from *New York Times*, July 26, 1974; Bob Woodward and Scott Armstrong, *The Brethren* (New York, 1979), 266–67, 283–85; Wilkinson, *From Brown to Bakke*, 216–49; and Mark Tushnet, *Making Constitutional Law* (New York, 1997), 86–89.

17 Douglas suffered a stroke in January 1975 and retired in November. At that time he had served thirty-six years and seven months, longer than any other Supreme Court justice in American history. He was replaced a month later by John Paul Stevens. Douglas died in January 1980, at the age of eighty-one.

18 Orfield and Eaton, *Dismantling Desegregation*, 291–94; *Newsday*, May 19, 1994; 901 F. Supp. 784, U.S. District Court, Delaware, Aug. 14, 1995.

19 The Court in fact had to decide such a case in 1976. It concerned Pasadena, which had adopted a court-ordered desegregation plan in 1970. The plan stipulated that no school could have a majority of minority group students. Rapid residential changes after 1970 meant that some schools in 1971 no longer complied with this stipulation, whereupon the city's school board asked the district court to lift or modify its order. The court refused, thereby confronting the city with the task of redrawing its districts. Pasadena carried the case to the High Court, which argued that the city had complied initially and did not have to redraw. It cited *Swann*, which had held that cities need not be held to any specific racial balance. The decision was six to two, with Brennan and Marshall dissenting. *Pasadena City Board of Education v. Spangler*, 427 U.S. 424 (1976).

20 *University of California Regents v. Bakke*, 438 U.S. 265 (1978); *Newsweek*, July 10, 1978, 18–21. For some of the many commentaries on this key case, see Erwin Chemerinsky, "Making Sense of the Affirmative Action Debate," in *Civil Rights and Social Wrongs*, ed. Higham, 86–101; and Nathan Glazer, "Why *Bakke* Won't End Reverse Discrimination," *Commentary*, Sept. 1978, 29–41.

21 Juan Williams, *Thurgood Marshall* (New York, 1998), 375. For a lower court challenge in 1996, see my Chapter 10.

22 Greenberg, *Crusaders in the Courts*, 394. See the next chapter for resegregation cases.

23 For statistics here and in the next paragraph, see Thernstroms, *America in Black and White*, 339–41; for modest optimism about the pace of desegregation in the 1980s see Orfield and Eaton, *Dismantling Desegregation*, 18. Orfield and John Yun, *Resegregation in American Schools* (Cambridge, Mass., 1999), 14, have similar but slightly different percentages from those cited by the Thernstroms. See also my Appendix II, Figures 1 and 2 and Tables 2 and 3.

24 Frederick Wirt, *"We Ain't What We Was": Civil Rights in the New South* (Durham, 1997), 92–93, 312; Robert Pratt, *The Color of Their Skin: Education and Race in Richmond, Virginia, 1954–89* (Charlottesville, 1992), 106–8.

25 For this kind of purposefulness in Columbus, Ohio, see Gregory Jacobs, *Getting around Brown: Desegregation, Development, and the Columbus Schools* (Columbus, 1998), 196–99.

26 Robert Carter, "A Reassessment of *Brown v. Board*," in *Shades of Brown*, ed. Derrick Bell (New York, 1980), 25.

27 Cautiously optimistic accounts include Greenberg, *Crusaders in the Courts*, 510; Orfield, "School Desegregation," 239, 247; David Tyack and Larry Cuban, *Tinkering toward Utopia: A Century of Public School Reform* (Cambridge, Mass., 1995), 27–28.

28 Thernstroms, *America in Black and White*, 341–42.

29 For Little Rock, *Newsweek*, May 4, 1981, 66; and Elizabeth Huckaby, *Crisis at Central High: Little Rock, 1957–58* (Baton Rouge, 1980); for Louisville, Wilkinson, *From Brown to Bakke*, 242–45.

30 Thernstroms, *America in Black and White*, 351. Figures for spending are in 1994 dollars, for public schools. For figures on college attendance see Thernstroms, "Reflections on *The Shape of the River*," *UCLA Law Review*, 46 (June, 1999), 1583. See also my Appendix II, Table 3.

31 David Armor, "Why Is Black Educational Achievement Rising?" *The Public Interest*, no. 108 (Summer 1992), 65–80; Greenberg, *Crusaders in the Courts*, 399.

32 Kantor and Brenzel, "Urban Education and the 'Truly Disadvantaged'," 385. See also Chapter 10.

33 James Traub, "What No School Can Do," *New York Times Magazine*, Jan. 16, 2000, 52ff; Diane Ravitch, *Left Back: A Century of Failed School Reforms* (New York, 2000); *New York Times*, July 26, 2000.

34 *New York Times*, May 18, 1979.

35 *New York Times*, May 17, 1984.

Chapter 9

1 Tom Dent, *Southern Journey: A Return to the Civil Rights Movement* (New York, 1997), 301–24.

2 The authors of these books, respectively, were Derrick Bell, Douglas Massey and Nancy Denton, and Carl Rowan. Some white writers, too, were pessimistic: Andrew Hacker, *Two Nations: Black and White, Separate, Hostile, Unequal* (New York, 1992); and Tom Wicker, *Tragic Failure: Racial Integration in America* (New York, 1996).

3 Bell, "Remembrances of Racism Past: Getting Beyond the Civil Rights Decline," in *Race in America*, ed. Herbert Hill and James Jones, Jr., (Madison, 1993), 74.

4 On the NAACP, Henry Louis Gates and Hendrik Hertzberg, "Requiem," *New Yorker*, July 7, 1997, 4–5; for poll data see *New York Times*, June 11 and Dec. 14, 1997.

5 *The Ordeal of Integration* (Washington, D.C., 1997), 48.

6 For optimism about race relations in the 1990s see Stephan Thernstrom and Abigail Thernstrom, *America in Black and White* (New York, 1997), esp. 493–545.

7 Nelson Rivers, cited by Peter Applebome, *Dixie Rising* (San Diego, 1996), 217.

8 Cited in *Washington Post*, April 29, 1995.

9 Wilson, "The Closing of the American City," *New Republic*, May 11, 1998, 3.

10 *New York Times*, July 8, 1989.

11 Joining these seven justices in 1992—Rehnquist, Stevens, O'Connor, Scalia, Kennedy, Souter, and Thomas—were two holdovers, Byron White and Harry Blackmun. They were replaced during the first term of President Bill Clinton by Ruth Bader Ginsburg and Stephen Breyer, who tilted the balance of the Court a little toward the left. Conservatives, however, still commanded a majority in most cases.

12 *Pasadena City Board of Education v. Spangler*, 427 U.S. 424 (1976). See chapter 8.

13 *Board of Education of Oklahoma City v. Dowell*, 489 U.S. 237 (1991). For commentaries on this and the other school cases considered in the next few pages see Hugh Davis Graham, "Legacies of the 1960s: The American 'Rights Revolution' in an Era of Divided Governance," *Journal of Policy History*, 10 (1998), 267–88; and John Harris et al., "The Curious Case of *Missouri v. Jenkins*: The End of the Road for Court-Ordered Desegregation?" *Journal of Negro Education*, 66 (Winter 1977), 43–55.

14 For Marshall and Starr, see *Washington Post*, April 29, 1995, also see James Traub, "Separate and Equal: School Segregation," *Atlantic Monthly*, 268 (Sept. 1991), 24ff.

15 With Rehnquist were Scalia, White, O'Connor, and Kennedy. Stevens and Blackmun joined Marshall's dissent.

16 *Freeman v. Pitts*, 503 U.S. 467 (1992). Also Julius Chambers, "Race and Equality: The Still Unfinished Business of the Warren Court," in *The Warren Court*, ed. Bernard Schwartz, (New York, 1996), 21–67; and Robert Carter, "Thirty-Five Years Later: New Perspectives on *Brown*," in *Race in America*, ed. Hill and Jones, 83–96.

17 Clark in *Washington Post*, April 11, 1992; Jackson in *New York Times*, April 2, 1992.

18 *United States v. Fordice, Governor of Mississippi*, 505 U.S. 717 (1992). Quotes from *Washington Post*, June 27, 1992.

19 *Missouri v. Jenkins*, 515 U.S. 1139 (1995). Also *New York Times*, Jan. 12, June 13, 14, 1995.

20 Joining Rehnquist were Scalia, Thomas, O'Connor, and Kennedy. The dissenters were Souter, Stevens, Bader Ginsburg, and Breyer.

21 For Thomas on the *Brown* case, see Juan Williams, *Thurgood Marshall* (New York, 1998), 393.

22 *New York Times*, April 23, 1997.

23 Brown in *Providence Journal*, May 11, 1998; Loury, *New York Times*, April 25, 1997.

24 Chambers, *"Brown v. Board of Education,"* in *Race in America*, ed., Hilland Jones, 186–87. See also James Liebman, "Three Strategies for Implementing *Brown* Anew," ibid., 112–66.

25 *New York Times*, Nov. 7, 1999. Exploration by Lise Funderburg.

26 *Los Angeles Times*, April 13, 1992.

27 Mark Tushnet, *Making Constitutional Law* (New York, 1997), 195. See also Williams, *Thurgood Marshall*, 397–98.

28 Ravitch, "Our Pluralist Common Culture," in *Civil Rights and Social Wrongs*, ed. John Higham, (University Park, Pa., 1997), 136.

Chapter 10

1 *Hopwood v. Texas*, 78 F. 3d 932 (1996); *New York Times*, March 20–25, 1996, Sept. 1, 1997.

2 *New York Times*, March 21, 1996; *Washington Post*, March 20, 1996. Texas quickly devised new procedures—requiring the university to admit the top 10 percent of graduates of every high school in the state—in order to circumvent *Hopwood*.

3 *Atlanta Constitution*, May 17, 1994; *Newsweek*, May 16, 1994, 26–31.

4 *Washington Post*, May 18, 1994; Brown-Thompson quoted in *Newsday*, May 15, 1994. For the long history of litigation in Topeka, see Paul Wilson, *A Time to Lose* (Lawrence, 1995), esp. 224–30. In 1998 the all-black Monroe School, where Linda Brown had gone to school in the early 1950s, became a national park. It is called the Brown v. Board of Education National Historical Site.

5 Jack Greenberg, *Crusaders in the Courts* (New York, 1994), 225–26.

6 Damon Freeman, "Reexamining Central High," *Organization of American Historians Newsletter*, Feb. 2000, 3ff; *New York Times*, Sept. 21, 1997; *Newsday*, Sept. 22, 1997; *St. Louis Post-Dispatch*, Sept. 28, 1997. See also Melba Pattillo Beals, *Warriors Don't Cry* (New York, 1994), xix–xxii, passim; and Elizabeth Huckaby, *Crisis at Central High* (Baton Rouge, 1980), 220–21.

7 Liva Baker, *The Second Battle of New Orleans* (New York, 1996), 478–80; *People*, Dec. 4, 1995, 104.

8 Kluger, *Simple Justice* (New York, 1975), 710; Wilkinson, *From Brown to Bakke* (New York, 1979), 49; Morris, "Centuries of Black Protest: Its Significance for America and the World," in *Race in America*, ed. Herbert Hill and James Jones, Jr., (Madison, 1993), 46.

9 Carter in *Washington Post*, May 28, 1994; Clark cited in William Bowen and Derek Bok, *The Shape of the River: Long-Term Consequences of Considering Race in College and University Admissions* (Princeton, 1998), xxiii; Orfield in *New York Times*, June 13, 1999.

10 For ambivalent public attitudes concerning affirmative action see Paul Sniderman and Edward Carmines, *Reaching beyond Race* (Cambridge, Mass.), 143–44. For liberal views, see Bowen and Bok, *Shape of the River*, 276–85; and Ronald Dworkin, "Affirming Affirmative Action," *New York Review of Books*, Oct. 22, 1998, 91–102. For a more conservative view, see Stephan and Abigail Thernstrom, "Reflections on *The Shape of the River*," *UCLA Law Review*, 46 (June, 1999), 1583ff. For an informative debate see Nathan Glazer and Abigail Thernstrom, "Should the SAT Account for Race?" *New Republic*, 22 (Sept. 27, 1999), 26–29.

11 For the Court in the 1990s, see Cass Sunstein, *One Case at a Time: Judicial Minimalism on*

the Supreme Court (Cambridge, Mass., 1999). For hiring by the justices, see *New York Times*, Oct. 6, 1998, and *USA Today*, March 15, 2000 (which noted modest progress by 2000— two African Americans and three Asian Americans among the thirty-four clerks hired). In this context, it is useful to note two things: first, that many young blacks did not wish to serve conservative justices; and second, that in 1990 only 3.5 percent of lawyers in the nation were black.

12 Especially large per student differences in school funding characterized New York City and suburban areas in Long Island. Some inner-city school districts heavily populated by blacks, however, offered higher per student financial backing than did surrounding suburban districts that were predominantly white. Newark, New Jersey, whose students scored poorly on academic achievement tests, was one prominent example. Money, in short, was not a panacea. See James Traub, "What No School Can Do," *New York Times Magazine*, Jan. 16, 2000, 52ff.

13 Orfield and John Yun, *Resegregation in American Schools* (Cambridge, Mass., 1999), 14, 24; Orlando Patterson, "What to Do When Busing Becomes Irrelevant," *New York Times*, July 18, 1999. See also Megan Twohey, "Desegregation Is Dead," *National Journal*, Sept. 17, 1998. In April 2000 the *New York Times* estimated that one-third of black public school students attended schools in which 90 percent of the students were non-white. Section IV, April 2, 2000. See my Appendix II, Table 5.

14 *New York Times*, Feb. 18, 1999; April 2, 2000.

15 *Boston Globe*, April 14, 1998; *New York Times*, Nov. 20, 1998, March 14, 1999; *Providence Journal*, July 15, 1999. In 1999, 15 percent of public school students in Boston were white (as opposed to 60 percent in the early 1970s), 49 percent were black, 26 percent were Latino, and 9 percent were Asian American.

16 Alison Morantz, "Desegregation at Risk: Threat and Reaffirmation in Charlotte," in *Dismantling Desegregation*, ed. Gary Orfield and Susan Eaton, (New York, 1996), 179–206; *Charlotte Observer*, April 5, Sept. 11, 1997; *New York Times*, April 25, Sept. 11, 1999.

17 *New York Times*, March 21 and April 2, 2000.

18 Achievement tests focused on in these pages are the federally sponsored National Assessment of Educational Progress (NAEP) tests, given to millions of American students at various ages in reading, mathematics, science, and other subjects. They measure cognitive skills. SATs, which until the late 1990s were misleadingly called "aptitude" tests, in fact reflect levels of cognitive development that depend on a host of social and environmental forces, not on innate "intelligence." See Stephan and Abigail Thernstrom, *America in Black and White* (New York, 1997), 348–85, 397–405.

19 Christopher Jencks and Meredith Phillips, "The Black-White Test Score Gap: An Introduction," in *The Black-White Test Score Gap*, ed. Jencks and Phillips, (Washington, 1998), 1–51. They note, 1, that the "typical American black still scores below 75 percent of American whites on most standardized tests." Data released in 2000, showed that the average black seventeen-year-old reads about as well as the average white thirteen-year-old on National Assessment of Educational Progress tests. *New York Times*, Aug. 25, 2000. See also my Appendix II, Table 6.

20 Much of the following discussion of test score gaps, including these observations, rests on conclusions in Jencks and Phillips, eds., "Black-White Test Score Gap"; and on Traub, "What No School Can Do."

21 Thernstroms, *America in Black and White*, 402–5; *New York Times*, Aug. 25, 2000.

22 Nonetheless, the tests do all right as predictors of performance by students in college.

23 For discussion of many of these critiques, see Nicholas Lemann, *The Big Test: The Secret History of the American Meritocracy* (New York, 1999), passim.

24 See Brent Staples, "How the Racial Literacy Gap First Opened," *New York Times*, July 23, 1999; Patterson, "What to Do."

25 For a description of inner-city black life that emphasizes economic problems associated with instability of employment see William J. Wilson, *When Work Disappears: The World of the New Urban Poor* (New York, 1996).

26 Average class sizes had declined since 1960. Indeed, spending per capita on public schools rose considerably faster than inflation every year between 1945 and 1997 (except during the recession years between 1978 and 1982). See National Center for Educational Statistics, U.S. Dept. of Education, *Digest of Education Statistics, 1997* (Washington, 1998), 172, and my Appendix II, Table 7.

27 *USA Today*, Nov. 12, 1999.

28 See Traub, "What No School Can Do." France, he argues, supports such a system. Head Start programs, he adds, have normally given relatively little emphasis to cognitive development and have had no lasting impact on the gaps.

29 Thernstroms, *America in Black and White*, 359.

30 Jencks and Phillips, "Black-White Test Score Gap"; *New York Times*, July 4, 1999.

31 Jencks and Phillips, "Black-White Test Score Gap," 43.

32 Cited in Twohey, "Desegregation Is Dead."

33 Orfield and Eaton, *Dismantling Desegregation*, 90–93, 297–345; and Orfield and Yun, *Resegregation*. For other solutions see James Comer, *Waiting for a Miracle: Why Schools Can't Solve Our Problem* (New York, 1998); Orlando Patterson, *The Ordeal of Integration* (New York, 1997), esp. 185–90; and Diane Ravitch, "Our Pluralistic Common Culture," in *Civil Rights and Social Wrongs*, ed. John Higham, (University Park, Pa., 1997), 134–48.

34 Traub, "What No School Can Do" estimates the cost of such a program as at least $25 to $30 billion per year, three times the amount spent on Head Start in 2000. A program of this sort that would also give substantial benefits to middle-class preschoolers would cost many times that much.

35 A study emphasizing the deep historical roots of these urban problems is Jean Anyon, *Ghetto Schooling: A Political Economy of Urban Educational Reform* (New York, 1997).

36 Blacks who dominated school boards in Yonkers, Seattle, and Prince George's County, Maryland, among other places, opted in the late 1990s to dismantle desegregation plans in favor of supporting better-financed neighborhood schools. Twohey, "Desegregation Is Dead."

37 These agendas varied, but many leaders continued to support an essentially integrationist set of goals, demanding that federal and state governments act firmly against segregated housing and schools. Most black leaders continued to be Democratic and to call for well-funded social legislation that would attack widespread black poverty, especially in the central cities.

38 See, for example, my Appendix II, Table 3.

39 Orfield and Eaton, *Dismantling Desegregation*, 108–9, cites a Gallup poll in 1994 revealing that 87 percent of Americans believed *Brown* to be appropriate.

40 For two of many studies that emphasize the staying power of liberal jurisprudence, especially as it has encouraged the efforts of an activist federal bureaucracy, see R. Shep Melnick, *Between the Lines: Interpreting Welfare Rights* (Washington, 1994); and Jeremy Rabkin, "The Judiciary in the Administrative State," *Public Interest*, 71 (Spring, 1983), 62–84.

41 Greenberg, *Crusaders in the Courts*, 401.

BIBLIOGRAPHICAL ESSAY

Although this book relies on considerable reading in contemporary materials, especially newspaper and magazine articles, I limit this bibliography to those books and scholarly articles that I especially recommend to readers who wish to pursue various themes in greater depth. As these references indicate, scholarship on race relations, especially concerning schools, has mushroomed since the 1970s. This book depends heavily on such writing, much of it since 1990.

The Court: The place to start is Richard Kluger, *Simple Justice: The History of Brown v. Board of Education and Black America's Struggle for Equality* (New York, 1975). This lengthy, deeply researched book is a key source for early chapters. Almost as useful, especially for my middle chapters, is J. Harvie Wilkinson III, *From Brown to Bakke: The Supreme Court and School Integration: 1954–1978* (New York, 1979). Wilkinson carefully analyzes cases and the context that helped to shape them. Throughout my book I relied also on Congressional Quarterly, *Guide to the Supreme Court* (2d ed., Washington, 1990). This is a massive reference work on the Court.

Other helpful books that focus on the Court and race relations include John Howard, *The Shifting Wind: The Supreme Court and Civil Rights from Reconstruction to Brown* (Albany, N.Y., 1999); David Armor, *Forced Justice: School Desegregation and the Law* (New York, 1995), a thoughtful evaluation of many decisions; Jack Greenberg, *Crusaders in the Courts: How a Dedicated Band of Lawyers Fought for the Civil Rights Revolution* (New York, 1994), an informative history by a leader of the Legal Defense and Educational Fund; Andrew Kull, *The Color-Blind Constitution* (Cambridge, Mass., 1992), a learned critique and analysis of many of the High Court's rulings concerning race; Constance Baker Motley, *Equal Justice . . . Under Law: An Autobiography* (New York, 1998), a memoir by a leading Defense Fund attorney; and Jennifer Hochschild, *The New American Dilemma: Liberal Democracy and School Desegregation* (New Haven, 1984), a strongly argued liberal critique of many aspects of *Brown* and *Brown II*.

I also relied in places on Gerald Rosenberg, *The Hollow Hope: Can Courts Bring About Social Change?* (Chicago, 1991). As his title suggests, Rosenberg does not think that *Brown* alone made a great difference. Excellent essays on *Brown* and the Court can be found in Austin Sarat, ed., *Race, Law, and Culture: Reflections on Brown v. Board of Education* (New York, 1997). Useful articles are collected in

Bernard Schwartz, ed., *The Warren Court: A Retrospective* (New York, 1996). A fine biography of Warren is Schwartz, *Super Chief: Earl Warren and His Supreme Court—A Judicial Biography* (New York, 1983). See also Ed Cray, *Chief Justice: A Biography of Earl Warren* (New York, 1997). Mark Tushnet has written much concerning the court and civil rights, including *The NAACP's Legal Strategy against Segregated Education, 1925–1950* (Chapel Hill, 1987), *Making Civil Rights Law: Thurgood Marshall and the Supreme Court, 1936–1961* (New York, 1994); and *Making Constitutional Law: Thurgood Marshall and the Supreme Court, 1961–1991* (New York, 1997).

Among the many other books concerning race and the law, the following are well worth reading: J. W. Peltason, *Fifty-Eight Lonely Men: Southern Federal Judges and School Desegregation* (New York, 1961), a very solid critical study; Jack Bass, *Unlikely Heroes: The Dramatic Story of the Southern Judges of the Fifth Circuit Who Translated the Supreme Court's Brown Decision into a Revolution for Equality* (New York, 1981), which covers some of the same ground; Bernard Schwartz, *Swann's Way: The School Busing Case and the Supreme Court* (New York, 1986), a clear account of the key case authorizing busing to achieve racial balance; William Harbaugh, *Lawyer's Lawyer: The Life of John W. Davis* (New York, 1973), an authoritative, well-written biography; and Paul Wilson, *A Time to Lose: Representing Kansas in Brown v. Board of Education* (Lawrence, 1995), a memoir by the reluctant legal defender of Topeka's segregated schools.

Also helpful are Melvin Urofsky, *Division and Discord: The Supreme Court under Stone and Vinson, 1941–1953* (Columbia, S.C., 1997); Morton Horwitz, *The Warren Court and the Pursuit of Justice* (New York, 1998), which is a brief and thoughtful reflection; Bernard Schwartz, ed., *The Burger Court: Counterrevolution or Conformation?* (New York, 1998); and Charles Lamb and Stephen Halpern, eds., *The Burger Court: Political and Judicial Profiles* (Urbana, 1991).

R. Shep Melnick, *Between the Lines: Interpreting Welfare Rights* (Washington, 1994); and Jeremy Rabkin, "The Judiciary in the Administrative State," *Public Interest*, 71 (Spring, 1983), 62–84, stress the large legacy of liberal jurisprudence in late twentieth-century America. Useful judicial biographies include Roger Newman, *Hugo Black: A Biography* (New York, 1994), which is a thorough research effort; Laura Kalman, *Abe Fortas: A Biography* (New Haven, 1990), an outstanding critical study; and Juan Williams, *Thurgood Marshall: American Revolutionary* (New York, 1998), which includes much information concerning personal aspects of Marshall's life.

A much debated revisionist article is Michael Klarman, "How *Brown* Changed Race Relations: The Backlash Thesis," *Journal of American History*, 81 (June 1994), 81–118. Other relevant scholarly articles are J. Morgan Kousser, "Separate but *Not* Equal: The Supreme Court's First Decision on Racial Discrimination in Schools," *Journal of Southern History*, 46 (Feb. 1980), 17–44; and Mark Tushnet, with Katya Levin, "What Really Happened in *Brown v. Board of Education*," *Columbia Law Review*, 91 (Dec. 1991), 1867–1930.

Articles by contemporaries and participants in legal battles include Kenneth Clark and Mamie Clark, "Racial Identification and Preference in Negro Children," in *Readings in Social Psychology*, ed. Eleanor Maccoby et al. (New York, 1952), 602–611; Charles Johnson, "Some Significant Social and Educational Implications of the U.S. Supreme Court's Decision," *Journal of Negro Education*, 23 (Summer 1954), 364–371; and Alfred Kelly, "The School Desegregation Case," in John Garraty, ed., *Quarrels That Have Shaped the Constitution* (rev. ed., New York, 1987), 307–334.

The South: I found the following to be especially relevant: David Goldfield, *Black, White, and Southern: Race Relations and Southern Culture* (Baltimore, 1994); Peter Applebome, *Dixie Rising: How the South Is Shaping American Values, Politics, and Culture* (San Diego, 1996); and Robert Margo, *Race and Schooling in the South, 1880–1950: An Economic History* (Chicago, 1990).

Fine state and local studies include David Cecelski, *Along Freedom Road: North Carolina and the Fate of Black Schools in the South* (Chapel Hill, 1994), concerning black attitudes toward change in eastern North Carolina; and Vanessa Siddle Walker, *Their Highest Potential: An African American Community in the Segregated South* (Chapel Hill, 1996), which also explores ambivalent reactions about desegregation among African Americans.

Other informative books about race and education in the post-*Brown* South, many of them published in the late 1990s, include Tom Dent, *Southern Journey: A Return to the Civil Rights Movement* (New York, 1997); Ronald Bayor, *Race and the Shaping of Twentieth-Century Atlanta* (Chapel Hill, 1996); William Chafe, *Civilities and Civil Rights: Greensboro, North Carolina, and the Black Struggle for Freedom* (New York, 1980); Frye Gaillard, *The Dream Long Deferred* (Chapel Hill, 1988), concerning Charlotte; Davison Douglas, *Reading, Writing, and Race: The Desegregation of the Charlotte Schools* (Chapel Hill, 1995); Bob Smith, *They Closed Their Schools: Prince Edward County, Virginia, 1951–1964* (Chapel Hill, 1965); Matthew Lassiter and Andrew Lewis, eds., *The Moderates' Dilemma: Massive Resistance to School Desegregation in Virginia* (Charlottesville, 1998); Robert Pratt, *The Color of Their Skin: Education and Race in Richmond, Virginia, 1964–1989* (Charlottesville, 1992); Adam Fairclough, *Race and Democracy: The Civil Rights Struggle in Louisiana, 1915–1970* (Athens, Ga., 1995); Liva Baker, *The Second Battle of New Orleans: The Hundred-Year Struggle to Integrate the Schools* (New York, 1996); and William Kellar, *Make Haste Slowly: Moderates, Conservatives, and School Desegregation in Houston* (College Station, Tex., 1999).

Two thoroughly researched, balanced books on southern reactions to *Brown* are Numan Bartley, *The Rise of Massive Resistance: Race and Politics in the South during the 1950s* (Baton Rouge, 1969); and Neil McMillen, *The Citizens' Council: Organized Resistance to the Second Reconstruction, 1954–1964* (Urbana, 1971). McMillen, ed., *Remaking Dixie: The Impact of World War II on the American South* (Jackson, Miss., 1997) includes many insightful articles by scholars. For essays concerning Little Rock see Elizabeth Jacoway and C. Fred Williams, eds., *Understanding the Little Rock Crisis: An Exercise in Remembrance and Reconciliation* (Fayetteville, Ark., 1999).

The North: Among the excellent sources concerning border state and northern cities are Elinor Pancoast and others, *The Report of a Study on Desegregation in the*

Baltimore City Schools (Baltimore, 1956); Gregory Jacobs, *Getting Around Brown: Desegregation, Development, and the Columbus Schools* (Columbus, Ohio, 1998); Arnold Hirsch, *Making the Second Ghetto: Race and Housing in Chicago, 1940–1960* (New York, 1983); and Thomas Sugrue, *The Origins of the Urban Crisis: Race and Inequality in Postwar Detroit* (Princeton, 1996). For Boston, site of great controversy over busing in the 1970s, see J. Anthony Lukas, *Common Ground: A Turbulent Decade in the Lives of Three American Families* (New York, 1986); and Ronald Formisano, *Boston against Busing: Race, Class, and Ethnicity in the 1960s and 1970s* (Chapel Hill, 1991).

Civil Rights: Scholars and others have devoted much attention to the civil rights movement. Some of the many strong books on the subject include Taylor Branch, *Parting the Waters: America in the King Years, 1954–63* (New York, 1988), a lengthy, but fast-paced narrative; John Dittmer, *Local People: The Struggle for Civil Rights in Mississippi* (Urbana, 1994), a prize-winning account; Hugh Davis Graham, *The Civil Rights Era: Origins and Development of National Policy* (New York, 1990), an indispensable analysis of its subject; and John Higham, ed., *Civil Rights and Social Wrongs: Black-White Relations since World War II* (University Park, Pa., 1997), which includes first-rate essays by scholars.

See also Charles Payne, *I've Got the Light of Freedom: The Organizing Tradition and the Mississippi Freedom Struggle* (Berkeley, 1995); Patricia Sullivan, *Days of Hope: Race and Democracy in the New Deal Era* (Chapel Hill, 1996); John Egerton, *Speak Now the Day: The Generation before the Civil Rights Movement in the South* (New York, 1994); John Salmond, *"My Mind Set on Freedom": A History of the Civil Rights Movement, 1954–1968* (Chicago, 1997), a fine, brief history; and Harvard Sitkoff, *The Struggle for Black Equality, 1954–1992* (New York, 1993). Michael Namorato, ed., *Have We Overcome? Race Relations since* Brown (Jackson, Miss., 1979) collects wide-ranging essays by scholars. A helpful article is Steven Lawson, "Civil Rights," in *Exploring the Johnson Years*, ed. Robert Divine, (Austin, Tex., 1981), 93–125.

Race Relations: A provocative book concerning attitudes about race is Daryl Scott, *Contempt and Pity: Social Policy and the Image of the Damaged Black Psyche, 1880–1996* (Chapel Hill, 1997). Excellent essays abound in Michael Katz, ed., *The "Underclass" Debate: Views from History* (Princeton, 1993). Two books that are informative about public attitudes toward race are Paul Sniderman and Edward Carmines, *Reaching beyond Race* (Cambridge, Mass., 1997), and Howard Schuman et al., *Racial Attitudes in America: Trends and Interpretations* (rev. ed., Cambridge, Mass., 1997). A positive account of affirmative action policies is William Bowen and Derek Bok, *The Shape of the River: Long-Term Consequences of Considering Race in College and University Admissions* (Princeton, 1998). A more negative view is Stephan and Abigail Thernstrom, "Reflections on *The Shape of the River*," *UCLA Law Review*, 46 (June 1999), 1583ff. Gary Orfield and Susan Eaton, *Dismantling Desegregation: The Quiet Reversal of Brown v. Board of Education* (New York, 1996) laments the trend of judicial interpretations in recent years and contains much data on trends. So does Orfield and John Yun, Civil Rights Project, Harvard University, *Resegregation in American Schools* (Cambridge, Mass., 1999). Christopher Jencks and Meredith Phillips, eds., *The Black-White Test Score Gap* (Washington, 1998) includes learned essays.

Other relevant books on race relations, especially during the 1990s, include Derrick Bell, *Faces at the Bottom of the Well* (New York, 1992); Herbert Hill and James Jones, Jr., eds., *Race in America: The Struggle for Equality* (Madison, 1993), a collection of scholarly articles; Douglas Massey and Nancy Denton, *American Apartheid: Segregation and the Making of the Underclass* (Cambridge, Mass., 1993); Orlando Patterson, *The Ordeal of Integration: Progress and Resentment in America's "Racial" Crisis* (Washington, 1997), a sophisticated book by an eminent scholar; and Andrew Hacker, *Two Nations: Black and White, Separate, Hostile, Unequal* (New York, 1992). Stephan Thernstrom and Abigail Thernstrom, *America in Black and White: One Nation, Indivisible* (New York, 1997), is both an effort at refuting Hacker and other pessimistic accounts of postwar race relations and a fount of statistical information. An authoritative earlier article is Herbert Hyman and Paul Sheatsley, "Attitudes toward Segregation," *Scientific American*, 211 (July, 1964), 16–23.

Schools and Race: An indispensable starting point concerning the impact of desegregation and other forces on educational achievement is James Coleman et al., *Equality of Educational Opportunity* (Washington, 1966). Frederick Mosteller and Daniel Moynihan, eds., *On Equality of Educational Opportunity* (New York, 1972), consists of well-informed essays on the Coleman report. Diane Ravitch, *The Troubled Crusade: American Education, 1945–1980* (New York, 1983), is a thoughtful survey that devotes considerable attention to racial matters. A superior study is Hugh Davis Graham, *The Uncertain Triumph: Federal Education Policy in the Kennedy and Johnson Years* (Chapel Hill, 1984). A collection of high-quality scholarly articles is Ravitch and Maris Vinovskis, eds., *Learning from the Past: What History Teaches Us about School Reform* (Baltimore, 1995). See also Gary Orfield, *The Reconstruction of Southern Education: The Schools and the 1964 Civil Rights Act* (New York, 1969).

I also learned a good deal from the following: Mwalimu Shujaa, ed., *Beyond Segregation: The Politics of Quality in African American Schools* (Thousand Oaks, Calif., 1996); Derrick Bell, ed., *Shades of Brown: New Perspectives on School Desegregation* (New York, 1980); Michelle Foster, *Black Teachers on Teaching* (New York, 1997); and David Tyack and Larry Cuban, *Tinkering toward Utopia: A Century of Public School Reform* (Cambridge, Mass., 1995), a well-informed history. A moving account of black parents' bold quest to place their children in a white Mississippi school is Constance Curry, *Silver Rights* (Chapel Hill, 1995).

Among the articles on race and schools that proved useful are Jack Greenberg, "Racial Integration of Teachers—A Growing Problem," *Journal of Negro Education*, 20 (Fall, 1951), 584–587; Hugh Davis Graham, "The Transformation of Federal Education Policy," in *Exploring the Johnson Years*, ed. Robert Divine, 155–184; David Armor, "Why Is Black Educational Achievement Rising?" *The Public*

Interest, No. 108 (Summer 1992), 65–80; Diane Ravitch, "The 'White Flight' Controversy," *The Public Interest*, No. 51 (Spring 1978), 135–149; James Traub, "Separate and Equal; School Segregation," *Atlantic Monthly*, 268 (Sept. 1991), 24ff; Abigail Thernstrom, "The Drive for Racially Inclusive Schools," *Annals of the American Academy of Political and Social Science*, 253 (Sept. 1992), 131–143; and Thomas Sowell, "Patterns of Black Excellence," *The Public Interest*, No. 43 (Spring 1976), 26–58. The article by W. E. B. Du Bois, "Does the Negro Need Separate Schools?" *Journal of Negro Education*, 4 (July 1935), 328–335, has stimulated decades of debate and remains well worth reading.

Other key articles on education include Carl Kaestle and Marshall Smith, "The Federal Role in Elementary and Secondary Education, 1940–1980," *Harvard Educational Review*, 52 (Nov. 1982), 384–408; Kaestle, "The Public Schools and the Public Mood," *American Heritage* (Feb. 1990), 66–81; Gerald Bracey, "What Happened to America's Public Schools? Not What You Think," *American Heritage*, (Nov. 1997), 39–52; and Patricia Albjerg Graham, "Educational Dilemmas for Americans," *Daedalus*, 127 (Winter 1998), 225–236; and James Traub, "What No School Can Do," *New York Times Magazine*, Jan. 16, 2000, 52 ff, which has influenced some of my arguments.

Among the many books that in recent years have stressed the necessity of high academic standards for *all* students are Miles Corwin, *And Still We Rise: The Trials and Triumphs of Twelve Gifted Inner-City High School Students* (New York, 2000); John McWhorter, *Losing the Race: Self-Sabotage in Black America* (New York, 2000); and Diane Ravitch, *Left Back: A Century of Failed School Reforms* (New York, 2000).

ACKNOWLEDGMENTS

In researching this book I had the great assistance of three enthusiastic and superior students at Brown University. Each devoted a summer to helping me move ahead. The first two, undergraduates at the time, were Justin Driver and John Snyder. They did outstanding work locating key books and articles and digging about in contemporary newspapers and magazines. The third, a graduate student in history, was Andrew Huebner, who not only assisted with research but also endured the laborious process of proofreading with me. His expertise with computers also saved me great amounts of time and trouble. I thank also Victoria Antonitis of the Brown History Department, who helped me deal at many stages with computer problems.

I am also indebted to numerous scholars. John Thompson of Cambridge University and Gareth Davies of Lancaster University offered good advice at key stages. Those who carefully read and criticized various drafts of the book included Melvin Urofsky of Virginia Commonwealth University, a foremost student of American legal and constitutional history; John Dittmer of DePauw University, an expert on American race relations and the civil rights movement; Tony Badger of Cambridge University, an authority on American political and southern history; Steven Gillon of the University of Oklahoma, who has written widely on aspects of modern American politics; Carl Kaestle of Brown University, a distinguished scholar of educational history; and David Hackett Fischer of Brandeis University. Their help has been invaluable. I also thank Peter Ginna, my editor at Oxford University Press. He not only encouraged me to write this book but also gave me detailed criticism at various stages of its creation.

Finally, my wife, Cynthia, offered help in all manner of ways while I struggled with this book, thereby keeping on a level track so that I could get it done.

INDEX

Page references in *italics* refer to illustrations or photographs